THE CYBERDIMENSION

the CYBERDIMENSION

A POLITICAL THEOLOGY OF
CYBERSPACE AND CYBERSECURITY

Eric Trozzo

CASCADE *Books* • Eugene, Oregon

THE CYBERDIMENSION
A Political Theology of Cyberspace and Cybersecurity

Copyright © 2019 Eric Trozzo. All rights reserved. Except for brief quotations in critical publications or reviews, no part of this book may be reproduced in any manner without prior written permission from the publisher. Write: Permissions, Wipf and Stock Publishers, 199 W. 8th Ave., Suite 3, Eugene, OR 97401.

Cascade Books
An Imprint of Wipf and Stock Publishers
199 W. 8th Ave., Suite 3
Eugene, OR 97401

www.wipfandstock.com

PAPERBACK ISBN: 978-1-5326-5119-9
HARDCOVER ISBN: 978-1-5326-5120-5
EBOOK ISBN: 978-1-5326-5121-2

Cataloguing-in-Publication data:

Names: Trozzo, Eric. |

Title: The cyberdimension : a political theology of cyberspace and cybersecurity / Eric Trozzo.

Description: Eugene, OR: Cascade Books, 2019 | Includes bibliographical references and index.

Identifiers: ISBN 978-1-5326-5119-9 (paperback) | ISBN 978-1-5326-5120-5 (hardcover) | ISBN 978-1-5326-5121-2 (ebook)

Subjects: LCSH: Religion computer network resources. | Cyberspace—Religious aspects—Christianity. | Internet. | Cybersecurity.

Classification: BL37 .T50 2019 (print) | BL37 (ebook)

Manufactured in the U.S.A.   APRIL 22, 2019

Scripture quotations are from the New Revised Standard Version Bible, copyright © 1989 National Council of the Churches of Christ in the United States of America. Used by permission. All rights reserved worldwide.

To Dante and Caedmon

Table of Contents

Preface ix
Acknowledgments xi
Abbreviations xii

Introduction 1

1   Cyberspace as a Dimension 21

2   Constant Conflict: Cyberwar and Just War Theory 60

3   Big Data, Data Mining,
    and the Reduction to Calculable Identity 102

4   Disruptive Resistance 145

5   Cyber-Tricksters: Digital Whistle-Blowing 188

6   The Hidden Church in the Cyberdimension 223

Bibliography 265
Name/Subject Index 275

Preface

This book is not a technical account of the Internet. Indeed, I have no background in Information Technology. I do little more on a computer than word processing, web browsing, and occasionally preparing PowerPoint presentations. I am not particularly active on social media. Yet I grew up hearing about the incredible possibilities that the Internet would bring. Growing up, I was the first of my friends to have a modem in the house when my father bought one in the late '80s/early '90s; I remember clearly those first forays into CompuServe. A few years later, I was in college as the World Wide Web became more and more accessible. In my four years of college my school went from text-only web access to using web browsers to access the Yahoo! search engine. I have not kept pace with the latest technologies since; in fact I did not even get a smart phone until I moved from the United States to Malaysia in 2012. It is beyond my talents, skills, and knowledge to give unique technical insights into cyberspace.

Yet as first WikiLeaks became well-known and then particularly as the Edward Snowden revelations came about, I was struck by the need to be involved. Though I had not kept up with the growth and evolution of cyberspace, I was still deeply shaped by the dreams of what the Internet could be and profoundly troubled by what was becoming clear that it had become. As I read about Snowden, I was struck by his insistence that his goal in revealing so many documents was to create a discussion about what cyberspace should be. In considering this, I realized that what was within my ability was to wrestle with the theological implications of the emerging portrait of cyberspace in its darkness as well as its potential.

One of the characteristics of writing on cyberspace issues, I have learned, is contending with the rapid pace of change that occurs in this area. Issues of cyberweapons and fake news, for instance, have a much higher profile in the public imagination than they did when I began undertaking this project, which was initially primarily focused on Snowden. On the one hand, this is a challenge in accounting for the latest developments. On the other hand, it is easy to become obsessed with the latest developments and not take the time to consider the more foundational structural and infrastructural issues inherent in the events that make the headlines. While I have endeavored to remain current with the news on specific issues, my true concern is the deeper structures of cyberspace, which do not shift so quickly.

In these pages you will find first my distillation of what is known about cyberspace and cybersecurity issues, along with my theological reflections on it. That is, my intention is to convey to a theological audience my understanding of what some scholars in other fields, as well as journalists, are reporting about the technical and theoretical issues of cyberspace, and then giving those reports a theological framing. In other words, I am not attempting to make any new technical claims about cyberspace or the details of what is known about cybersecurity issues like cyberwar, data mining, or activism in cyberspace. I am drawing from what is publically available, particularly through technology writers who make the technical issues understandable for the nontechnically trained. These technical details are essential for engaging the debates about cyberspace, and too often create a barrier to those of us in the humanities lending the perspectives of our fields of study. Thus from the technical issues, I endeavor to contribute some theological reflection. My hope is to foster greater theological debate about the theological significance of the cyberdimension.

Acknowledgements

My heartfelt thanks to all of those who have helped bring this project to completion. Foremost in this is my wife, Wendolyn. Thank you for making "writing weekends" possible and being supportive of the time writing a book takes away from other aspects of life.

My thanks also go to those who have given thoughts and feedback on the words that I put to the page. I particularly thank Chris Rodkey for reading an early draft and giving helpful ideas for refining my thoughts. I also thank Josh Drescher for giving me a perspective from someone on the IT side rather than the theological side. I also appreciate the friendly intellectual conversations with Sivin Kit and Cheong Weng Kit.

An early draft of chapter two was presented to the faculty and advanced students at Gurukul Lutheran Theological College and Research Institute in Chennai in 2015. My thanks to Gurukul for the opportunity to share and the lively conversation in response, among all of the other forms of hospitality you have shown me and my family. A version of chapter three, meanwhile, was presented through the Centre for the Study of Religion and Society in Kuala Lumpur in 2017. Again I am grateful for the opportunity and for responses I received in that conversation.

Abbreviations

BC   *The Book of Concord: The Confessions of the Evangelical Lutheran Church,* eds. Robert Kolb and Timothy J. Wengert, trans. Charles Arand, Erick Gritsch, Robert Kolb, William Russell, James Schaaf, Jane Strohl, and Timothy J. Wengert (Minneapolis: Fortress, 2000).

LW   *Luther's Works,* eds. Jaroslav Pelikan and Helmut T. Lehman, 55 vols. (Philadelphia: Fortress; St. Louis: Concordia, 1955–86).

ST1   Paul Tillich, *Systematic Theology Vol. 1: Reason and Revelation, Being and God* (Chicago: University of Chicago Press, 1951).

ST3   Paul Tillich, *Systematic Theology, Vol. 3: Life and the Spirit; History and the Kingdom of God* (Chicago: University of Chicago Press, 1963).

Introduction

The digital dream, it seems, is broken. The promise of a new age of shared ideas and greater democracy through the spread of the Internet has turned to a barrage of news about data theft, election interference, cyberwar, and Big Brother references in response to mass surveillance. Add to this the push at the end of 2017 in the United States to end net neutrality regulations, and the hope of the bright cloud of computing too often feels as if it has darkened into a raging storm. Rather than excitement, for many people discussions about cyberspace has become increasingly filled with fear. Can we engage these fears and find a new source of hope for our existence that increasingly depends on engagement with the online world? Can we deal hopefully but nonetheless realistically with this new dimension of human existence, or are we bound to be controlled by it?

Many studies have engaged the content of this new world. Some continue to tout the promise and greater connections that the online world brings, while others worry about how large-scale media consumption affects our brains and the quality of our day-to-day relationships. In other words, there are digital optimists and digital skeptics. Yet too often the undergirding structures that enable this interaction are not considered, but rather only the online content. Such a content-only approach, I suggest, leaves a truncated picture of how the emerging online world intersects with a broader sense of the world. It not only misses the technical details, but it is disembodied not only in ignoring the physical components of computer networks, but also from the political, ecological, and economic underpinnings of cyberspace. Beyond that, I contend that there is a spiritual significance not only to the content of the online world, but also to its physical aspects.

In this book, then, I endeavor to take a broad view of cyberspace by looking through the lens of cybersecurity issues. In a sense, these are the issues that have broken the dream of an idealized realm of online hope. At the least, to put it more personally, the rise of concern with cybersecurity issues has been responsible for my own shift from being a digital optimist to a cyber-cynic. That is, I am not a full-blown skeptic about the value of cyberspace, but rather disillusioned by its unfulfilled potential. More pointedly, I find that a space of potential renewal has been co-opted and colonized by political, military, and commercial interests. An arena that I had hoped would bring a greater horizontal sense of mutual participation and interdependence has been revealed to be dominated by the same old vertical structures of power that have long dominated human existence. Yet I remain an optimistic cynic. In this book I intend to tease out how the hope of the cloud has come to be colonized, and then to seek a framework for a postcolonial hope that some of the promised potential may be reclaimed. In other words, I seek to engage the ambiguity of cyberspace and to point towards positive potential within that ambiguity, or what theologian Paul Tillich would call a metaphor of unambiguous existence.

Too often a stumbling block to discussions of the problems, ambiguities, and potentialities of cyberspace among those of us within the humanities is a lack of understanding of the technical foundations of the Internet. Without a basic of understanding of how this phenomenon works, any discussion of the issues surrounding it is bound to be superficial. Thus before delving further into my argument in this book, it is important to give a basic overview of what is meant by the Internet or cyberspace, as well as what cybersecurity is and how it functions.

How Does the Internet Work?

As I have suggested that the nuts and bolts of the functioning of the Internet is an essential aspect of understanding cyberspace, let us take a moment to sketch the basics of how these computer networks function. Indeed this basic outline of the structure is also essential for understanding the key issues of cybersecurity. The Internet itself is a massive network of digitized information. Some two and a half quintillion bytes of information are added daily.[1] At the same time individual users are increasingly able to tailor the information that they receive to suit their

---

1. To give a visual sense of this scale, that number is 2,500,000,000,000,000,000 bytes of information added daily.

personal tastes. In addition to this raw information, however, cyberspace also includes e-commerce and the functioning of critical infrastructures, such as power grids or water treatment facilities, of modern civilization. All of this relies on the networking of computer systems.[2] Thus considering cyberspace is about more than sharing memes on Facebook or watching movies on Netflix. It is intertwined with nearly every aspect of life for a large portion of the world's population. Yet too frequently this undergirding is forgotten about in discussions of cyberspace.

Key to the exchange of information through the internet are "packets." Packets function as envelopes for data being transmitted. The packet contains a "header" with information about the source, destination, and some information about the contents, much like the outside of a "snail mail" envelope. Information being sent from one computer is broken up into many packets. This allows each packet to travel independently to its destination, before being reassembled at the endpoint. The flow of the data is thus flexible and decentralized. Packets can take an infinite number of routes from the origin to the destination. Rather than creating a direct link from one computer to another, which is impractical, this network allows fewer links to carry a constant flow of information between many computers. In fact, the Internet is not a single network but rather a network of networks each capable sharing information with one another. Packets can be sent through any of these networks. The largest of these networks are called "network service providers," or NSPs, and they form the backbone of the Internet's infrastructure.

The networks work together by using a protocol known as TCP/IP. This protocol consists of two elements. The IP, or Internet Protocol, establishes a unique numeric address for each system that is part of the Internet. The IP allows for labeling data so that the packets can be sent in the most efficient manner. These numeric IPs are connected to more memorable web addresses (like google.com, for instance), through what is known as the Domain Name System (DNS). The TCP, or Transmission Control Protocol, meanwhile, manages the path of the packets. Packets arrive at their destination via a system of routers. As cyberspace ethicist Richard A. Spinello explains:

> When a packet arrives at a router, the router looks at the IP address and checks the routing table, and if the table contains the network included in the IP address the message is sent to

---

2. Singer and Friedman, *Cybersecurity and Cyberwar*, 16.

that network. If not, the message is sent along on a default route (usually the next router in the backbone hierarchy). If the address is in another NSP, the router connected to the NSP backbone sends the message to the correct backbone where it is sent along by other routers until it reaches the correct address.[3]

These exchanges happen at an incredibly rapid speed. Yet it is important to note that the packets are transmitted from one physical computing location to another. The transfers do not simply occur "in the cloud" of an electronic ether. Yet because the number of these physical locations is virtually uncountable, there are innumerable paths that a packet could possibly take in getting from source to destination, and the path taken may not correspond to a geographical sense of the most direct path. The many access points to the Internet give it a great openness to novelty. Cyberspace can incorporate many types of computing (laptops, smart phones, refrigerator sensors, and so forth) and also many types of applications (emails, MP3 and MP4 files, instant messages, FitBit data, etc.) This flexibility allows cyberspace to be viewed as an open system that can constantly incorporate new technology into its network of networks, allowing cyberspace to continually evolve.[4] This decentralized structure is also why cyberspace is generally considered to be somewhat chaotic and difficult to censor, though this assertion will be questioned somewhat in the first chapter.

A great challenge for conceiving how the Internet works is the size of these interconnected systems. With thousands of networks that are constantly shifting their interconnections, it is impossible to map the full system of the Internet. Rather, through what is known as the "control plane," nodes in this vast network share some of the essential information about how they are networked with other routers, which in return share their current connection status. Using this information, each router is then able to create its own temporary route to get its information to its final destination. Along with the information, the router also passes along this "map" of the intended route so that other routers know how the others are directing traffic.

As P. W. Singer and Allan Friedman, in their immensely helpful book *Cybersecurity and Cyberwar: What Everyone Needs to Know*, sum up the relevance of this complicated technical process: "The takeaway for cybersecurity is that the entire system is based on trust. It is a system

3. Spinello, *Cyberethics*, 32.
4. Ibid.

that works efficiently, but it can be broken, either by accident or by maliciously feeding the system bad data."[5] As an example of feeding the system bad data, they point to an incident that occurred in February 2008. The Pakistani government considered some of the content available on the video-sharing website YouTube objectionable and so ordered Pakistan Telecom to block access to the site within Pakistan. To do so, the telecom company fed false information to their customers' computers, tricking them into believing that the most direct route to YouTube was through Pakistan Telecom, where the company could then block access to the real YouTube website. However, through the control plane, routers outside of Pakistan began to pick up this route map and began directing their attempts to reach YouTube through Pakistan Telecom. Before long, more than two-thirds of the world's Internet traffic attempting to reach YouTube was being directed to Pakistan Telecom. This heavy traffic load overwhelmed Pakistan Telecom's computers and temporarily "broke the Internet," as some phrased it. The problem was only resolved by Google engineers aggressively advertising the correct routes throughout the web.

Again Singer and Friedman explain that the decentralized architecture of the Internet has two essential insights in considering cybersecurity. One is that the Internet does not need top-down coordination to function. It is by nature a grassroots system, so to speak. At the same time, the second point is that this decentralization underscores, "the importance of the Internet's users and gatekeepers in behaving properly, and how certain built-in choke points can create great vulnerabilities if they don't."[6] Again, we see that the Internet is a decentralized system built on the ability to trust others in the web to give accurate information. To have cybersecurity is, in a sense, to have trust in the cyberdimension.

Because of the decentralized architecture, the Internet has historically been a space that has defied traditional governance models. Cyberspace has had a bit of an unruly or even anarchic streak. That is, as Singer and Friedman note, political philosophy has most often been centered on the issue of proper distribution of limited resources. Digital resources do not become "scarce" in the same way that traditional physical resources do, however. Thus, "the main questions of Internet governance are of interoperability and communication rather than the classic issue of distribution," the two claim. In 1992, Internet pioneer David Clark of MIT

---

5. Singer and Friedman, *Cybersecurity and Cyberwar*, 25.
6. Ibid.

set forth a dictum that has become rather famous as a statement of the ethos of the early Internet:

> We reject: kings, presidents and voting.
> We believe in: rough consensus and running code.

Thus there is a bit of anarchy woven into the history of the Internet. At the same time, Clark followed up this statement with a lesser-known one on the following slide: "What are we bad at? Growing our process to match our size."[7] As the Internet has grown, new processes have indeed needed to be created in order to govern and safeguard trust within cyberspace.

Interoperability is guaranteed through basic rules known as standards, currently overseen by a voluntary organization called the Internet Engineering Task Force (IETF). This group creates standards through specific working groups that primarily operate through open forums and mailing lists and rely on consensus. The IETF is but one group now under the Internet Society, or ISOC. The ISOC was established in 1992, as the Internet was growing rapidly, as an independent international organization to help safeguard the standards process. In particular there was concern because of the central role that the United States government had played in the development and running of the Internet.

While many resources do not become scarce on the Internet, there are some aspects that are indeed limited. In particular, identifiers such as IP addresses and domain names must be unique. As the commercial component of the Internet increased, competition for domain names also increased. In 1998, the Internet Corporation for Assigned Names and Numbers (ICANN) was created to decide on domain names and who gets to use them. ICANN navigates a range of commercial, political, intellectual property rights, and other issues. ICANN follows an approach where decisions are supposed to be made by consensus. However, some argue that governments and large commercial interests can afford to pay staff to participate in the forums while smaller groups cannot. Likewise, some feel that ICANN remains captive to US interests because the control of assigning names officially belonged to the US Department of Commerce, which delegated the power to ICANN by renewable contract, until September 2016.

---

7. Ibid., 30.

What is "cybersecurity"?

Central to the operation of the Internet is trust. One site in the network must trust the other parts sufficiently in order to interact with them. Yet in such a vast system, what basis is there for trust? This is the basic question behind the idea of cybersecurity. How can one be sure that those with whom one interacts online are not malicious? This is especially important in cyberspace not just because of the size of the network but also because there is no way of knowing the full extent of the web of relationships with which you are interacting every time you engage in anything in cyberspace. Nobody takes the time to track down the paths of every packet of information involved in your online interactions. Cybersecurity, then, deals with how to establish trust in cyberspace as well as how to protect oneself against damaging and malicious uses of cyberspace.

Singer and Friedman hold, "Security isn't just the notion of being free from danger, as it is commonly conceived, but is associated with the presence of an adversary."[8] Thus we see that in cybersecurity, two sides are needed. Human intentionality creates a cybersecurity situation. Singer and Friedman report that cybersecurity traditionally has three goals, known as the "CIA Triad": Confidentiality, Integrity, and Availability. To these three they add a fourth: Resiliency. Each of these marks a type of security needed to retain trust in cyberspace.

Confidentiality has to do with keeping information private. As they note, in the cyberdimension, data has power, and thus there are significant ramifications as to which data are known and which are not known. We will return to this theme throughout the book. Confidentiality is maintained through legal protections but also through technical tools such as encryption software and access control measures, such as passwords. *Integrity*, meanwhile, is the ability to have confidence that the system will be available and behave as expected. This means the ability to assume that the system and the data within it have not been changed or altered without proper authorization. Because we depend on computer systems to tell us if they are functioning properly, the consequences of being unable to trust the information we receive via cyberspace can be grave. We will explore this topic more, particularly in our discussion of cyberwar. *Availability*, then, is the ability to use the system as anticipated. This would mean, as an example, the ability to access a website when we want. In terms of cybersecurity, the issue is not a matter of technical

8. Ibid., 34.

breakdowns but rather of, for example, intentionally overwhelming and thus shutting down websites, as we shall see in our discussion of hacktivism. *Resilience*, finally, has to do with the ability to repel or endure against outside threats. Resilience, for them, is the ability to remain operational even if threats are successful in penetrating online defenses. [9]

While cybersecurity is related to these four aspects of computer systems, it is otherwise an incredibly diverse concept. Singer and Friedman note a *Washington Post* op-ed written by three US senators who were sponsoring a cybersecurity bill in 2011. The column referenced three recent high-profile incidents as evidence of the need for cybersecurity legislation: attacks against Citigroup, RSA companies, and the Stuxnet worm's targeting of Iranian nuclear research. Singer and Friedman note, "The problem is that these three cases reflected wildly different threats. The Citigroup attack was about financial fraud. The RSA attack was industrial theft, and Stuxnet was a new form of warfare. They had little in common other than they involved computers."[10] How, then, do we differentiate between these types of events that commonly get lumped under the category of cybersecurity?

A distinction needs to be made here between a vulnerability and a threat. A vulnerability is a weakness in security, but a weakness does not in and of itself constitute danger if there is nobody interested in exploiting that weakness. Having someone interested in exploiting a vulnerability constitutes a threat. A single vulnerability may have multiple threats. It is thus the person who intends to attack cybersecurity that creates a cyberthreat. While such people are often referred to with a general term of "hacker," there is in fact a wide range of motivations behind the many possible cyber threats.

Singer and Friedman note that there are basically three things that you can do to a computer: steal its data, misuse credentials, and hijack resources. They further point out, however, that because we are now so dependent upon computers a great deal can be done with any one of those three things. Thus understanding the intentions of the actors behind security threats is essential to understanding cybersecurity. Some of the actors behind cyber threats commit them in order to engage in warfare on behalf of their country officially or unofficially, for patriotic reasons. Others act out of a sense of justice. Still others do so

---

9. Ibid., 35–36.
10. Ibid., 37.

for monetary gain. We will explore some of these in later chapters. For our purposes, I find little theological insight to be gained in considering crimes of the physical dimensions that happen to be conducted with the aid of computers and the cyberdimension. For example, I see nothing novel in stealing online bank account information in order to take money from those accounts. That is old-fashioned bank robbery utilizing the new technology of the cyber realm. Similarly, industrial espionage may take new forms in the cyberdimension but other than new technology there is little difference between cyber forms and older forms of it. What is of interest are the cybersecurity forms that are substantially different in the cyberdimension. For me, this particularly includes warfare, social activism, and surveillance.

Cyber Defenses and Attacks

Central to keeping a computer system and its data safe is the ability to allow those who should have access to the system that access while keeping those who should not have it out. In computer-world terms, "identification" is the term for matching a person or entity with information about that person or entity. This might be, for example, connecting a bank account number with the name of the owner of that account. Identity tells who should have access to what data. "Authentication," meanwhile, is proof of the identification. That is, authentication is proving that someone who says they should have access to a certain system or data is indeed a person who ought to have access to that system or data. Traditionally, authentication comes through "something you have, something you know, or something you are." Something you know is often knowledge of a correct password or similarly secret information. Something you have refers to a physical object such as an ATM card or more recently a unique Internet banking security device for inputting a PIN number along with Internet banking transactions. Finally, something you are is called "biometric" authentication, where something like a fingerprint or retina scan is required to as proof of identity. Lastly comes the level of authorization. That is, once a person is recognized the following question is what portions of a system they are entitled to use.

The challenge in proving identity is central to many of the unique features of cyberspace. There is a tension between the need for authentication and the ability to be anonymous online, which was a cherished aspect of the early days of the Internet. There is also a tension between a sense of ownership of property of certain online data, such as messages intended to be private, and the ideal of consensus coming from the decentralized nature of Internet architecture. These tensions will prove to be crucial to the issues we encounter in the following chapters. Because cyberspace interconnection is not a face-to-face interaction, it brings forth questions of what constitutes identity in an online space. What is the relationship between an online presence with which you interact and an embodied person with whom you interact?

Yet even with the level of uncertainty about the identity of the person sitting at a keyboard, quite a bit can actually be known about this person. All Internet activity is routed from a unique IP address. For most people, this IP address is not constant. Rather the Internet service provider (ISP) dynamically reassigns numbers after a customer disconnects. However it is possible to correlate the IP address with a specific date and time to a pinpoint a specific customer within the ISP's data. This does not give a specific identification of an individual, but it does provide geographical location and means of accessing the Internet. When this information is combined with other data, who was doing what and in which location at which time can be ascertained with a high-probability guess. At the same time, identity cannot be known with certainty, particularly because skilled individuals can mask the IP address they are using. These aspects become important as we turn to questions of surveillance and data mining.

Cyberattacks, meanwhile, aim to take information from a system, take control of a system, or change data within a system. Different types of attacks aim at different vulnerabilities within the structure of computer systems and allow achievement of different goals within these three basic areas of cyberattack. "Cyberattack" thus covers a range of different motives and tactics for in some way controlling or manipulating a portion of the network of cyberspace that is not intended to be available to the attackers. These tactics can range from a simple deceitful request for information, such as through an email posing as coming from a bank and asking for confirmation of bank account number and password, to complex techniques for bypassing Internet security systems.

An example of a more sophisticated approach that hackers might exploit is identifying mistakes in the systems themselves. Given the millions of lines of code in current operating systems, it is inevitable that there will be some vulnerabilities yet undiscovered. Hackers will search the code for weaknesses that can be exploited. An attack that uses a previously unknown weakness in the system is known as using a "zero day" because it occurs the day before the first day the rest of the world is aware of the weakness and so no patch exists to fix the hole. Zero days are highly prized by hackers, as we shall explore in chapter 2.

Once into the system, a variety of choices can be made by an attacker for how to use this advantage. One common approach is to set the computer to respond to the attackers' commands rather than the programs' commands. This can be done, for example, through an SQL injection attack. Such an attack takes advantages in weakness in software code in order to inject SQL commands into login forms or other data entry. An SQL query occurs when a legitimate user enters their information into the login space on a website; it is the process of connecting the entered username and password, for example, with those on file for that site. By injecting SQL commands, the attackers can bypass the SQL procedures and go directly into the system. The attackers thus gain access to the database.[11] It is then possible to access, control, delete, or change the data on the system. This allows the hackers to alter websites or computers to perform actions not intended by the owners.

While these types of attacks are difficult to design, once the design is created it is relatively simple to make the "exploit" available to other, less savvy attackers. The prepackaged exploitation of a vulnerability is known as malware. Malware can compromise a system and insert a "payload" of instructions as to what the system should do once it has come under the malware's control. Malware is sometimes designed to automatically spread itself across the network; this is known as a "worm." Perhaps the most malicious form of malware are programs designed not just to provide access to a computer system but to take and keep control of a computer in order to use its computing and networking abilities. Attackers can gain control a vast array of computers and coordinate their activities. These "zombie" computer armies are known as "botnets." A user rarely has any idea that their computer is part of a botnet. Yet these computers can be used to launch attacks. Not only do botnets give huge computational power to their users, but they also work to shield the attacker's identity, as it is the unsuspecting users' IP addresses that the attacks are traced back to, and not the controlling hacker's address.

One of the most powerful uses of a botnet is a "distributed denial-of-service" (DDoS) attack. A denial-of-service (DoS) attack works much

11. Open Web Application Security Project, "SQL Injection."

like calling someone's phone number repeatedly. The repeated calls would make the phone impossible to use because it is tied up constantly receiving calls. Similarly, a DoS attack continually attempts to access a website in an attempt to overwhelm it. A DoS attack is easy to block, however, by simply blocking the IP address that is sending the continual requests. In a DDoS attack, however, the full resources of the botnet can be employed to overwhelm the website. With thousands or possibly even millions of computers sending in requests, it is incredibly difficult to stop the attack. A DDoS attack will generally shut down a website while the attack is going on. Often this type of attack is done with larger goals in mind, however. The goals may be criminal, but this type of action is also commonly being employed for political reasons, whether by social activists or to suppress political activism. We will explore these uses more in chapter 4.

Perhaps the form of cyberattack that has most grabbed the popular imagination are what is known as Advanced Persistent Threats (APTs). These attacks are the work of a highly advanced and organized team that is able to conducted complex attacks. While there is evidence to suggest that these threats are becoming more common, for the majority of people they are no cause for concern. Singer and Friedman explain that an APT always has a specific target chosen because of their high strategic value. Targets have ranged from military jet designs to oil company trade secrets. These attacks are done by teams of specialized experts, each taking a specific role in a long-term project that may take months. The target is studied in detail until vulnerabilities are understood, then the system is breached. Information may be extracted or the system controlled. The relevant point here is that these are highly sophisticated attacks done by skilled and well-funded hackers.

Defending against malware is an important part of cybersecurity. Probably the most familiar and widely used form of defense is anti-virus and anti-malware software. While most people hopefully are used to having some form of anti-virus software on their computers, few stop to think about the details of how it works. The fight against malware is constantly evolving, with new types of malware being identified literally every second.[12] Attackers are constantly attempting to identify and exploit vulnerabilities. Defenders, meanwhile, seek to block the attacks and fix the vulnerabilities. When the defenders succeed, the attacks adapt and seek out new vulnerabilities, and the cycle continues.

12. Singer and Friedman, *Cybersecurity and Cyberwar*, 61.

Traditional anti-virus software simply keeps track of the ways that hackers have attacked systems before and watches for the "signatures" of these kinds of attacks. If it detects any of those signatures on the files of the computer or in the in the data coming in from online, it tells the computer to avoid that bit of code. The limitation of this approach is that the list of attacks continually grows, meaning that it takes longer and longer to compare the files on the computer to the list of malware that the defense software recognizes. Even though hackers are unlikely to use any of the old vulnerabilities, they must still be defended just in case someone does try to use one. More than this, attackers are also able to create programs that alter the features of malware so that one type of malware may have many different signatures, all of which must be included in the anti-virus database.

To combat this large number of signatures needed to defend against, newer anti-virus software incorporates another approach. "Heuristic" detection employs advanced analysis to identify suspicious behavior by computer code. If it detects something that seems amiss, it can test the suspicious code by simulating its operations without actually putting the system at risk.

Along with screening the computer for attacks, another basic approach to cyberdefense is to block unwanted material from reaching the computer. Firewalls are code filters that reject any activity that does not meet preset conditions. "Intrusion detection systems," meanwhile, are systems within the computer or network that monitor the operations for anomalous activity or signatures that might signal outside infiltration of the network or computer. These systems can often close down suspicious connections or activities. A third form of blocking unwanted material is the "software patch." A patch is sent out when a vendor identifies a vulnerability and builds a fix into the code. A weakness of patches is that they rely on the user to download the security update, which many users fail to do. Many vendors now counter this problem by having automatic updates. This can backfire, however, as sometimes the patch can cause other problems with the software.

The final line of defense for a computer system is the "air gap." That is, critical computer systems can be physically separated from the network. Essentially, the theory here is that if the computer is not online it is not susceptible to cyberattack. Thus critical infrastructure, such as power companies, often separate their core computing centers from their networked computers. Air gapping is also important in keeping data secret.

Air gaps, however, have some significant limitations. For example, power companies that keep their computers offline may be less vulnerable to attack, but they are also unable to run "smart" power grids that are more efficient. Likewise, air gaps often simply do not work. Singer and Friedman report that the National Cybersecurity and Communications Integration Center has surveyed hundreds of air-gapping attempts by private American businesses. None of the cases managed to completely separate the desired network from the business's other networks.[13]

Along with these defensive tactics, there must also be a way to confirm trust between networks, since as we might recall the working of the Internet is predicated on trust. The means for establishing trust between computers is through cryptography. Cryptography, of course, is an ancient practice of communicating in code so that sensitive information can be kept confidential. Online cryptography is built upon the "hash." As Singer and Friedman explain, "A hash function takes any piece of data and maps it to a smaller, set-length output, with two specific properties."[14] The first property is that this function has a single direction, meaning that it is difficult to differentiate the original data from what is sent out. Second, it is incredibly rare that two input pieces of data would generate the same output hash. These two properties thus allow the hash to "fingerprint" a document or email so their integrity can be verified. "If a trusted fingerprint of a document does not match the fingerprint that you generate yourself using the same method, then you have a different document."[15] Thus the hash allows for verification of data through the fingerprint. However, to build trust there must also be a means of giving identity. This is done through "asymmetric encryption."

In "symmetric encryption" data is encrypted and multiple parties share the same key for decrypting it. This gives everyone with a key equal access to data. This is fine if everyone involved knows each other and trusts each other. For example, if a group is coediting a document it is helpful to all have equal access. However, in most online situations such a level of familiarity and trust is not possible. Asymmetric encryption tackles this issue by giving different keys. Thus for example, my email address has two keys, a public one and a private one. My friend also has two keys for his email address. When we exchange addresses, we are giving

13. Ibid., 63–64.
14. Ibid., 46.
15. Ibid.

each other our public keys. When this friend sends me a message, he encrypts it with my public key, but I must decrypt it with my private key, and vice versa.

When a digital fingerprint is combined with a public key to send a message, a digital signature is created. Thus if my friend emails me a document, that email is signed with his private key along with the unencrypted document. I use his public key to compare the fingerprint of the document he sent with the document I have received. If they do not match, someone has changed the document enroute; if they do match then I can trust the document I have received. In order for this system to work, however, I must trust the public keys that I possess. The Internet relies on third parties to verify the keys. Organizations known as "certificate authorities" do this and produce signed digital "certificates" that tie an entity to a public key. The public keys to those authorities are widely known and cannot be spoofed; thus trusting the public key of these authorities provides the basis for trusting other public keys that they sign. Few of us notice using this system, but it is the basis for online interactions. When our browser tells us that it has verified a secure connection and we are using a HTTPS web address, our browser has checked the public key and the signed certificate from a certificate authority.[16]

These third parties issuing certificates thus play an essential role in the functioning of the Internet by providing a sense of trust. Yet we can also see here where problems may arise in this system. If, for example, the signing key of a certificate authority could be co-opted, whoever took control of it would have access to all of the supposedly secure traffic using sites verified by that certificate authority. This has, in fact, happened before. In 2011 a Dutch certificate authority's keys were stolen and used to intercept Iranian users' access to Google's Gmail. Later leaks identified the NSA as being behind this theft.

Because there are some ways to abuse the trust built into the Internet system, some people opt for more advanced security. Perhaps the most infamous of these approaches is Tor, an acronym for "The Onion Router." Encryption only secures the content of what communicated. It does not keep private who is involved in the conversation. As we shall see in later chapters, this information about who one communicates with, when one communicates with them, and where the parties are when the communication happens can be extremely potent information from which a great

---

16. Ibid., 47.

many conclusions may be extracted. One can obscure this information by using a "single-hop" proxy. This is where traffic is first sent to another computer before being sent to its final destination. Yet to do this requires putting a great deal of trust in the ability of this second computer to keep its information secure. Tor provides an answer to this dilemma. It is an "overlay network;" that is, a network laid overtop the internet with its own structure of nodes and links maintained by volunteers who offer their machines for this purpose. Traffic through the Tor network is broken into chunks, just as the packet approach of the underlying network is, and encrypted. Tor uses a multiple hop approach where each hop is separately encrypted, however, so that the full route is disguised, thus preventing eavesdroppers from determining the source or the endpoint of the communication.[17]

As we shall see later, Tor is controversial. On the one hand, it provides anonymity that allows social movements to engage in activism. Indeed it was widely used by dissidents in the 2009 "Green Revolution" in Iran and in the 2011 "Arab Spring" for collaboration. At the same time, this anonymity has been used for criminal activity. Tor has been connected to cases of child pornography, bank fraud, malware distribution, and black market sales of guns and drugs. It is thus perhaps not surprising that Edward Snowden revealed that use of Tor is considered automatic grounds for surveillance by the NSA.[18]

A Colonized Space

From this technical background, we can begin to consider questions of our relationship to cyberspace and the security issues raised within it. Part of this is the question of naming cyberspace. Certainly the Internet is a helpful naming of the network of computers that is at the heart of what we are discussing, but the term does not include all aspects of cyberspace. A key component it misses, for instance, is the users who engage with the computers. Thus it is too limited a term. Another possible term is "digital," but by definition this is a binary framework that I find to be problematic. Another possibility is "virtual," but for me this minimizes the physical infrastructures that are essential to understanding the

17. Ibid., 109.
18. Ibid., 108.

phenomenon of cyberspace. Thus I find the term *cyberspace* most appealing. Yet even this term is controversial in its connotations. It is the preferred term of governments and Internet security agencies. Many who advocate for a more open sense of the online aspect of life feel that the "cyber" prefix denotes a policy-based and authoritarian understanding. Yet part of my intention is to take seriously the reality and problems stemming from the more hierarchical understandings of cyberspace, and so employing the term *cyberspace* helps to highlight this reality.[19] At the same time, I agree with those who feel that this term is too reductive to describe the ways that online and physical overlap with one another.[20] Thus in the first chapter I argue for the use of the term *cyberdimension*. In this I follow Tillich's understanding of a dimension as an aspect of life that is interpenetrated by other dimensions of life. Thus cyberspace cannot be isolated from other realms of life, including the inorganic, organic, and spiritual aspects of existence.

In coming to frame cyberspace as a dimension, I engage a variety of philosophical and theological constructions of what is meant by cyberspace. In particular, I look at early Internet theorist John Perry Barlow's breathless anticipations of the new world heralded by the Internet, as well as more recent attempts to impose traditional authority structures on the Internet by Vladimir Putin. Between extreme materialist views of the Internet and disembodied ideological constructions of it, I find most helpful the recent move within media studies towards a focus on infrastructure. In particular I am swayed by John Durham Peters's "infrastructuralism" as a framework for conceptualizing the complexity of cyberspace's web of connections. At the same time, I find that a theological supplement is needed to account for the spiritual significance of cyberspace. Thus I turn to the dominant theological speculation on cyberspace, which is predominately Teilhardian in outlook. Yet I find this framing to be insufficient for an infrastructural account of cyberspace, and thus argue to adjust the framing to Tillich's understanding of dimensions. From this viewpoint, cybersecurity emerges as a manifestation of the ambiguity of reality that the spiritual dimension strives to transcend. As such, questions of cybersecurity become essential to engaging the religious significance of cyberspace.

19. Segal, *The Hacked World Order*, 26.
20. Meyer, "Cyberspace Must Die."

Thus in chapter 2, I begin to turn towards cybersecurity issues and the theological significance presented by them. I look first at cyberwar and cyberweapons. Military ethicists debate whether cyberweapons can be accounted for by Just War Theory, but this debate has not spread far beyond them. After reviewing what cyberweapons are and the shape of debate over the ethics of this form of warfare, I turn to Daniel M. Bell, Jr.'s account of what is distinctive about a Christian understanding of Just War. For him, Christian Just War thought is a means of shaping the Christian community into being a loving community even when it finds itself in a situation of war. Drawing on his approach, I find that cyberweapons cannot fit within a Christian understanding of Just War. More importantly, however, is the realization that the entirety of cyberspace is potentially weaponized by cyberweapons. As such this constitutes a military colonization of a dimension of existence. This militarization is of even greater concern than the more specific question of cyberwar and cyberweapons.

Having considered the military colonization of cyberspace in the second chapter, in chapter 3 I turn to commercial and government colonization through big data surveillance. After discussing how big data and data mining can be a form of social control, I turn to surveillance studies. Particularly key here is theorist Andrea Smith's insistence that we not disconnect our consideration of Internet surveillance from the history of colonial sexual surveillance as a means of disappearing from view those whose existence would delegitimize the state itself. I also explore in this chapter how cyberspace challenges Foucaultian conceptions of surveillance through the panopticon model and instead calls for a turn to a more Deleuzian understanding of "power assemblages" as alignments of forces of power, such as governments and commercial interests, acting together to maintain the status quo. Together these forces act to reduce individual identity to calculable predictability in order to retain control and cultivate ideal docile consumers. Philosophically this can be understood as an attempt to corral the excess of Otherness. Theologically I turn to postcolonial theologian Mayra Rivera's insistence that divine glory is not a glory of rendering individuals transparent in order to control them, but rather an illuminating of their opacity in order to highlight and honor the excess that lies beyond what is seen. This requires a theological reorientation beyond a God of omnipotent surveillance to a sense of immanent transcendence that works to resists attempts to eliminate the excess of Otherness.

This sense of resistance to the colonizing tendencies of the power assemblages takes us in chapter 4 to a history of digital activism and hacktivism. In particular I turn to theorist Molly Sauter's defense of DDoS actions as a legitimate form of social protest. What we find in this history is the centrality of irony and aesthetics as a means of protest within the cyberdimension. This is particularly drawn out through the work of Italian scholar/activist Tatiana Bazzichelli's engagement with performance art. Theologically this opens us to the importance of aesthetics as an opening to excess that allows for political resistance to attempts to reduce reality to the calculable. In particular, I find valuable poet Glyn Maxwell's understanding that the poetry of language that distinguishes a poem from prose is the "white space" that surrounds the letters of the words rather than the words themselves. It is here in the absence that the excess of meaning is expressed. So too, theologically, the dimension of Spirit is expressed in absences that indicate excess.

From this general consideration of online activism, chapter 5 then turns more specifically to digital whistle-blowers such as Chelsea Manning and Edward Snowden. After detailing the stories of these whistle-blowers, I consider their significance first through the exchange of correspondence between Slavoj Žižek and Nadezhda Tololonnikova. This framing leads us to consider the intertwining of economics, technology, and culture more closely, which I do through the theory of Marxist philosopher of technology Bernard Stiegler. In Stiegler's thought we again find a connection between resistance and aesthetics, although in his case the metaphor is of rhythm rather than sight or word. The resistance seeks to form a challenge to dominating systems not through direct confrontation, which would simply mirror the logic of domination, but rather through ironically exposing the limits and pretensions of the power assemblages. Such irony can be understood as a form of trickery working within systems of domination. This is precisely the argument put forward by theologian Marion Grau, who sees the theological task as being one of playing the trickster in the face of the power systems of the world. Following Grau, then, we can understand whistle-blowers as playing a trickster role in challenging the power assemblages of the cyberdimension from within.

Having encountered the ways in which the cyberdimension has become colonized and approaches to resisting that colonization, chapter 6 then offers up the metaphor of the invisible or hidden church as a metaphor for transcending the ambiguity of the cyberdimension. I draw this metaphor from my own Lutheran tradition, both in its classical form in the theology of the Reformers and in the contemporary form of theologian Deanna Thompson's articulation of the "virtual body of Christ" in the Internet age. I constructively retrieve it through the lens of contemporary theologian Catherine Keller's use of postcolonial theory in her political theology, as well as in engagement with the thought of decolonial thinker Édouard Glissant. In particular I draw on Glissant's contrasting of transparency and opacity to understand the hidden church as a metaphor for a community that not only makes visible those that are marginalized and thus made invisible by digital surveillance, but does so in a way that honors the opacity of those individuals and communities.

In general, each of the chapters begins with examples of how the relevant issues for that chapter operate within the cyberdimension. Following the explanation, I turn to theoretical concerns to better understand the dynamics at play in that aspect of the cyberdimension. Building on the relevant theory, I finally turn to theological reflection in engaging the participation of the dimension of spirit within the cyberdimension.

As we turn in the final chapter to the symbolic participation in the tiny boat of the church as a metaphor of the hidden church in the cyberdimension, I suggest that we will come to the possibility of a reforged dream of cyberspace. It is a more limited dream of the cloud, not reaching the stratosphere or noosphere of earlier articulations. Rather it rises as the transpiration of the chaotic waters of the deep, into a wispy cloud of hope guiding the tiny boat by day across the ambiguous abyss as a hint of glimmering opacity. The blank space holds out a poetic promise of possibility even as the storm of colonizing calculability swarms around us and threatens to swamp us. It is a dream woven from the broken bits and pieces of earlier visions of cyberspace that have been dashed by the surf(ing of the web). It is a dream of technology infused with artistry in order to mediate the infinite depths of meaning rather than cultivating consummate consumers docilely attenuated to the status quo. Such a dream constitutes participation in the life of spirit within the cyber dimension. It is the quest for the meaning of cyberspace.

Chapter 1

Cyberspace as a Dimension

What does cyberspace mean? This is, of course, a double question. On the one hand, it asks what exactly we are talking about when we speak of cyberspace. How do we understand cyberspace ontologically? More than that, however, there is the question of the meaning, value, or transformative potential of cyberspace. Is cyberspace unique, or simply another form of human communication? This latter question certainly contains social, political, and economic ramifications, but there is also a theological component to it. Is the divine involved in cyberspace at all, or, more importantly, involved differently than through other forms of media? There has been quite a bit of speculation in various disciplines about this second type of meaning, including some philosophical and theological discussion, but surprisingly little on the first. Yet in important ways our answers to the second question of meaning rely on our assumptions about the first. Cyberspace, I contend, should be understood as a dimension, following Paul Tillich's understanding of the dimensions of life. As such, we must understand cyberspace to be a locus for a unique manifestation of Spirit. Before unpacking this contention, however, let us first reflect on why our understanding of cyberspace matters and examine what theoretical frameworks are currently operating.

The Ramifications of Our Understanding of Cyberspace

Our understanding of the nature of cyberspace has important political and social consequences. In their book *The Red Web*, for instance, journalists Andrei Soldatov and Irina Borogan examine the tensions in Russia between those who see the Internet as a means to greater democracy and freedom of expression and those who see it as a means to control. This tension is hardly unique to Russia, of course. In various forms it simmers in many countries, including Iran, Brazil, Egypt, China, India, and the United States, to name but a few. Yet it has, perhaps, been expressed in its clearest form in Russia. Much of this comes from the head of the government. "Vladimir Putin was certain that all things in the world—including the Internet—existed with a hierarchical, vertical structure," Soldatov and Borogan explain. "He was also certain that the Internet must have someone controlling it at the top."[1] In other words, we can say that Putin's worldview defines how he understands cyberspace. Which worldview shapes the understanding of cyberspace, once again, has immense political and social consequences, but I would further suggest that the cosmological framework here also has theological relevance. After all, a cosmology holding that all things exist with a vertical, hierarchical structure and someone controlling it from the top would be at home in more than a few articulations of Christian theology.

Yet the assertion that someone is controlling the Internet or that cyberspace is a vertically arranged system runs counter to much of the American narrative about cyberspace. Certainly for me, as someone who grew up in the 1980s hearing about the possibilities that having a modem could provide and then later was in college in the mid-1990s as the World Wide Web came to prominence, Putin's understanding seems an affront to all that I had understood the Internet to be. Much more influential to me were the ruminations of early Internet theorists such as John Perry Barlow.

For Barlow, the Internet is a space of infinite possibility, promising true democracy and social change. He is perhaps best known for his 1996 "A Declaration of Independence for Cyberspace." In it, he writes,

> Cyberspace consists of transactions, relationships, and thought itself, arrayed like a standing wave in the web of our communications. Ours is a world that is both everywhere and nowhere, but it is not where bodies live.
>
> We are creating a world that all may enter without privilege or prejudice accorded by race, economic power, military force, or station of birth.

---

1. Soldatov and Borogan, *The Red Web*, 223.

We are creating a world where anyone, anywhere may express his or her beliefs, no matter how singular, without fear of being coerced into silence or conformity.

Your legal concepts of property, expression, identity, movement, and context do not apply to us. They are all based on matter, and there is no matter here.

Our identities have no bodies, so, unlike you, we cannot obtain order by physical coercion. We believe that from ethics, enlightened self-interest, and the commonweal, our governance will emerge.[2]

Barlow thus challenges any vertical understanding of cyberspace. He is specifically writing in response to the US Telecommunications Reform Act of 1996, which brought the Internet under telecommunication regulation, but he also attacks attempts by other countries to impose traditional legal controls on cyberspace. His basic contention is that cyberspace is a separate realm where the tactics of the old world have been put aside and new egalitarian possibilities are opened. He concludes the Declaration by saying, "We will create a civilization of the Mind in Cyberspace. May it be more humane and fair than the world your governments have made before."[3] We find here the fundamentally idealistic and optimistic impulse at the heart of many understandings of cyberspace from this era.

Yet there is much evidence from recent years to support Putin's viewpoint. To give a few examples, in 2014 Putin signed a law that required bloggers with more than 3,000 followers to register with the government. As Soldatov and Borogan note, "Registration was more than a mere formality; it would give the security services a way to track them, intimidate them, or close them down."[4] Later in 2014, Twitter blocked accounts of Pravy Sector, a Ukrainian party critical of the Russian annexation of Crimea, for Russian users. Twitter held that this was in response to a Russian court order. Russia also passed a law stipulating that global platforms such as Twitter, Google, and Facebook would be required to store Russians' personal data on servers located in Russia by September 2015.[5] The point here is that Putin's worldview, and others sympathetic to his way of thinking, is reshaping cyberspace. Again, because this is a political and social reshaping based on cosmological assumptions, I contend there is

2. Barlow, "A Declaration of Independence for Cyberspace."
3. Ibid.
4. Soldatov and Borogan, *The Red Web*, 215.
5. Razumovskaya, "Russia Moves Some Servers."

a theological significance to this movement that needs to be considered. Indeed, I contend that it is an urgent necessity to theologically engage the importance of cyberspace and its relationship to understandings of divinity. The failure to do so is already leading to significant social consequences. To that end, let us consider some of the most prominent philosophical and theological constructions of the meaning of cyberspace.

Theoretical Frameworks for Understanding Cyberspace

David Koepsell's Materialist "Common Sense Ontology"

There has been surprisingly little philosophical reflection on the nature of cyberspace. As legal analyst and philosopher David R. Koepsell notes in his book from the year 2000, *The Ontology of Cyberspace*, "No serious philosophical approaches to the ontology of cyberspace have been made to date."[6] This situation has changed little until recent years. Even a definition of cyberspace is somewhat elusive. It originates from science-fiction novelist William Gibson's "cyberpunk" fiction. In his 1984 novel *Neuromancer*, he describes it as "a consensual hallucination experienced daily by billions of legitimate operators, in every nation . . ."[7] who "jack in" to computer networks in order to share experiences. Yet cyberspace has come to refer to a wide range of networked computer interaction, most notably through the Internet.

For Koepsell, the most interesting previous philosophical account of cyberspace is offered by Michael Heim in his book *The Metaphysics of Virtual Reality*. In it, Heim writes, "cyberspace suggests a computerized dimension where we move information about and where we find our way around data."[8] Koepsell, however, is disturbed by the description of cyberspace as a "dimension." He holds: "The use of the word 'dimension' shows that this definition is rough and ready at best. It is imprecise and begs all of the ontological questions [of the exact nature of cyberspace] . . . although it captures a sort of general understanding of the pop-cultural notion of cyberspace."[9] As we shall see, I propose to reclaim the concept of dimension for considering cyberspace, but with a specifically

---

6. Koepsell, *The Ontology of Cyberspace*, 13.

7. Gibson, *Neuromancer*, 128.

8. Heim, *The Metaphysics of Virtual Reality*, 78. Quoted in Koepsell, *The Ontology of Cyberspace*, 12.

9. Koepsell, *The Ontology of Cyberspace*, 12.

Tillichian sense. For now, however, let us focus on Koepsell's critique of Heim. Koepsell argues that despite Heim having some vague notions of a Platonic or Leibnizian framing of cyberspace, he does not ultimately offer an ontology of cyberspace.

Despite his insistence on the need for an ontology of cyberspace, however, Koepsell himself fails to offer one. Instead, he sidesteps the issue after raising it. Rather than attempting to answer any questions of what cyberspace is in its own right, his primary focus is on providing legal definitions. Thus he advocates what he calls a "common sense ontology," that "account[s] for phenomena in a metaphysically neutral manner—that is, without regard to whether or not the objects of our common perceptions are real in some ultimate sense."[10] In other words, he wants to clarify how cyberspace should be understood and thus regulated in the context of the US legal system rather than attempting to understand what cyberspace is. Thus the very nature of his inquiry presupposes a vertical view of cyberspace as something that can indeed be regulated. As we have seen, this runs counter to Barlow's vision of cyberspace as a radically egalitarian plane.

From this legal point of view, Koepsell's fundamental thesis is that cyberspace is simply machines that happen to be connected. That is, he takes a drastically materialist and reductionist view of cyberspace as purely an outgrowth of electronic computations and software. For him, there is no broader existence that occurs through these connections. More specifically, he argues that all aspects of computer-mediated phenomena are sensible experiences that can be categorized into the following groups: bits, bytes, words, algorithms, and programs. Each of these categories is a type of digital information stored in some form of computer memory. "[Storage media] are all objects which take up space and which may be directly perceived," he explains. "But," he further contends, "storage media are also a substrate for cyber-objects such as those discussed above. In this way, cyber-objects are ontologically dependent upon storage media for their existence. Storage media do not exist in cyberspace, but rather cyberspace may be said to exist in, or by virtue of, storage media."[11] Thus he is arguing that the reality of cyberspace is the existence of the informational components that it relies upon stored in

10. Ibid., 26–27.
11. Ibid., 80.

memory devices. It exists as a "physical" entity in that its components are imprinted on the media storage components.

Koepsell further points out that the law treats machines differently from ideas. Put simply, this is the difference between patent law and copywrite law. For him, the challenge of understanding cyberspace is not a matter of comprehending revolutionary interactivity, but rather that it involves machines that blur the distinctions between what is patentable and what is copywritable and therefore makes the distinction untenable. Thus he dismisses suggestions that networked computers bring something different from individual ones. "Computation may occur over a network just as it may on a single computer," he avers. "All that is involved in either is the movement of bits among processors, storage and input or output devices."[12] Again, for him cyberspace is simply a matter of the storage and movement of data from one machine to another.

Koepsell is thus dismissive of rhetoric of the emergence of pure thought freed of physicality through cyberspace. He criticizes Barlow, for example, who rather poetically expounds, "Once . . . all the good of the Information Age . . . will exist either as pure thought or something very much like thought: voltage conditions darting around the Net at the speed of light, in conditions which one might behold in effect, as glowing pixels or transmitted sounds, but never touch or claim to 'own' in the old sense of the word."[13] To this, Koepsell retorts, "It is simply not accurate that one cannot touch or own bits. I own the hard drive on which this manuscript is encoded in the form of bits."[14] To him, while digitally encoded ideas are easier to reproduce, they are not functionally different from ideas recorded in analog, so that the "old sense" of ownership remains very much valid. The debate around ownership within cyberspace is central to our concerns. It would seem that seeing a vertical organization to cyberspace means that it is an extension of the terms of the "old" world. Therefore concepts such as ownership or national sovereignty are still in power in the same sense that they have been in modernity. Koepsell's view works to provide a framework for Putin's approach to governing cyberspace.

On the one hand, Koepsell provides some important reminders for not getting carried away in a poetic mythology of cyberspace without also recognizing its mundane aspects. As will come up repeatedly in

12. Ibid., 82.

13. Barlow, "Selling Wine Without Bottles." Quoted in Koepsell, *The Ontology of Cyberspace*, 87.

14. Koepsell, *The Ontology of Cyberspace*, 87.

our considerations, the foundation of cyberspace is indeed a network of computers that exist physically in locations under the jurisdiction of various regulatory agencies and are largely owned by governments and private corporations. While Barlow's rhetoric of a civilization of the mind located everywhere and nowhere may be inspiring for some, it too easily omits this basic physical reality of cyberspace.

At the same time, Koepsell's definitional meaning of cyberspace ignores deeper questions of meaning. He takes no account of how cyberspace does indeed blur many boundaries and distinctions that had previously held sway. Questions of the nature of national power, legal ownership, and human identity—to name but a few—are indeed raised by cyberspace, as we shall see in later chapters. Koepsell's reductionist approach in ignoring these issues serves only to re-inscribe the status quo into cyberspace. To be sure, in issues of cyberwar, data mining, digital surveillance, and so forth, the continuation of the status quo in fact intensifies the vertical authority of the powers that be. Bracketing these issues, then, serves to bolster authoritarian impulses.

Theologically, this brings us to the question of whether cyberspace must follow the rules the old world, or whether it brings new possibilities. Might we even dare to ask whether it might be an opening to a "new creation"? To be clear, I am not suggesting that cyberspace is the new creation in the sense of it being the arrival of the kingdom of God in its fullness, as it were. Yet, more modestly, might the arrival of cyberspace be a means by which encrusted human structures that perpetuate injustice—that is, the old creation—be challenged and cracked open so that in the new openings created something new might emerge? Might it be that through cyberspace room for the kingdom of God might appear? If so, then cyberspace may be a conduit through which healing, justice, and a new vision of human relationships might come. The question, then, is how the divine might work through cyberspace and what might resist this working. To help in uncovering the nuances of the possibilities and limitations of cyberspace, then, let us turn to the ways cyberspace is described in media studies, and more specifically in its attention to the role of infrastructure.

Cyberspace as Media Infrastructure

In recent years, a new wave of thinking about cyberspace has emerged within media studies, focusing on the material infrastructures of media.

This approach applies interdisciplinary thought to conceptualize vast interrelated systems while also highlighting the importance of materiality. In the introduction to their edited volume *Signal Traffic: Critical Studies of Media Infrastructures,* Lisa Parks and Nicole Starosielski explain, "As a suggestive concept, then, signal traffic demarcates a critical shift away from the analysis of screened content alone and toward an understanding of how content moves through the world and how this movement affects content's form."[15] In other words, the media infrastructure approach denoted by the term *signal traffic* attempts to understand the dynamic interconnections of the media systems in its broad sense. It thus requires conceptualizing the many layers of interaction effected by networked systems.

An essential aspect of media infrastructure is the physical components necessary for cyberspace to operate, as Koepsell has noted. Certainly this includes individual computers involved in networks, but it extends beyond them as well. For instance, in a chapter of *Signal Traffic,* Paul Dourish reexamines the infrastructure of Internet routing, with a greater focus on its materiality. That is, he is similar to Koepsell in his skepticism of the Internet as a realm of Platonic ideals. One clear example of this is the fact that all aspects of cyberspace are electronic, and electricity itself requires conductive material in order to be used. The material necessities of using electricity must be accounted for within an understanding of cyberspace. Dourish also considers the vaunted decentralization of cyberspace. Yet, he notes, "one thing that an examination of Internet routing reveals is that the flexibility of decentralized routing depends on many other components that may not have the same degree of decentralized control."[16] Here we can include issues such as network addressing, agreements on a standardization of programming languages so that different systems can understand one another, and other such issues of standardization that make networking possible but also create limitations. Thus Dourish holds that it is not that there is a centralizing tendency of autocratic power involved in cyberspace but a certain vertical aspect is present simply as a matter of material consequence. As we have already noted, however, these material limitations may provide opportunities for autocratic authorities to impose centralization onto cyberspace. Indeed, Dourish rightly points to the entanglement of politics,

---

15. Parks and Starosielski, "Introduction," 1.
16. Dourish, "Protocols, Packets, and Proximity," 192.

protocols, and pragmatic decision-making in shaping the cyberspace infrastructure.[17]

To be sure, the media infrastructure approach gives an opportunity to see how vast the reach of cyberspace and other media technologies actually is. For example, the hardware required for cyberspace must be built, maintained, and repaired. Thus labor is involved, and so consideration of training, payment, and working conditions of laborers must be accounted for in relation to cyberspace. The machines themselves when operating require power, and therefore, as we have noted, consume electricity; this in turn has an environmental impact.[18]

As a further example, Parks and Starosielski cite the "Telephone Cable Channel" in Hawai'i. When the first trans-Pacific cable was laid in the 1950s, a landing station was built at Hanauma Bay. To connect the landing station to the open ocean, a path was blasted through the coral reef. This hole in the reef is now a major nature reserve and ecotourism site for divers and snorkelers; the cable has meanwhile been repurposed for scientific research, sensing aquatic life and seismic movements. As Parks and Starosielski note, "Critical studies of such sites draw attention to media infrastructures' entanglements with environmental and geopolitical conditions, from the moment of installation through their residual uses."[19] In her individual chapter in the book, Starosielski explores the impact of undersea cables. She notes, "Almost 100 percent of transoceanic Internet traffic is carried via fiber-optic undersea cables and, at times, is transmitted this way when it is moving between locations on the same continent."[20] This means that these cables are central to the global flow of digital information, and therefore an essential part of cyberspace. These physical cables are deeply intertwined in physical environments, human power dynamics, histories of imbalance and injustice, and a host of other local realities. Indeed because so much data flows through these cables, their efficiencies and inefficiencies control the flow of time in cyberspace, as inefficiencies can produce processing time lag that can, for example, transform a seamless Skype conversation into a choppy or even an incomprehensible one.[21]

17. Ibid., 201.
18. In 2007 between 2.5–3 percent of greenhouse gas emissions came directly from media technologies. See Parks and Starosielski, "Introduction," 14.
19. Ibid., 4.
20. Starosielski, "Fixed Flow," 54.
21. See ibid., 56.

Thus from considering fiber-optic cables we see that along with the material aspects of cyberspace, critical media infrastructure studies also considers political and social realities created by cyberspace. On the macro and meso scales, this involves considering the massive relational webs created by infrastructures, with their rippling and overlapping effects. These webs span continents and oceans and can have long-lasting effects. Meanwhile, on the microscale unique local manifestations must also be considered. Parks, for instance, in her individual chapter of *Signal Traffic*, examines the wide ranging social, economic, and environmental impacts of attempts to provide Internet access in rural Zambia. Her fascinating investigation points to the ways that digital technologies can both open new opportunities but also creates digital divides between those with high speed connections and those with limited or sporadic access.[22]

Parks and Starosielski also note that media infrastructure studies must further consider psychological components such as affect theory. They contend, "To be sure, infrastructures are part of such 'force-relations' [considered by affect theory], since our encounters with them can elicit different dispositions, rhythms, structures of feeling, moods, and sensations."[23] Thus media studies has helpfully shown that any consideration of cyberspace must take into account a host of dynamics that are built upon an existing foundation of infrastructural systems encompassing materiality, subjectivity, and relationality.

Infrastructuralism

Perhaps the best way to appreciate the strengths and limitations of critical media studies is to move from the general introduction given by Parks and Starosielski, and to look more closely at what I find to be perhaps the most philosophically interesting work within the movement, John Durham Peters's *The Marvelous Clouds: Toward a Philosophy of Elemental Media*. Peters suggests that in the wake of structuralism and then

---

22. See ibid., 12. My own personal awareness of these issues has been sharpened by living in Malaysian Borneo since 2012. Although living in the state capital, my Internet access is fairly slow and can go out unexpectedly for days or weeks at a time. Meanwhile some of my students come from villages with limited electricity and no Internet access. They navigate between a rural, Internet-free existence and a wired, academic and city experience, while as a teacher I have had to learn to be sensitive to a variable and unpredictable level of access.

23. Ibid., 15.

post-structuralism, the next movement may perhaps be infrastructuralism. He understands infrastructuralism as focusing on the often-mundane infrastructural elements that underlie the possibilities of structures and the breakdown of the structures. "Infrastructure in most cases is demure," Peters writes. "Withdrawal is its modus operandi, something that seems a more general property of media, which sacrifice their own visibility in the act of making something else appear."[24] He suggests that infrastructures are hidden or invisible ontologies that allow for the production of meaning, or, more specifically, that "Ontology, whatever else it is, is usually just forgotten infrastructure."[25] Infrastructure is so commonplace as to go unnoticed but allows the actions that fill life to take place.

Central to Peters's understanding of infrastructures is his quest to understand media. He notes that until a relatively few decades ago, the word *media* carried most strongly the connotation of the four basic elements of water, fire, earth, and air. He thus uses these elements as a trope for developing an expansive understanding of media, maintaining, "The elemental legacy of the media concept is fully relevant in a time when our most pervasive surrounding environment is technological and nature—from honeybees and dogs to corn and viruses, from the ocean floor to the atmosphere—is drenched with human manipulation."[26] Thus for instance he turns to the element of water, and more particularly the ocean, as a medium in which a great diversity of life exists.

As an illustration of Peters's notion of infrastructuralism, he particularly highlights dolphins for the great hold they have on the human imagination. For him, they especially represent life without infrastructure. Dolphins have great intellectual abilities but no ability to build infrastructure in order to create enduring civilization. They do not have hands or paper for writing and sharing ideas or memories. In the depths, sun and moon do not move through the sky as a means of keeping time. Fire does not burn in water, and so they have no access to controllable energy sources for the development of technological advances. Thus dolphins live without these basic infrastructures that Peters suggests are foundational to how humanity processes the world and intuits meaning within it.

---

24. Peters, *The Marvelous Clouds*, 34.
25. Ibid., 38.
26. Ibid., 2.

This is not to say, Peters would add, that dolphins are without culture or communication. He points out several techniques that he considers dolphins to have. For example, they communicate with each other through sounds travelling across vast distances of water. Thus the water becomes a medium full of meaning. He posits, "Cetaceans could certainly be capable of what Hannah Arendt calls 'action,' the bringing of new political orders into being.... They are also capable of what she calls 'labor,' tasks that reproduce life itself."[27] In other words, they have techniques of social structures and conceivably some form of art, but nothing that lasts. In this, Peters sees the blessing of infrastructure for humanity.

Infrastructure, for Peters, is what allows techniques to lead to technologies. Technology, he tells us, is distinguished from technique by having durable materiality.[28] Thus he explains, "In cars, detailing and diagnostics are techniques, but camshafts and crankcases are technologies."[29] A technology externalizes a technique into a durable form. This robust exteriority allows our techniques to endure our absence so that others can benefit from them even when we are not there.

Yet Peters does not conceive of technology as being limited to human creations. As we will see below, this is a significant distinction from Tillich's understanding of technology. Peters notes that the marking of those that have gone before us are inscribed in our bodies, "whose structure and DNA testify to a long history of the departed and absent."[30] Indeed bodies are essential to technology. They are, for Peters, the fundamental infrastructural medium for humans, as they are a matrix of interdependent ecosystems that are in constant nonverbal communication with each other as well as the environments and ecosystems that surround the body. The mind, he suggests, is a technology for managing and coordinating the unfathomable and chaotic mix of semiotic systems at play within the body, so that "our bodies and minds are technical and cultural in their anatomy and physiology. They have evolved to flourish in artificial habitats in which we can burn meanings from plants, animals, the earth, and ourselves."[31] The structures of our bodies shape the meanings we take from the systems that we are immersed in, and these meanings are passed on through cultural means that in turn shape our bodies

27. Ibid., 85.
28. Ibid., 87.
29. Ibid., 90.
30. Ibid., 91.
31. Ibid., 267.

in various ways, such as through a learned recognition of which plants to take into our bodies as food or medicine. Of course, this same argument could be applied to dolphins and a multitude of other animals to insist that they have technologies as well. Peters himself seems to vacillate a bit on whether bodies are a technology or the medium of technology.

Embodied technology is an important point for Peters, because, he argues, "technology in patriarchal societies (i.e. civilization) has been conceived in a masculinist fashion, as tools of governing and organizing matter rather than as techniques of producing and caring for people and their bodies."[32] Thus Peters's arguing for bodies as technologies is an attempt to recognize the power dynamics of gender, class, and other divisions, even while also recognizing that historically elite males have dominated the production and use of externalized technologies as a means of control. It is a helpful reminder not just to consider embodied aspects of technology, but also not to limit our understanding of technology to devices allowing control and mastery but to include means of nurturing life. Indeed, Peters lifts up Leroi-Gourhan's identification of the feet as the defining characteristic of humanity. Human bipedal feet free up the hands for gestures and writing, while at the same time "enabl[ing] dance and poetry (whose basic unit is the foot),"[33] Peters explains. Such increased options for communication meanwhile helped provide an impetus for the development of the human brain to recognize these means of communication.[34] Thus human bodily infrastructure enables art as we know it. Art expresses human intuitions of meaning; what is the ramification, then, of understanding cyberspace as a disembodied plane? Is art negated in the realm of ones and zeroes? The magnitude of this question will become clearer in later chapters, and so we will return to it later. Yet it is important here to see art as being among the examples of technologies that do not seek to subdue others but rather to nurture the depth of meaning of life.

We must deal now with what is meant by "media." Media functions as a storehouse of meaning. Meaning in this sense is not simply mental content organized for human communication, Peters contends. Rather, he understands meaning as "repositories of readable data and processes

---

32. Ibid., 99.
33. Ibid., 268.
34. Peters also references Daniel Lieberman's *The Evolution of the Human Head* on this point; ibid., 268.

that sustain and enable existence,"[35] so that technologies are a means for nature (in an encompassing sense that includes humanity) to engage media and thereby express itself and engage in processes whereby it is altered. A medium is thus a space in which the give and take of life occurs, though it is not immediately recognized as such. Instead, Peters suggests, "A medium reveals a medium—as medium. Without other media, a medium is not a medium. Is the ship or the sea the medium? To dolphins the sea could be a medium: they are their own ships. But only nondolphins can see that the sea is a medium to them."[36] Thus a medium unveils a space in which meaning is shared. There is an endless web of media in which nature and technology are intertwined, where the inorganic, organic, and human play off one another. Infrastructure—natural and technological, if the two are indeed distinct—provides the basis for the media soup.

This leads us to the relationship between technology and media. Technology, Peters contends, creates media. That is, for example, he suggests that the ocean only becomes a medium—at least for humans—with the invention of a ship. "In contrast to dolphins," he observes, "humans can live and flourish at sea only by ship, and the same is true a fortiori for the sky. The ship is thus an enduring metaphor of the ways in which we stake our survival on artificial habitats amid hostile elements—that is, our radical dependence on technics."[37] Ship metaphors recur whenever we ponder the ontology of environments. Along with seacraft, aircraft, and spacecraft, it is hard to miss the oceanic metaphors of cyberspace—a computer's docks and ports, surfing the web, navigating websites, even the "net" conjures up images of fishermen, and so forth. Returning to our water image, the technology of the ship allows humans to enter into the media of the sea. Indeed, Peters argues, "[the ship] is an arch-medium that reveals the ontological indiscernibility of medium and world. Your being depends radically on the craft."[38] The ship is an artificial ground on which being can stand. It is the means of entry to the ocean; a technology of human civilization that mediates the experience of the more-than-human world. Further technology, such as scuba diving, allows for greater submersion (quite literally) in the media of the ocean. This greater sub-

35. Ibid., 4.
36. Ibid., 111.
37. Ibid., 101.
38. Ibid., 102.

mersion allows entry into greater access into the meaning communicated through the media. Instead of the ocean being viewed as vast emptiness, submersible technology has allowed us a glimpse of the vast array of life in it, the whale songs that reverberate about it, and through fiber-optic cables also traverse the sea communicating meaning to those that have the technology to decode it. Technology thus allows entry into the depths of meaning present within media. The production of technology, meanwhile, requires the backbone of infrastructure.

Having taken this elemental detour into media and infrastructure, how does this aid our quest to understand the meaning of cyberspace? Cyberspace is a medium accessed by technology. It is a realm of information that can be shared through the access of a variety of devices and technologies. It and those who engage in it are altered through the shared interaction. In this Peters sees digital technologies as a means of return to more fundamental elemental media of water, air, earth, and fire that a focus on communicative media overlooks. Indeed, for Peters, despite the nautical imagery and pretensions of being an ethereal "cloud," cyberspace is essentially an earth-and-fire–bound technology. It is built on computational power of computers and cables and other earthy materials and fueled by electricity predominately produced from the fires of fossil fuels. The infrastructural technology transforms stored data into a media web of shared meaning. It is a medium rich in potential for altering the life forces of the world—indeed perhaps even transforming them, as Barlow and others hope—but that meaning must be accessed by human created technologies, which brings with it the infrastructural realities of imbalances of power, injustice, gender issues, ecological issues, and all of the other issues of the old creation.

An important aspect of media technology for our discussion is that it is marked by the characteristic of nonsimultinaity. The transmission of meaning and its reception are nonsimultaneous. The message must travel through the medium. The difference in time may be imperceptible, as when the sound of the words spoken by the person sitting next to me travel through the medium of the air and reach my ears even as I see their lips moving. Yet the difference can also be large. Peters wonders about how dolphins perceive messages sent through the water across vast distances. Within cyberspace there is also a processing lag that occurs in communication, so that even direct conversation is not simultaneous: "The circumference of 'now' is defined by signal speed," as Peters frames it.[39] Thus there is a distortion of time through media. Yet it is more than a slight difference in processing times. Media technology brings into question what is meant by presence as well as time. Writing, for example, is a simulation of presence that crosses time and distance. Ideas and people from long ago and far away appear in the present tense as we read words by them. It does more than simulate presence, in fact: it creates a new type of absent presence. Cyberspace heightens this blurring of the line between past and present and circumventing distance through its speed. It allows for an experience of "real-time" communication across the globe. Yet it can also distort or stop time. We have mentioned lag time due to processing time that disrupts the feel of real time connection. Yet online communication such as through social media can also have a timeless quality. Peters mentions the ability to stall time in order to compose one's thoughts in a text message in a way that would be impossible in a face-to-face conversation as an example of this. While Peters discusses these issues at length in terms of the social ramifications of these forms of communication, for our purposes what is important is that time functions differently within cyberspace. As we shall see, this is an important aspect of Tillich's definition of a dimension of life. What is unique in cyberspace is the mixing of types of telepresence, including written, audio, video, images, data, with their different flows of time, along with the infrastructural fluctuations of data transmission speeds. Peters's theory of infrastructuralism thus opens theological possibilities and a helpful framework for understanding the breadth of cyberspace.

Peters further contends that the capacity for making meaning accessible at such a vast scale gives cyberspace unique religious significance. Indeed, he attempts to point to some theological implications of this media.[40] In particular he points to a connection between Google's attempt to categorize all human information into a database with the concept of divine omniscience.[41] Elsewhere he engages briefly in more philosophically sophisticated theological discussion, in particular discussing negative

---

39. Ibid., 93.

40. Peters is a self-professed Mormon and has done interviews linking his academic work with his faith. Yorgasan, "The Gospel in Communication."

41. We do not have space here to discuss the long history of debate over whether omniscience is a divine attribute and if so what the nature of that omniscience is. However, few of its defenders would equate divine omniscience with being a mere database in such simplistic fashion. Peters himself notes that this equation is a trend of popular culture decried by many traditional churches. See Peters, *The Marvelous Clouds*, 335.

theology and Scotus Erigena's definition of God as *nihilum*. He dismisses this approach, arguing, "All things that exist are particular, including deity. From this finitist view follows a theology not of nonexisting entities but of superhuman ones, a theology absolutely central to the question concerning technology."[42] For him, then, the god of a technological theology is one that can transcend human limitation. I appreciate the gesture of recognizing the tradition of negative theology, even as I find little use for his inclination to preference God as a being or deity over a more Tillichian sense of the divine as the Ground of Being. Indeed here I see the theological limits of the infrastructuralist approach. It cannot speak of the excesses and forces and callings that provide the wellspring for the accumulation of infrastructure. It lacks a space for the *potentia absoluta* of God, which for Tillich was a powerful articulation of a sense of the divine lying behind the structures and infrastructures and thus highlighting the contingency of existence, a "perennial threat to any given structure of things."[43] Infrastructuralism cannot speak to the abyss of structure such as is found in a theology of the cross paired with the concept of the deep hiddenness of God. Such theology contends that divine meaning is encountered in the cracks and fissures created by the limitations of cultural and physical structures and infrastructures.[44] We cannot deal fully with these theological objections here, however; nor are they central to the helpfulness of the infrastructuralist approach for understanding the nature of cyberspace. We will, however, return to these themes in the final chapter.

More theologically interesting to me in drawing from Peters's analysis is the blurring of presence and distance. Such blurring, I would argue, is crucial to Christian theology, in that it is a theology of the Word. A word is a media technology that simulates presence or creates an absent presence. Christian theology arises through an ongoing engagement with the words of Scripture as a means of mediating the presence of the divine. At the same time, it proclaims Christ as the Word of God, the divine communication made flesh. Drawing on Peters, then, we can understand Christ, incarnate and resurrected, as an embodied *technology* that communicates and creates a new form of presence of divinity that has durable

42. Ibid., 370.

43. Tillich, ST1, 168.

44. For more of my theological reflection on the *potentia Dei absoluta*, the hiddenness of God, and the theology of the cross in engagement with Tillich's thought, see Trozzo, *Rupturing Eschatology*, especially chapter 3.

materiality (sacramentality). The Word becomes an infrastructure enabling the engagement with the divine.

We can thus see, then, that infrastructuralism opens the door for theological rumination. In order to return to the issue of the meaning of cyberspace and the role of the divine within it, however, let us turn next to the specifically Christian theological attempts to grapple with this question, followed by a discussion of Tillich's understanding of the dimensions of life. This will then allow us to see how Peters and Tillich can be useful in sharpening the theological analysis of cyberspace.

Cyberspace and Christian Theologies of Evolution

One of the first specifically theological investigations into the nature of cyberspace was Jennifer Cobb's book *Cybergrace: The Search for God in the Digital World*, published in 1998, at a time when the World Wide Web was just beginning to become ubiquitously part of day-to-day life for a large number of people. She is writing not long after Barlow's "Declaration," for example. The book is aimed at a popular audience and so, as we shall see, is somewhat fuzzy or simplified on many of the details; her goal is more in provoking thought about cyberspace than giving a precise academic account. For her, a reductionist view of cyberspace as merely machines running software is simply wrong. She insists, "By definition, cyberspace is what happens when software and hardware are joined together and put *into motion*."[45] In the working together, something new is created. It is this novelty that emerges from the interaction that is essential to Cobb's thought on cyberspace. We find some resonance here with Peters's sense of technology being a space where processes of life occur.

While not as exuberant as Barlow, Cobb is certainly optimistic about the possibilities being opened by cyberspace. She writes, "Although still in its early stages, cyberspace appears to be coevolving with a more global worldview, one that transcends the limitations of the democratic nation-state."[46] At the same time, she also notes that it is far from given that cyberspace will indeed deliver on its promise, and may in fact only serve to further the needs of corporate interests. She contends, "The process of fully integrating cyberspace in a healthy manner will require enormous

---

45. Cobb, *Cybergrace*, 50. Author's italics.
46. Ibid., 110.

consciousness from each of us. This is the great evolutionary test."[47] Thus she sees cyberspace as presenting a unique new opportunity for human development even while harboring potential danger.

Cobb frames cyberspace as fundamentally an interactive immersive experience. That is, it differs from other immersive experiences such as reading a book or watching television in that the flow of information is multidirectional. Cyberspace grants agency to users. It is this interactive ability that gives cyberspace a quality of fluidity, where new experiences constantly emerge and immerse us in their flow. For Peters this would be the way that cyberspace calls us back to the more fundamental elemental aspect of media, rather than the communicative media such as writing or television. Cobb notes that for a computer, the basis of reality is the computational process, thus underscoring process as the ultimate reality of cyberspace. Theologically, then, she contends, "The continual movement of self through cyberspace—processes leading to processes—undermines the tidy, rational linearity of the purely scientific worldview."[48] By this she means that computer reality is not ruled by a stereotypically Enlightenment sense of linear material cause and effect but rather by the relationality of a network, so that in cyberspace something "more than" mere materiality is experienced. One might question Cobb on the role that data plays in the reality of a computer. Recalling Peters, meanwhile, we can note that cyberspace is hardly the only interactive immersive media experience; scuba diving would be an example of a literal interactive immersion in media that contains a surplus of meaning. Cobb here comes across as being a bit breathlessly caught up in the romance of cyberspace, along the lines of Barlow.

Indeed for Cobb there is no room for the divine within the realm of material cause and effect. Again here her reference to material cause and effect is a trope for a rather clichéd sense of Enlightenment thought. For her the divine is best understood as creativity itself. Cyberspace likewise is not confined by material cause and effect, but rather is a realm of rapid creative emergence, in Cobb's analysis. Thus even though cyberspace can be considered a human creation, it allows for the pure creativity that is the domain of the divine. Here we might question her about the withdrawal of infrastructure from her analysis of cause and effect in cyberspace. At any rate, Cobb argues that cyberspace is theologically important because it transcends the limits of physicality and allows for a renewed

47. Ibid., 113.
48. Ibid., 11.

engagement with the divine. Specifically, it allows her to reconsider God and cyberspace from a variety of idealistic and evolutionary philosophical frameworks, including Platonic, Whiteheadian, and Teilhardian.

From a Platonic viewpoint, Cobb suggests that cyberspace can be seen as a space that seems removed from the physical world. It is, she holds, a realm of pure information, images, and symbols that can be seen as the realization of the Platonic realm of the forms. She further points to the binary mathematical basis of computers as the creation of a realm where ideas are regnant and directly experienceable. She writes, "The software that forms the technical heart of cyberspace, the instructions that make it run, are all coded in binary sequences of either 0s or 1s.... These glorified calculators use mathematics to create a palpable world of experience analogous to Plato's world of forms."[49] Here we see a resonance with Barlow's civilization of the mind that exists everywhere and nowhere with no need for bodies. Cobb is appreciative of this framing.

Yet the Platonic viewpoint is insufficient for fully comprehending cyberspace, Cobb holds. She writes, "One moves through the Web on an almost infinite variety of pathways that are related and connected by virtue of their participation in the network of cyberspace. As we move through this computational space, our fundamental notions about the world are challenged, and even Plato's classical image only partially satisfies our desire to understand."[50] There are two factors that challenge the Platonic framework for understanding cyberspace. One is its linking a physical network with an electronic ecosystem, thus challenging Platonic dualism between the forms and the physical world. The other is that cyberspace is an abstract realm that is nonetheless filled with human experience. In these we see some appreciation for the ideas raised by the consideration of infrastructure in more recent media studies. Because human interaction is poured into the abstract space, Cobb holds, it is not a static realm, as the Platonic realm of the Forms is. Cyberspace is continually forming new connections and encompassing new materials. In short, it evolves. Thus Cobb turns to theologies with an evolutionary sensibility to supplement her Platonic vision of cyberspace.

Cobb's focus on the reality of cyberspace being one of process naturally lends itself to Whiteheadian process thought. She thus engages the work of John B. Cobb, Jr. (no relation), even while noting that it is no

49. Ibid., 31.
50. Ibid., 33.

small irony to employ the thought of a theologian particularly known for the ecological importance of his work for considering a human-made environment like cyberspace. In particular, she draws on John Cobb's Whiteheadian notion of the divine as the creative force of life. The power of life is more than a biological concept. Rather, John Cobb holds, "The power of life is not limited to clearly living things, and we may think of life as exerting its gentle pressure everywhere, encouraging each thing to become more than it is."[51] Life is the process of unfolding novelty. Such novelty need not be limited to the biological sphere, but may include inanimate things as well. Life is concerned with the production of creative novelty. Even inanimate objects can participate to a degree in the creative process of novelty. Novelty here is more than mere change; rather it is the possibility of change that runs counter to the basic force of entropy. Novelty is thus a transcending of the forces of the past in bringing forth creative newness. Such forces of emergence are not restricted to organic entities. Thus Jennifer Cobb contends, "Computers are infused with emergence, with novelty, with life as [John] Cobb understands it."[52] Indeed, as cyberspace continues to evolve it becomes more self-organizing and self-generating, and thus to Jennifer Cobb a space through which divine creative persuasion flows.

In other words, Jennifer Cobb uses John Cobb's thought to suggest that the divine is therefore also active within cyberspace. Cyberspace is a realm of creativity, where human ideas take on an active force. Cyberspace is a phenomenon that emerges out of interactions between computers that together bring new connections and behaviors to fruition. To be clear, the argument is not that computers are alive in a biological sense, but rather that they are sites of creativity and so have a vibrancy through which novelty emerges. Together, then, computers create cyberspace, which is a realm in which creativity might be experienced. Experience in these Whiteheadian terms is participation in its surrounding environment. The degree to which participation is possible in cyberspace is what differentiates it from other forms of media. It is a realm in which ideas participate in their surrounding environment and interactively create virtual forms. Yet again, however, Cobb's focus is primarily on the growth of content within cyberspace. It is also worth noting how similar this understanding of cyberspace as a space of creative interaction that brings

---

51. Birch and Cobb, Jr., *The Liberation of Life*, 189. Quoted in Cobb, *Cybergrace*, 56.
52. Cobb, *Cybergrace*, 58–59.

forth novelty is to Peters's understanding of media as a space where the give and take of life occurs.

After engaging with process metaphysics for comprehending cyberspace, Jennifer Cobb turns to Pierre Teilhard de Chardin for framing the theological implications of the emergent nature of cyberspace. More recently, Italian Catholic theologian Antonio Spadaro, in his book *Cybertheology*, has also pointed to ways in which the Teilhardian vision might be illuminative of the nature of cyberspace. Indeed, given that Spadaro gives the most sustained theological reflection on cyberspace since Cobb and the Teilhardian vision is central to both of their reflections, it is worth taking the time to review the basic contours of his thought.

Spadaro notes passages where "Teilhard de Chardin attributed to technological communications a fundamental role in the creation of a communal consciousness, of a sort of brain constituted by interconnections, not of nonthinking fibers, but of other thinking brains."[53] This web of thinking interconnections constitutes what Teilhard de Chardin terms the "noosphere." The noosphere is a type of collective consciousness that progressively encircles the globe through the process of evolution. The divine in this thought drives evolution to ever-greater consciousness. There is a link between this collective consciousness and telecommunications technology. He ponders:

> how can we fail to see the machine as playing a constructive part in the creation of a truly collective consciousness? It is not merely a matter of the machine which liberates, relieving both individual and collective thought of the trammels which hinder its progress, but also of the machine which creates, helping to assemble, and to concentrate in the form of an ever more deeply penetrating organism, all the reflective elements upon earth.[54]

He goes on to specify that the machines he has in mind are radio, television, and electronic computers. Such speculation is certainly prescient, given that it was first published in 1959.

For Teilhard de Chardin, we move through history towards the Omega Point in different stages. The lithosphere is the lifeless inorganic base that forms the bedrock of life. From it, the biosphere emerges, where dynamic life—including plant, animal, and eventually human life—appears and evolves. According to N. M. Wildiers, in his introduction to

---

53. Spadaro, *Cybertheology*, 99.
54. Teilhard de Chardin, *The Future of Man*, 161–62.

Teilhard de Chardin's thought, this phase "is characterized by the emergence and marvellous upsurge and progress of life, which added an entirely new aspect to our earth, encircling it with a wonderful covering of plant growth and populating it with an infinite variety of changing forms of life."[55] Beyond the biosphere comes the noosphere. This is the realm of knowledge and thought, with is shared ever more communally. This realm of the mind began to appear, for Teilhard, over the past several hundred years. As greater levels of abstract thought and the ability to share thoughts and knowledge has increased, the earth has slowly been "enveloped" by this cloud of thought. Eventually its destination is the Omega Point of history. At the Omega Point the resurrection of Christ encapsulates the meaning of history. Wildiers explains, "The point Omega is indeed the element that imparts to the whole of cosmic evolution its final unity—the point at which multiplicity is reduced to unity and on which all the threads of history converge. It is just such a function that we are to ascribe to Christ."[56] Yet even more than this unity of multiplicity, in the Teilhardian vision Christ is in fact the goal of evolution. The lithosphere reaches its fullness in providing the ground for the biosphere, and the biosphere culminates in humanity. Humanity produces the noosphere, and this mind is centered on Christ. Christ is centered on the divine. Thus evolution is a process of maturation towards divinity that reaches fullness in Christ. Again turning to Wildiers, "As Teilhard envisaged it, we could say that the world is an instrument for realizing the total Christ."[57] Thus we see in Teilhard a hierarchical arrangement of movement from inorganic towards divinity as well as a system that is not ever-expanding but rather directed towards convergence.

For Spadaro and others, it is no great leap to jump from this cloud of thought of the noosphere to the digital cloud of cyberspace. He points to Teilhard de Chardin's question, raised in the 1940s: "What would humanity become if, to be absurd, it had perhaps been free to thin out and expand indefinitely on an unconfined surface, in other terms, if it had perhaps been abandoned only to the one game of interior affinities?"[58] For Spadaro this question is prophetic of the reality of cyberspace, which he sees as an unlimited realm of human consciousness and cognitive

---

55. Wildiers, *Introduction to Teilhard de Chardin*, 65.

56. Ibid., 138.

57. Ibid., 139.

58. Teilhard de Chardin, *The Phenomenon of Man*, 264. Quoted in Spadaro, *Cybertheology*, 101.

interconnectivity. Indeed, he appreciatively notes Jennifer Cobb's use of the Teilhardian vision. In particular, he echoes her contention: "The levels of information and of global connectivity that are available through cyberspace can strengthen our experiences of 'harmonized complexity,' the experiences of being at the same time free to express the uniqueness of our 'I' while we participate in a context that is synthetic and global."[59] For both Spadaro and Jennifer Cobb, such connectivity of consciousness while retaining individual identity is constitutive of cyberspace as well as the enactment of the Teilhardian vision.

The image of cyberspace as the realization of a Teilhardian noosphere takes us back to Platonic thinking, as it conjures up the image of the Platonic *khora*. For Plato, *khora* was the placeless place of potentiality. It was that from which all possibility emerges. It is tempting to construe cyberspace in this manner, as a disembodied space of possibility. There is a certain sense in these Teilhardian schemes of a movement away from the body towards a pure consciousness, even though as we have seen that cyberspace itself cannot be disconnected from the physical components that support it.

I worry, however, about this close connection between consciousness and divinity. I am troubled by the relegation of embodiment to a phase that must be transcended within both evolution and the process of the divine spirit, even as we consider what the theological significance of non-embodied space might be. If we recall Peters's argument that the mind is a technology for managing the various ecosystems of the body, then a disembodied mind becomes obsolete technology. It no longer serves a purpose. Turning aside questions of divinity for a moment, human minds without bodies or cyberspace without its earthbound infrastructure would constitute a loss of the infrastructural essence of humanity and cyberspace, respectively. Theologically, meanwhile, the equation of the divine with consciousness constitutes a transcendence without immanence. It is a fantasy of an unmediated God; it loses the sacramental presence of the Word.

All in all, these Teilhardian images of cyberspace seem rather optimistic. To be sure, as we have noted, Jennifer Cobb recognizes some potential dangers within the growth of cyberspace. Most notably, she warns of the economic domination of cyberspace. She notes, "The worldwide communications systems of cyberspace work primarily to serve the

---

59. Cobb, *Cybergrace*, 96; quoted in Spadaro, *Cybertheology*, 103.

economic needs of first-world countries.... Global marketing and media are blurring cultural and local specificity, creating a homogenized world based on the lowest common denominator of economic advantage."[60] Yet in these theories these problems seem to be but a temporary roadblock on the path to the Omega Point. At the very least, Jennifer Cobb seems to believe that it is at least possible to overcome these issues of justice within cyberspace through a turn to greater consciousness. If that were ever possible, twenty years later it seems much less likely that humanity will find in cyberspace the realization of such idealism. I would, in fact, argue more strongly that the ambiguities of cyberspace have never been possible to fully overcome for humanity because the justice issues of humanity are built into the infrastructures that allow the presence of cyberspace. Recent concern with cybersecurity has only made clear what had already been true. While there is certainly potential within cyberspace to challenge the imbedded injustices of the old creation in a unique manner, such challenges can appear in a transitory manner only due to cyberspace being forged within the confines of that old creation.

Indeed, the loss of materiality haunts the consciousness-based visions of cyberspace. What of the physical infrastructure that holds up the existence of cyberspace? Spadaro, for instance, ruminates on the nature of virtual existence. He offers, "It leaves aside the physical, but offers a form, that is sometimes also vivid, of social presence. This is unquestionably not simply a product of the conscience, an image of the mind; nor is it a *res extensa*, an ordinary, objective reality, because it also exists only when there is interaction."[61] This would seem to suggest that he is only considering the social interaction of cyberspace and not its infrastructural aspects, though he does go on to suggest that cyberspace is a hybrid reality. Part of what he wishes to highlight here, it would seem, is the collapsing together of reality and information about reality that occurs in cyberspace. Cyber reality is an interactive informational reality. It is in this sense that cyberspace challenges simple understandings of the "metaphysics of presence," Spadaro notes.[62] Presence, that is, is virtual and mediated through avatars and other digital means in cyberspace. Yet if we recall from Peters, all presence is mediated to some extent, even if only over a short distance and through the medium of air. I have also sug-

60. Cobb, *Cybergrace*, 111.
61. Spadaro, *Cybertheology*, 81.
62. Ibid.

gested theologically that Christian theology is meditation on the mediation of the divine through the Word, creating a type of absent presence. Thus through media telepresence, time, and distance are mediated in new ways that foster new forms of presence.

For Spadaro, cyberspace is ever available but not located anywhere. Yet he seems more concerned about the mediated access to this reality and social interaction as a hybrid of virtual and concrete than he is about a hybridity of machine and cloud. That is, his concern for understanding the nature of cyberspace seems to focus on the *content* of the Internet rather than cyberspace in its fullness. To be sure, on the theological side he does affirm the necessity of physical matter in the sacraments and ultimately considers cyberspace to be but one component of the space through which God may be active within the world and in which Christianity may express its faith. Thus he does not argue for a simple theological dualism. Nonetheless, his framing of cyberspace and its relation to divinity focuses on the content of cyberspace and thus remains somewhat disembodied. This would seem to be a limitation of the focus on an eschatology of pure consciousness inherent in the Teilhardian scheme.

Jennifer Cobb, however, does not abandon the physical facet of cyberspace entirely. Rather, she offers up Ken Wilber's conception of holoarchies. This is a framework for understanding complex interconnecting systems. It is a similar paradigm to Tillichian dimensionality, though Cobb does not offer a compelling theological account from the holoarchic system that one would find in a Tillichian scheme.[63] Thus the specific details of this particular framework are of less importance than the recognition that for Cobb there is an important element of materiality in cyberspace that is not inherently of lesser value than its aspects of consciousness. That is, for her, the computer machine, the software it runs, and the human interactivity and the novelty it creates are all independently real but equally essential to cyberspace.[64]

In fact, the exact details of Cobb's religious vision have some difficulties in holding together, as she seems content to accept each of the metaphysical systems she considers: Platonic, Whiteheadian, Teilhardian, and

---

63. I am not giving complete account or critique of Wilber here, but rather am focused on how his thought is utilized by Cobb. Cobb does indeed discuss Wilber's understanding of Spirit, but I find Tillich's ideas to be of greater use in this inquiry than what she presents of Wilber, even as they seem to have some significant resonances with one another.

64. See Cobb, *Cybergrace*, 102–4 for her discussion of Wilber and holons.

Holoarchic. More pointedly, her discussion of the movement towards what she dubs the "theosphere" draws equally from each of them. She draws the term *theosphere* from the Teilhardian vocabulary, noting that "theos" transcends "noos" just as "noos" transcends "bios." In speaking of spirit, however, she quotes Wilber discussing that the ultimate Omega point as the utter formlessness of transcendent spirit.[65] Yet again she turns to the process vision of John Cobb, holding that "Spirit is, by its very definition, that which moves through all aspects of ourselves in the form of emergent creativity."[66] Thus she leaves considerable ambiguity on where exactly she stands on these issues. To be fair, she is not attempting to work out a complete metaphysics of cyberspace so much as to insist that there is spiritual significance to it. Yet while there is indeed a considerable amount of resonance between the proposals in that they are attempts to understand the dynamism of increasing systemic complexity, they are not identical. Further, I would argue, the differences between them make a difference in how we comprehend the meaning of cyberspace. Before moving forward with these issues, however, it is necessary to add in another theological theoretical framework for dynamism, Paul Tillich's discussion of "dimensions" of life, in order to fully lay out the concerns we are facing.

Tillich's Dimensions of Life

Tillich contends that life is characterized by "multi-dimensional unity." This is specifically a rejection of hierarchical terms such as "levels" of existence. He employs, rather, the metaphors of "dimension" and "realm" as preferable as better descriptions of differing aspects or forms of life. No dimension is "better" or "more real" than the others. Rather, the dimensions have a type of mutual interdependence. As Tillich scholar Frederick J. Parrella explains, "In one dimension of life, therefore, all dimensions are potentially present, while some may be actualized; they cut through each other and do not interfere with each other."[67] Thus for Tillich there is an interpenetration of dimensions yet still distinctions between them.

More specifically, some dimensions require other dimensions in order to be actualized, such as the organic requiring the inorganic to first be

---

65. Ibid., 122.
66. Ibid., 123.
67. Parrella, "Tillich's Theology of the Concrete Spirit," 76.

actualized. Yet, Tillich holds, other conditions are also required in order to actualize a new dimension. For example, he holds, "Billions of years may have passed before the inorganic realm permitted the appearance of objects in the organic dimension, and millions of years before the organic realm permitted the appearance of a being with language."[68] A host of conditions must be met before a potential dimension may be actualized. When the conditions arise, then the potentiality in one dimension for another dimension is realized and this additional dimension appears as a distinct dimension or realm. Indeed, Tillich includes "realm" as an equally preferred metaphor because it holds to the unity and yet distinctness of the various dimensions. He notes, "One can use the term 'realm' to indicate a section of life in which a particular dimension is predominant."[69] That is, again, all dimensions are potentially present in all aspects of life for Tillich, but a realm indicates an aspect of life particularly characterized by the presence of one particular dimension.

While all dimensions are present in all other dimensions, not all dimensions are of equal value. Tillich contends, "That which presupposes something else and adds to it is by so much the richer."[70] Thus the actualization of a dimension increases the value of a form of life. For Tillich, humanity in adding the historical dimension to all of the previous dimensions achieved the highest level of being, and as such is "the highest being in the realm of our experience."[71] Highest here does not mean more perfect, Tillich hastens to add. Perfection has to do with the degree to which a being actualizes the potentialities available to it. Thus a rock or an insect or a dog may well be more perfect than a human. Rather, humanity should be seen as the being that has the most potentiality that can be actualized, and in this sense has more value available to it.

Tillich discusses several dimensions of being, although he does not give a definitive list of dimensions. He focuses on the inorganic, the organic, the spiritual, the psychological, and the historical. He in fact holds that there is no definite number of dimensions, and outlines what he calls "flexible criteria" for a dimension. He elucidates, "One is justified in speaking of a particular dimension when the phenomenological description of a section of encountered reality shows unique categorical

---

68. Paul Tillich, ST3, 16.
69. Ibid., 16.
70. Ibid., 17.
71. Ibid.

and other structures."[72] For our purposes, the question is whether or not the cyber might be considered as an additional dimension.

Tillich suggests that the character of a dimension "can best be seen in the modification of time, space, causality, and substance under its predominance. These categories have universal validity for everything that exists."[73] He continues to explain that all things have a definite time and space but that different dimensions have time and space differently. Thus for example, "In historical time or causality, all preceding forms of time or causality are present, but they are not the same as they were before."[74] On the one hand, we can see the challenge in speaking of cyberspace here, in that it does not fully exist in an objective form in which time, space, causality, and substance exist. Yet might that in fact be an argument for understanding cyberspace as a dimension, in that it challenges the way we frame these concepts as universal? As we have seen, time, space, causality, and substance certainly cannot be thought in the same way in cyberspace as they are in other dimensions, yet at the same time because it is supported by a physical computer network the preceding forms are indeed still present to cyberspace.

Before pursuing this question further, however, let us recall that Tillich is discussing here dimensions of life. Thus before answering these questions, the first questions are how Tillich defines life and how this definition might apply to the cyber realm. For him, everything alive has three basic movements: self-identity, self-alteration, and a return to oneself. Parrella explains, "These movements, which create the pattern of going out from one's self-identity and returning to oneself, takes place in life's three functions: self-integration, self-creation and self-transcendence."[75] Tillich laments the lack of a "theology of the inorganic" in much religious thought, insisting that it must be included in discussions of life and the ambiguities of life because all dimensions presuppose the inorganic. He notes that concepts such as "becoming" and "process" are essential to the concept of life, but wants to further emphasize that also characteristic of all life is the creation of something new. Thus even a non-organic chemical reaction, for instance, in creating something new participates to a degree in life, and in that such reactions are required for

---

72. Ibid.
73. Ibid., 18.
74. Ibid.
75. Parrella, "Tillich's Theology of Concrete Spirit," 76.

organic life the chemicals hold within them the potential of actualizing other dimensions of life.

Yet it is the spiritual dimension that is Tillich's primary focus. For him, Spirit is the ultimate, all-embracing dimension of life. Spirit infuses the other dimensions and brings meaning from them. Spirit, for Tillich, is seen in humanity alone, and comes as a transcending of the historical and psychological dimensions, rather than a dualism opposed to them. Thus the spiritual dimension is more than self-awareness; it is the process of actualizing potentialities and overcoming the ambiguity of estranged existence. Yet he adds, "There is no straight and certain way to the norms of action in the dimension of spirit. The sphere of the potential is partly visible, partly hidden." Thus any concrete movement in or explanation of the dimension of spirit is a risk subject to failure; in fact failure is at least partly assured as the dimension is always only glimpsed, not fully revealed. The full revelation of the dimension of spirit as the unambiguous life is only anticipated, known through metaphors such as the kingdom of God.

In turning, then, to the three basic movements of life, we see the spiritual dimension at work in humanity. In the spiritual dimension, the unity of being and meaning is found. That is, the power of being (God) and the New Being (Christ) is unified in life as Spirit. Or again, Spirit is the fulfillment of creation and salvation, making the unambiguous life possible. Parrella describes, "The divine Spirit creates unambiguous life within the spirit's centre; it elevates the human spirit into the realm beyond the distinction of subject-object."[76] The divine Spirit, then, is the ground on which all of the dimensions rest. The Spirit works through the dimensions, including but not limited to the spiritual, historical, and psychological.

Underlying all of Tillich's theological thought is his distinction between essence and existence. Essence is how things ought to be, but the existential reality is a separation from that essence; he calls this separation "estrangement." Human existence is estranged from its essence. In terms of his understanding of the dimensions of life, the tension between essence and existence must be manifested in each dimension. Looking to his three functions of life—self-integration, self-creation, and self-transcendence—we see the tension at play through all three.

---

76. Ibid., 79.

Self-integration is the maintenance of a centered sense of individualized self. Tillich describes this function as a circular direction, in that the self circles around that which is indivisible within itself, thus coming to a sense of its own identity. He holds that this process occurs in all dimensions. As Parrella explains, "In the inorganic realm, it is a process of concentration and expansion; in the organic realm, the tension between integration and disintegration."[77] Disintegration is the death of self-identity or the ability to incorporate new elements into the centered whole. Disintegration is a force of estrangement constantly threatening healthy and fulfilled life. In the spiritual dimension, self-integration is expressed as morality. Morality here is not following a divine or human law, but rather the overcoming of estrangement. Morality requires a strong sense of self that can view the world as an Other with which there can be an ethical relationship.

Self-creation, meanwhile, is the production of growth and re-creation. In this function, we find the polarity of dynamics and form. Dynamics is the process of becoming something new; form is structure that makes a thing what it is. In order for growth to occur, old forms must be destroyed so that new forms may be built. For Tillich, in the inorganic dimension growth is largely metaphorical, while in the organic realm it is expressed as the tension between vibrancy and the inevitability of death. The tension between life instinct and death instinct bring forth the ambiguities of existence as part of self-creation. Self-creation for Tillich is metaphorically the horizontal direction of life, reaching out for newness. In the spiritual dimension, this is manifested in culture. Culture seeks new expressions of meaning but thus meaning is also continually destroyed due to the various forms of estrangement known through the ambiguities of life.

Of particular interest in this function of life is Tillich's discussion of technology. For Tillich, a "thing" is an object that has no subjectivity. It is only an object for use. Things do not occur naturally but only appear when created through a technical act. The technical act destroys the previous form and re-creates it as a thing: "trees into wood, horses into horsepower, men into quantities of workpower."[78] Yet Tillich notes an ambiguity here: humans create things with which there can be no interrelationship, and thus turn themselves into things as well. "[The]

---

77. Ibid., 77.
78. Tillich, ST3, 74.

self becomes a thing by virtue of producing and directing mere things, and the more reality is transformed in the technical act into a bundle of things," Tillich argues, "the more the transforming subject himself is transformed, [the self] becomes a part of the technical product and loses [its] character as an independent self." Technology is intended to give humanity greater freedom, but for Tillich its actuality in fact brings enslavement. Yet the ambiguity here, he continues, is that it would be unnatural to seek a pretechnical naturalism. Rather, he concludes, this ambiguity of life joins with other ambiguities in seeking unambiguous relations in the kingdom of God.

Tillich, we can see, posits technology as a human creation and as such an aspect of the dimension of Spirit because its creation is an act of human creativity. Yet as we have seen, Peters' infrastructuralist approach problematizes this understanding of technology. Such a framework for technology is disembodied and does not account for the necessary framework required for technologies. In particular, Peters's consideration of technologies of nurturing life functions as a helpful corrective to Tillich's construal of technology. Drawing on Peters as a supplement to Tillich's understanding of dimensions, we might see technology as a dimension in its own right. In fact, it could be seen as coming prior to the psychological and historical dimensions. Indeed, following Peters we might say that the emergence of each new dimension of life requires first the development of the necessary infrastructure to sustain it. Thus for example complex organic life—whether human or not—requires some form of mind to manage its complexities. The mind, we may recall, is for Peters a technology in that it is a durable and material form of perpetuating a technique. Such a technology is a necessary condition for the development of human life that can cultivate psychological and historical dimension. Peters's infrastructural approach thus gives a more fundamental and positive role to technology. Embodied technologies do indeed give humanity identity and freedom, even as they also open up avenues for ambiguity. Technology for him is a means for unlocking meaning held within media.

The third function of life for Tillich is self-transcendence. As Parrella explains, "Properly speaking, self-transcendence is not a function beside the other two functions of the spirit, but a quality of all of them."[79] Self-transcendence is the vertical direction in that it is striving from total bondage to the constraints of finitude towards the freedom of infinite being. This is the religious function of life, and it is the source of unity

---

79. Parrella, "Tillich's Theology of Concrete Spirit," 78.

between morality and culture. Religion provides ultimate seriousness to morality and depth to culture. The religious sphere brings an anticipation of unambiguous life; that is, life as the overcoming of the limitations that separate essence from existence in those other spheres. This unambiguous life is known for Tillich through the metaphors of spiritual presence, the kingdom of God, and eternal life. All three point to the anticipation of unambiguous life that are present in all dimensions of life. They are mutually immanent to one another, Tillich points out, and due to the multidimensional unity of life all three refer to all realms of life, though more directly in some dimensions then others.[80] We might see, for instance, the spiritual presence referring more specifically to the spiritual dimension, the kingdom of God to the historical, and eternal life to the psychological.

The religious life is also subject to ambiguity, however. On the one hand, it faces ambiguity from the profane; that is, that which resists transcendence. On the other hand, ambiguity comes from the demonic, which is a distortion of transcendence. Profanation occurs through the denial or dismissal of the transcendent element. This could occur through a secular reduction of life to morality and culture, or through the indifference of religious institutions to transcendence. Demonization, meanwhile, occurs when the conditional or finite is treated as infinite, unconditioned, and unambiguous.

Tillich and Teilhard de Chardin

James E. Huchingson argues that in Tillich's discussion of dimensions his thought draws quite close to Teilhard de Chardin's. Huchingson employs a third concept, that of "system," as a means of comparing the two. Huchingson defines a system as "a bounded arrangement of parts or components and the relationships between them."[81] He suggests that systems are hierarchically arranged so that simpler units integrate so as to create the next level of a system. He finds Teilhard to be in agreement with him on this, in his statement, "Each element of the cosmos is woven from all others; from beneath itself by the mysterious phenomenon of 'composition,' which makes it subsistent through the apex of an organised whole: and from above through the influence of unities of a higher order which

---

80. Tillich, ST3, 107–9.
81. Huchingson, "Dimensions of Life," 752.

incorporate and dominate it for their own ends."[82] Thus we see for both Huchingson and Teilhard a vertical arrangement of organization.

Yet as we have seen, Tillich resists the language of hierarchy in his preference for the metaphors of dimension and realm. Tillich employs the term *dimension* because of the connotation that multiple dimensions can exist without interference with one another. Huchingson, however, argues, "It is not clear that Tillich has advanced the issue significantly through his introduction of this new cluster of dimensional metaphors to replace those of hierarchy and levels."[83] He continues that he feels Tillich overemphasizes the distinction between levels and underemphasizes the interaction between the levels. For Huchingson it is the mutual interactions of the components of a system that allow for greater levels of complexity, which thus makes more complex systems richer entities. As we have seen, Tillich agrees on this point, and indeed Huchingson admits that Tillich and Teilhard are close together in valuing the complexity while also wanting to honor the integrity of the constituent parts of a system. Indeed, Huchingson notes that "The process Tillich calls life is for Teilhard the universal process of ingathering in which the radically disconnected elements of a field of infinite multiplicity enter into an ever greater and more inclusive association tending towards and finally culminating in a cosmic arrangement of unsurpassable complexity and centeredness, the Omega Point."[84] Thus for Huchingson, Tillich's sense of the emergence of new dimensions can be seen as movement towards a Teilhardian noosphere.

While Huchingson notes a few divergences between the two thinkers that he considers to be minor, one worth closer consideration is the concept of spirit. Huchingson contends, "With respect to the dimension of spirit, Teilhard frequently associates spirit with . . . self-consciousness, sometimes even using this term and others, such as thought, as synonyms."[85] He clarifies that Teilhard does not limit spirit to such consciousness, however, at times speaking of it as something of a spiritual energy that drives towards complexification. As we have seen for Tillich, meanwhile, the dimension of spirit is more of an animating power of life. In fact, Tillich specifically holds that spirit is a transcending of the psy-

---

82. Teilhard de Chardin, *The Phenomenon of Man*, 44. Quoted in Huchingson, "Dimensions of Life," 753.

83. Huchingson, "Dimensions of Life," 753.

84. Ibid., 754–55.

85. Ibid., 755.

chological. Teilhard may at times move close to Tillich's understanding of spirit here, but it would seem that his thought—certainly as employed by the discussions we have seen of Teilhard's thought as a resource from understanding cyberspace—preferences the cognitive more strongly than Tillich does. For Tillich meaning and actualizing potentiality cannot be restricted to the cognitive aspects of existence. Huchingson minimizes this distinction, however, suggesting that Tillich's power of animation can be seen as a drive towards complexity.

Yet I would suggest that these differences on hierarchy and spirit that Huchingson notes are indeed of significance for our question of the meaning of cyberspace. We have seen the tension between those that view cyberspace as a radically egalitarian plane and those that view it as a plane where the hierarchies of the world are continued. Is there a theological stake in this question? Does the Teilhardian sense of movement towards an Omega Point threaten the openness of cyberspace? Conversely, might it be that Teilhardian hierarchy of consciousness over other levels is related to a more horizontal view of cyberspace? This seems at first glance counterintuitive. Yet it is worth noting that Barlow was an early advocate of employing Teilhardian thought to understanding cyberspace.[86] The reasoning could be as follows: because the cognitive is higher than the physical and cyberspace is a cognitive realm, cyberspace should be a higher level of existence than traditional space. Yet as we have seen this way of considering cyberspace downplays physical realities in ways that are theologically troubling. Further, considering cyberspace to be a higher plane of existence has frankly lost credibility today given the amount of attention everyone engaged in cyber activities must give to online self-defense and in considering other cybersecurity issues.

Meanwhile, Teilhard's focus on consciousness in terms of the dimension of spirit is likewise problematic specifically because of its hierarchical nature. Again such a framing risks a de-emphasis on embodiment and the value of multiplicity. In terms of considering cyberspace, meanwhile, if we do not consider its physical elements we are ignoring a wide section of reality in our theologizing. Tillich's sense of the multidimensional unity is helpful here in not excluding any dimension of life from the spiritual presence. Thus I find Tillich's understanding of dimensions to be a more helpful way forward in describing cyberspace as a cyberdimension.

86. Cobb herself wrote about the Teilhardian influence on Barlow and others in a 1995 article for *Wired* magazine, Cobb Kreisberg, "A Globe, Clothing Itself with a Brain."

Cyberspace as Cyberdimension

Given this structure of dimensions and the function of life, how might Tillich help us in understanding cyberspace? First off, we must recall the basic tension in Tillich's theology between essence and existence, with the gap of ambiguity or estrangement. This division can help us to understand the differing approaches to cyberspace. Seen in this light, Barlow and other cyber idealists are presenting a vision of the essence of cyberspace, and indeed more radically a vision of the nature of reality as directed towards a particular religiously understood end. Yet the infrastructural realities of cyberspace make it more complex than a Platonic form or an evolutionary step of humanity towards shedding the bonds of materiality. Indeed one need only consider the reality of the need for cybersecurity in order to recognize the estranged character of the existence of cyberspace. Whatever cyberspace might be essentially, existentially it is filled with danger and mixed motivations and unjust structures. Dourish, though not writing with a consideration for religious dimensions, perhaps puts it best: "Precisely which Internet do we talk about when we celebrate openness, diversity, and decentralization as characteristics of the Internet when compared to mass media as forms of communication? Certainly, we can celebrate the potential for these properties, but perhaps not their practical embodiment within the Internet as we know it—our Internet rather than a possible Internet."[87] Dourish is here pointing to what Tillich would identify as the gap between essence and existence. Cybersecurity issues such as cyberwar, the effects of data mining and identity theft, and a host of other related issues are specifically the manifestation of the estrangement of cyberspace. Likewise, ecological concerns about cables or energy production are marks of the estrangement of cyberspace, as are labor issues surrounding those who work to maintain cyberspace, and so forth. These infrastructural concerns mark the estrangement from a possible Internet to our actual Internet, as Dourish puts it.

Being a part of estranged existence suggests that cyberspace could be a dimension of life. To consider it as such would mean to ponder how the three functions of life might be manifested through cyberspace. The cyber dimension would need to participate uniquely in self-integration, self-creation, and self-transcendence, if we follow Tillich's definition. Let us contemplate, then, how these three functions might be present in cyberspace.

---

87. Dourish, "Protocols, Packets, and Proximity," 199.

The function of self-integration brings forth the tension between the individual and the network. Questions of identity in cyberspace are of immense importance. On the one hand, there is the ability to create an avatar or virtual identity that may or may not have direct correspondence to a person sitting behind the computer. There is a plasticity to human identity in cyberspace, as a person's telepresence can separate their constructed identity from physical characteristics that could be interpreted as markers of race or gender, for example. In cybersecurity, this is known as the "attribution problem." At the same time data mining by governments and corporations create data-driven profiles of those who engage in activities within cyberspace. Such reduction of identity to the accumulation of data about activity and the inferences that can be made based on that data threatens the complexity of identity, especially as it is interpreted through algorithms that may incorporate the biases of its programmers.[88] More broadly, we can find here the tension between discrete concrete aspects of the infrastructure of cyberspace and the meaning accessed through the networking of systems. We can recall Peters's contention that technology creates media and media unveils other media as media. Technology is required for entering into the medium of cyberspace and its flow of information, and through the networking of that medium it is possible to engage a variety of media that all enable connection and interaction. Yet as Koepsell rightly notes, the individual machines that allow the connection are individual devices and the data is stored on individual hard drives. Digital self-integration arises from individual technological devices recognizing the interconnection.

Self-creation, meanwhile, is the function of growth. Certainly through cyberspace an unprecedented accumulation of data about the world becomes possible. Whether about human spending habits, fluctuations in sea temperatures, or the total distance run by each soccer player in a match, data collected and stored about the world is increasing exponentially through cyberspace. Humanity is indeed enabled to analyze the world and engage in the growth of reflection and knowledge in new ways through cyberspace technology. This growth in data enables new practices to be formed. So, too, the nature and shape of cyberspace is constantly evolving through new technologies and new content added by users. There is indeed a mutual shaping occurring between humanity and technology. That is, while the forms of cyberspace have incredible

---

88. See Owen, *Disruptive Power*, especially chapter 8.

plasticity and are destroyed and re-created at a rapid pace, it does indeed occur as growth. Meanwhile, through environmental impact such as the Telephone Cable Channel in Hawai'i, growth and change is instigated through cyberspace infrastructure.

Finally, what of self-transcendence? Thus far in terms of cyberspace the vertical dimension has been equated with the old regime of power politics and authoritarian control. Might there be a positive sense of verticality, as Tillich employs it of this function? For instance, might we understand Putin and Koepsell as each in their own way denying a transcending function to cyberspace, and thus falling into the distortion of profanation? Might there be a way in which the unambiguous life can be anticipated through the cyberdimension? As I suggested earlier, I believe that cyberspace may indeed crack open a space through which the kingdom of God may be glimpsed. Let us recall that for Tillich the function of self-transcendence is a quality of the other functions. It is the quality of striving to overcome the ambiguities of reality. In this sense, the appeal to what Dourish calls the potential Internet is a sense of the self-transcending potentiality in cyberspace. In this sense, Barlow is not an analyst of what the Internet is but rather a prophet of what it could be. He renders a glimpse of the dimension of Spirit offering healing and deliverance from the ambiguity of the estranged existence of reality.[89] Putin, meanwhile, recognizes the political realities of our Internet as it is, full of the ambiguities of existence. It would be naïve to expect Barlow's vision to come in its fullness, but at the same time to give up the vision of what is possible, even if only partially and in glimpses, is to deny the intersection of the dimension of Spirit within the cyberdimension.

Thus we see that cyberspace can indeed be understood through the lens of Tillich's definition of dimension. As such it functions in a distinct manner from other dimensions. Time, presence, identity, and interrelationships all grow and exist in unique forms through cyberspace. Because of this, the dimension of Spirit can also be uniquely manifested, thereby producing new possibilities for understanding divine activity within the world. These possibilities cannot be separated from the infrastructures that are an integral component of cyberspace. The cyberdimension is indeed a nexus of meaning and existence, where the give and take of life occurs. Perhaps, then, a different metaphor of unambiguous life might emerge alongside the kingdom of God, spiritual presence, and eternal

---

89. At the same time, his sense of the Internet as disembodied, with the mind explicitly seen as overcoming the limitations of bodiliness, remains problematic.

life as having the capacity to speak of the manifestation of spirit in the cyberdimension. Indeed, I will suggest that the metaphor of the invisible or hidden church may hold such potential, a possibility that we will consider more fully in the final chapter.

Ultimately, of course, it does not matter whether cyberspace constitutes a new dimension or if it is simply the latest emergence of infrastructure in the technological realm. These are metaphors that allow for some slippage. The key issue for us, rather, is the multidimensional unity of life. That is, whether cyberspace is considered a new dimension or not, we must consider how Spirit may be manifested through cyberspace. Provisionally, then, let us consider cyberspace as the cyberdimension as a means of homing in on the distinctiveness of the cyber realm as a locus of the action of Spirit.

Thus the above questions in Tillich's three functions of life will help guide us through the issues of cybersecurity that we will explore in the next chapters. We will take something of a circuitous route through the issues, noting the theological stakes as we pass by. Yet through our strolling we may come across some insights into if, and if so how, the cyberdimension contributes new ways of participating in these functions of life. Along the way, as we pass through cyberwar, data mining and surveillance, hacktivism and digital activism, and digital whistle-blowing, we will also enter political and social matters as elements of life, before returning to considering these questions again with a deeper understanding of how cybersecurity helps us better understand the meaning of cyberspace.

Chapter 2

Constant Conflict: Cyberwar and Just War Theory

Stuxnet came to international attention in 2010. It was a computer virus of extreme complexity that appeared on computers, particularly around the Middle East. While at first it did not seem to do anything, over time its purpose, design, and designers became apparent. It was designed to affect a particular model of Siemens operating system. Specifically, it was the type of machine used by Iran for its nuclear centrifuges. As documents released by Edward Snowden eventually confirmed, Stuxnet was designed by American and Israeli forces in order to derail the Iranian nuclear program. Thus Stuxnet became the first publicly known cyberweapon to be employed, thereby moving the idea of cyberwar from the realm of speculation and science fiction into a contemporary issue. Stuxnet has many important features that can allow us to consider the issues presented by the concept of cyberwar more broadly. As we have seen, it is a program in existence in the cyberdimension aimed at physical results, thus demonstrating the blurred lines between the cyberdimension and the physical dimension.

Finding a definition of what we mean by "cyberwar" is elusive. The term has been applied to a wide range of events in cyberspace. Simple cyber vandalism, for instance, has been deemed by some to be cyberwar. A 2010 cover story in the magazine *The Economist* included credit card fraud as a type of cyberwar.[1] The current US government definition of cyberwar, however, is a cyberattack that "proximately result[s] in

---

1. Briefing, "War in the Fifth Column." The article is noted in Singer and Friedman, *Cybersecurity and Cyberwar*, 120

death, injury or significant destruction."[2] Singer and Friedman, for their part, hold that the key elements of war are a political goal and violence. Johannes J. Fruhbauer, meanwhile, distinguishes between infowar, cyberwar, and netwar.[3] For our purposes, a precise definition of cyberwar is not essential. What is relevant for us in this chapter is that a new, unseen dimension of warfare done in the name of nation-states has opened up. Attacks may be going on at any moment, unknown to all but a handful of computer system operators. Yet this unseen dimension of war is not disconnected from the physical dimensions. Conflict in one dimension cannot be disconnected from conflict in other dimensions. For theology, then, the question is how existing discussions of the Christian response to war translate into this added dimension.

Stuxnet and Cyberwar

Stuxnet is notable for being the first significant known use of a cyberweapon, but it is also notable for how subtle and complex the attack was. Stuxnet included at least four "zero days"; that is, previously unexploited software vulnerabilities. Such zero days are prized by hackers and not used unless necessary; thus to incorporate four was not only extraordinary but indicated the level of resources and determination its designers had. Because they target vulnerabilities that are unknown to vendors, cybersecurity experts, and hackers, using zero days allows malware to penetrate cyber defenses undetected. Having a zero-day weakness gives the upper hand to cyber attackers because while defenders seal off known weaknesses and create virus protection against known types of attacks, a zero day attacks a weakness that is not known to the defenders. That is, indeed, where the term *zero day* comes from: it is the day before the first day that the vulnerability is known. Once a zero day is used, defenders can devise ways to combat that type of attack. To use more than one zero day on a single project is to risk exposing a great deal of strategically valuable information.

Zero days play an important role not only in hacking, but perhaps even more so in cyberwar. Possession of knowledge of a vulnerability in

2. Singer and Friedman, *Cybersecurity and Cyberwar,* 120.

3. For Fruhbauer, infowar is the broadest of the terms, dealing with aggressive action against an opponent's communications systems, while cyberwar is similar but has an explicitly military component. Netwar, meanwhile, targets an enemy's knowledge and self-image. Fruhbauer, "'Cyberwars,'" in Borgman et al., eds., *Cyberspace,* 49–59.

software that others do not know about gives an incredible advantage to those who wish to go on the offensive in cyberspace. Conversely, they are the biggest threat for those concerned with cyberdefense. That government forces would hoard so much knowledge of software weaknesses indicates a great many things, including deep technical expertise, funding, and an offensive mind-set. It also indicates a willingness to risk civilian safety for the sake of national political objectives. To understand why the use of so many zero days indicates all of these things requires unpacking a variety of aspects of cyberweapons.

Holding on to the knowledge of a zero day reflects offensive priorities. This is because a zero day is a danger to all computer users, military or not. A zero day is a defensive liability because anyone who possesses knowledge of the zero day has the ability to attack another computer covertly because the attack is directed at an unknown vulnerability. Thus traditionally when a cyberdefense company, such as ones that provide anti-virus software, uncovers a zero day, not only do they set their defensive software to be aware of the vulnerability in its scans, but they also report the vulnerability to the maker of the software for which they discovered the zero day. Thus if they discover a zero day for an iPhone, for instance, they would inform Apple. That way the company can issue a patch to shore up the vulnerability. This makes the Internet safer for all users. It is in the best interest of users, companies, and governments to minimize cyber criminal activity by improving cyber security. Yet the decision to keep silent about the knowledge of a zero day reflects a disregard for this sense of the common good. It reflects a decision to not give valuable defensive intelligence for the sake of retaining an offensive advantage. As journalist Kim Zetter argues, "In amassing zero-day exploits for the government to use in attacks, instead of passing the information about holes to vendors to be fixed, the government has put critical infrastructure owners and computer users in the United States at risk of attack from criminal hackers, corporate spies, and foreign intelligence agencies who no doubt will discover and use the same vulnerabilities for their own operations."[4] In Stuxnet's use of at least four zero days, we have evidence that American and Israeli forces have a cache of zero days stockpiled for offensive operations. Indeed, some officials have hinted that there are many more zero days in the offensive arsenals.

In fact, there are indications of conflicting agendas within the United States government. Richard Clarke, who served as cybersecurity czar

---

4. Zetter, *Countdown to Zero Day*, 221.

during the Bush administration and a member of a surveillance reform board called by the Obama administration in the wake of the Snowden leaks, has argued, "If the US government finds a zero-day vulnerability, its first obligation is to tell the American people so that they can patch it, not to run off [to use it] to break into the Beijing telephone system. The first obligation of government is to defend."[5] Yet such a philosophy has not held sway throughout the entirety of the United States government. Indeed, Zetter and other observers point to the Department of Defense's split of offensive and defensive cyber operations in 2004 as the beginning of the militarization of cyberspace.[6] Zetter further reports that a "cult of offense" truly took hold the following year when General Keith Alexander became the director of the NSA.[7] We will return again to the fact that cyberwar programs were centered in an espionage agency rather than the military itself. Meanwhile, Sean McGurk, who directed the NC-CIC, which is the Department of Homeland Security computer emergency response team, at the time that details of Stuxnet began to come to light publically, reported that while giving briefings on the findings about Stuxnet to various high ranking officials, he never had the impression that Stuxnet had come from within the government itself.[8] Even those in the government tasked with defense seem to have been unaware of the offensive focus.

In fact, it would seem likely that anyone tasked with defense would balk at the offensive use of zero days. This is because cyberweapons have one clear difference from other types of weapons: once a cyberweapon is used it is essentially handed over to all others to use. Using a zero day and creating a code to go with it is expensive and difficult, but copying an existing code and using a known vulnerability is easy. Thus once a virus is unleashed into "the wild" of cyberspace, it is rather simple for not only other nations but possibly even lower-level criminal hackers to make copycat versions of the weapon. Once the difficult work of development is done, the code acts as a blueprint for others to follow. Even if a

---

5. From Clarke's speech at the RSA Security Conference in San Francisco, February 2014, quoted in ibid., 390–91.

6. Ibid., 214. The two were recombined in 2010 with the creation of US Cyber Command, which will be discussed below.

7. Ibid.

8. See ibid., 186–89.

sophisticated program like Stuxnet cannot be fully replicated, the ideas and zero days contained in it become readily available.[9]

Because zero days are so valuable, there is a large market for them. Zetter reports that there is an underground market for selling zero days. While it has been around for some time, she asserts, "In the last few years, however, it has gone commercial and exploded as the number of buyers and sellers has ballooned, along with prices, and the once murky trade has become legitimized with the entry of government dollars into the arena to create an unregulated cyberweapons bazaar."[10] In this "gray market" of government purchasing of zero-day vulnerabilities we see a glimpse of the blurring of militarization and commercialization of the cyberdimension that we will consider more fully in later chapters. Indeed we also see a bit of the blurring between military and espionage that we will return to later as well, as Zetter notes that "one person's national security tool can be another's tool of oppression, and there's no guarantee that a government that buys zero days won't misuse them to spy on political opponents and activists or pass them to another government that will."[11] Furthering this point, for 2013 the NSA budgeted $25.1 million for "covert purchases of software vulnerabilities" from the private sphere; in other words buying zero days from the cyber military commercial complex. As a more recent example, in 2016 an iPhone was recovered from a terrorist in San Bernardino, California. Apple, however, refused to provide the FBI with the means for breaking through the iPhone's security in order to examine the data held on the phone. There was great public controversy over whether Apple should give this kind of information or not, but before the issue was resolved with Apple the FBI decided to pay professional "gray hat" hackers to break through the phone's defenses. Once this was done, the FBI did not immediately reveal to Apple the vulnerability that was used, in part because the hackers did not sell all of the technical details of how they hacked the phone.[12] Thus the vulnerability in that particular type of iPhone could conceivably have been subsequently offered for sale by those same hackers to any interested parties.

After Stuxnet, several other related examples of malware have been uncovered, so that it seems that Stuxnet was but one program in a family of weapons employed. The scenario pieced together by various researches

9. Ibid., 388.
10. Ibid., 99.
11. Ibid., 101.
12. Yadron, "FBI confirms."

seems a likely conjecture. Malware that came to be known as Flame first worked as an espionage tool, perhaps as early as 2005. In 2007 or 2008 another tool, which came to be known as Duqu, was used to scout and steal information. The earliest versions of Stuxnet, then, began to operate in 2009. It has been suggested that Flame was created by a team from the United States, while Duqu came from Israeli sources. Portions of Stuxnet came from each of these earlier programs.[13] Another tool, labeled Gauss by antivirus researchers, has also been identified as sharing code with Flame. Gauss includes a Trojan program designed to steal bank account login credentials, particularly in Lebanese banks. There is no sign that Gauss was used in connection with Stuxnet—or used at all, in fact—but rather its existence demonstrates that there are likely many undiscovered nation-state-created cyber programs for offensive operations.

One ploy contained in this family of malware that is of particular concern is its attempts to subvert the trust that underlies the functioning of the Internet. Recall from the Introduction that trust is essential to the communication between machines, and that trust is predicated on the certificate system. Flame was shown to be attempting to steal certificates. In fact, it contained a forged Microsoft certificate. This allowed the program to infect the Windows Update tool. If hackers could gain control of the Windows Update system, which Microsoft uses to distribute patches against vulnerabilities, they would be impervious to anti-virus software because they could control the patches. Indeed, there would be few limits on what could be done in this scenario; it is more powerful than a zero-day attack. Zetter points out, "The Windows Update hijack was a brilliant feat that pushed the boundaries of mathematics and could only have been achieved by world-class cryptographers."[14] Flame did not actually go so far as to subvert the patch servers themselves, instead only controlling Windows Update on the machines it infected, but it was still a dangerous precedent to set. In fact, Microsoft engineers managed to use the exploit they discovered in Flame to create a less sophisticated version of the Flame attack on Windows Update in just three days, demonstrating the danger of copycat attacks after a cyberweapon is used.[15] As Zetter argues, the agencies behind Flame worked to subvert the foundational trust between Microsoft, the largest software maker in the world, and

13. See Zetter, *Countdown to Zero Day*, 284.
14. Ibid., 288.
15. Ibid., 89.

its customers.[16] Stuxnet, meanwhile, employed certificates stolen from Taiwanese companies as a means of slipping through security.

In terms of Stuxnet, it is important to note that it was designed to exploit vulnerabilities in what are known as Programmable Logic Controllers, or PLCs. PLCs are widely used but not widely known systems. They are used to control a broad range of automated systems. They are, for instance, used in keeping power plants running smoothly, dams and water treatment plans functioning, factories operating efficiently, controlling traffic lights and elevators in buildings, regulating agricultural production and food distribution, and in countless other automated regulatory functions. From the time they were first developed in the 1960s until the late 1990s these computers tended to be isolated systems, but more recently have become networked by having commercial operating systems such as Windows overlaid onto them. Yet while they had been brought into the cyber domain, their security was quite weak.

Prior to Stuxnet there were a few close calls of hackers accessing critical infrastructure computers. Fortunately no damage was done in these incidents, but it also led to lack of action on improving security for PLCs.[17] On March 4, 2007, the Department of Homeland Security, concerned about the vulnerability of PLCs, held the Aurora Generator Test at the Department of Energy's Idaho National Lab. A stream of malicious code was sent to a generator with a 5,000-horsepower diesel engine before a crowd of government and power industry officials. Within three minutes, the machine was reduced to essentially scrap metal and a plume of smoke, with a level of force that surprised even the engineers who had planned the demonstration. Thus three years prior to the discovery of Stuxnet, the potential for physically damaging industrial machinery through malware had been demonstrated.

Along with the zero days for accessing Windows, Stuxnet exploited the security holes in the PLCs. Yet even with these security holes, a great deal of knowledge of the exact setup of the Iranian centrifuges was required to pull off the attack. The attacks did not destroy the centrifuges, however. Rather, they interfered with the proper functioning of the machines. It manipulated the speed of the machines' rotors so that the speed fluctuated and sometimes surpassed the speed for which they were

---

16. Former government officials told *The Washington Post* that the NSA, CIA, and Israel's military were behind Flame. Nakashima et al., "U.S., Israel Developed Flame Computer Virus."

17. See Zetter, *Countdown to Zero Day*, 129–65.

designed to withstand. Thus the centrifuges frequently broke down and failed to produce enriched uranium. On top of this, the malware caused the displays to indicate that everything was functioning normally, so that the scientists were not even aware of the cause of the breakdowns. This continued for over a year, possibly devastating the morale of the Iranian scientists because they could not even make centrifuges work. Indeed there seems to have been at least 1,000 centrifuges that were damaged during the time period that Iran later claimed that Stuxnet was active.[18] It was designed specifically to make the Iranians feel stupid.[19]

In considering Stuxnet, then, we see a multidimensional attack, which I suggest is a hallmark of cyberwar. It created damage to machines and processing capabilities, thus attacking at an inorganic level. Because it was also designed to taunt and belittle the scientists, it could be considered an attack with a spiritual dimension. Finally, because it was done through digital means, it also had a cyber component.

Many cyber theorists consider Stuxnet to be a "game-changer," as Mikko Hypponen puts it. He continues, "We are entering an arms race where countries start stocking weapons, only it isn't planes and nuclear reactors they're stocking, but it's cyberweapons."[20] Likewise, cybersecurity policy expert Adam Segal asserts, "Just as historians consider 1947 as the year that two clear sides of the Cold War emerged, we will look back at the year that stretches roughly from June 2012 to June 2013 as Year Zero in the battle over cyberspace."[21] He points to a June 2012 newspaper article about Stuxnet as the beginning of Year Zero. As we shall see, there are indeed debates over the ethics of Stuxnet specifically and cyberwar more generally. Some critics focus on the precision of the code in Stuxnet, which meant that only the very specific set-up of the Iranian laboratory was affected, while others are concerned about how widespread the virus nonetheless became and how much worse could be done with cyberweapons. Singer and Friedman ask, "Do you focus on the fact that this new kind of weapon permitted a preemptive attack and in so doing touched thousands of people and computers who had nothing to do with Iran or nuclear research? Or do you focus on the fact that the cyber strike caused far less damage than any previous comparable attack and

18. Ibid., 247.
19. Singer and Friedman, *Cybersecurity and Cyberwar*, 117, and Deibert, *Black Code*, 179.
20. Quoted in Singer and Friedman, *Cybersecurity and Cyberwar*, 118.
21. Segal, *The Hacked World Order*, 1.

that the weapon was so discriminating it essentially gave new meaning to the term?"[22] This is indeed the challenging question raised by cyberwar.

In fact, much of the debate about Stuxnet is less on Stuxnet itself and more on what it may herald. Key issues include the fact that Stuxnet was essentially an act of war in order to avoid war, on the one hand, and on the other hand the precedent it sets. Indeed, it is worth knowing that Stuxnet was launched in the first place because of President George W. Bush's refusal to use air strikes against Iran. Israel and hawks in the Bush administration were pushing the president to take military action against Iran in 2003, even though the United States was already involved in wars in Iraq and Afghanistan. Bush refused, and so Stuxnet, or "Operation Olympus," as it was called within the administration, was devised as an alternative plan. Bush endorsed it enthusiastically.[23] The project was ongoing when President Barack Obama took office. The Obama administration not only continued the program but increased its scale, even while Obama gave a series of speeches about the importance of increasing the defense of cyberspace as a national security interest. From this we see that there was bipartisan presidential support for the cyberattack. We can also see that while public rhetoric was on defensive measures against possible attack, the United States was actually engaged in an attack itself.[24] At the same time, we also see that it was indeed intended to limit kinetic war. Thus we can see the moral ambiguity.

Again, however, the most trenchant criticism is not about Stuxnet itself, but about what it could pave the way for. For instance, cybersecurity expert James A. Lewis argued in testimony before the United States Congressional Subcommittee on Cybersecurity, Infrastructure Protection and Security Technologies in 2012, "The day a terrorist group gets cyberattack capabilities, they will use them."[25] In other words, while Stuxnet was quite discriminating, there is no way to ensure that other nations, let alone other groups online, will be as restrained if they engage in cyberattacks. This is all the more disturbing because, as we have noted, once malicious code is in the wild anyone can study it and employ its

---

22. Singer and Friedman, *Cybersecurity and Cyberwar*, 119.

23. See Zetter, *Countdown to Zero Day*, 191–94.

24. The political backdrop behind Stuxnet is detailed in journalist David Sanger's book *Confront and Conceal*.

25. Lewis, "Thresholds for Cyberwar." Quoted in Zetter, *Countdown to Zero Day*, 384.

techniques. Thus each cyberattack raises the danger level for potential new attacks.

To further the point, because the most powerful nation has been confirmed to have engaged in a cyberattack outside the boundaries of wartime, it makes it much easier for other nations to justify their need to engage in such actions. In addition, as we have seen, cyberwar is not confined to designated war zones. In fact, it takes place over equipment—computers—designed for a wide variety of uses, the vast majority of which are civilian and most of which are owned by and produced by civilians or for public infrastructure needs. As General Kevin Chilton, the commander of the US Strategic Command, informed the House of Representatives Strategic Forces subcommittee at a hearing in 2009, there are no "protected zones" or "rear areas" in cyberspace. All are equally vulnerable. Every computer is potentially on the front line of battle.[26]

Also of note in considering Stuxnet is the extremely limited public and congressional response provoked by it. There has been little debate over the ethics of cyberwar. To this day there has been little formal discussion of what is acceptable in this arena. After the Snowden revelations, the White House did organize a surveillance reform board, which touched on some cyberwar issues. Notably, it recommended that "US policy should generally move to ensure that Zero Days are quickly blocked, so that the underlying vulnerabilities are patched on US Government and other networks,"[27] and that only in very rare instances should zero days be used for espionage purposes. A month after the report, Obama issued a new policy on zero-day vulnerabilities. If the NSA discovers flaws in software, it must report them to the vendor. However, this only applies to flaws discovered by the federal agencies, not contractors or other groups, including ones that might sell their discovery on the gray market to the government, let alone those discovered by the US military. Further, a flaw that has "a clear national security or law enforcement use" can be kept secret and used by the government, giving the NSA great leeway in deciding which vulnerabilities to actually report, as we have also seen with the FBI in the San Bernardino iPhone example. Further, no mention is made of whatever stockpile of zero days was already on hand. Meanwhile, the reform committee did not address subversion of the digital certificate

26. Chilton, Testimony, 47. Quoted in Zetter, *Countdown to Zero Day*, 377.
27. Clarke et al., "NSA Report," xxxvi. Quoted in Zetter, *Countdown to Zero Day*, 390.

system or the military use of cyberweapons.[28] Again, this board operated within the executive branch of the government. Discussion has not reached the legislative branch in any widespread manner, reaching beyond subcommittees.

On the flip side of this, the Snowden documents revealed a 2012 secret presidential directive stipulating that outside of wartime the use of cyberweapons requires presidential approval, while during war military officials have the authority to take quick action at their own discretion, provided digital attacks are proportional to the threat and seek to limit civilian casualties and collateral damage. Presidential authorization is not needed for espionage operations that simply collect data or map a network, though some parameters are provided. What is notable in this directive is that it only addresses military operations, and specifically excludes intelligence and law enforcement agencies from these restrictions. Thus we can see from these two sets of policies instituted by Obama, there is a veneer of regulation on government cyber activities by the United States, but in practice the restrictions are quite superficial.

Broader Examples of Cyberwar

Cyberwar need not be confined to such cloak and dagger assaults, however. War occurring in the cyberdimension can occur in conjunction with conventional military operations as well. For example, in 2007 seven Israeli F-5I fighter jets crossed into Syrian airspace and dropped several bombs. This attack destroyed a plutonium processing facility at al Kibar. The Syrian air defense network did not fire a shot at the Israeli planes. Reportedly, the Israelis had been able to hack into the Syrian military computer network and were thus able to direct their own data streams into the air defense computer. They were consequently able to show the radar offices false images so that they did not know the attack was occurring until the bombs began to fall. Known as Operation Orchard, this is an example of a cyber operation with a military component.

Another important feature of cyberwar is that it cannot be confined to government agencies as easily as conventional warfare can be. A key example of this is the so-called "Estonian Cyberwar." In 2007, Estonia's websites were hit with a denial of service (DoS) attack that shut down their public websites for several days. Estonia felt it was an attempt to

---

28. Zetter, *Countdown to Zero Day*, 390.

damage its economy and weaken its government, and they believed that Russia was behind it. In fact, Urmas Paet, the Estonian foreign minister, accused the Russian government of being behind the attack: "Russia is attacking Estonia. . . . The attacks are virtual, psychological, and real."[29] In other words, they were multidimensional. Yet in response, Sergei Markov, the Russian parliamentary leader, denied that the government was behind it. Rather, he slyly replied that the attack "was carried out by my assistant."[30] The assistant in question was a leader in the Nashi (or "Ours") movement. This movement, boasting some 120,000 Russians aged between seventeen and twenty-five, is not officially part of the Russian government but rather is organized by pro-Putin regime supporters. Along with activities like running summer camps, the group also took initiative in cyber activities against "Nazism and liberalism." Estonia had relocated the *Bronze Soldier of Tallinn*, a memorial from the Soviet era, along with the remains of Soviet soldiers, inciting the Nashi response.[31] While perhaps not technically cyberwar, these initiatives were certainly cyberattacks.

A year later, war broke out between Russia and Georgia over the disputed territory of South Ossetia. In addition to Russian tanks entering that territory, Georgia's websites and a significant amount of its information infrastructure, including banks and emergency services, came under a large-scale DDoS attack. After the war came to an end, researchers tracked the domains of the botnets involved in the cyber attack. The network of zombie computers spanned the globe, with most concentrated physically in the United States and Germany. Indeed at one point Georgian officials turned over their website hosting to a Georgian ex-pat based in Atlanta. With the websites and so many of the botnets located physically in the United States, some of this cyberbattle raging in the *country* of Georgia was actually happening between computers in the American *state* of Georgia. Thus we see not only the porosity of borders in the cyberdimension, but also how difficult it is to pin down who exactly is involved. The Russian military may have been involved directly, though this cannot be said with certainly. It is highly likely, rather, that Russia made use of "patriotic hackers."[32]

29 Quoted in Singer and Friedman, *Cybersecurity and Cyberwars*, 110.
30. Singer and Friedman, *Cybersecurity and Cyberwars*, 110.
31. Ibid., 111.
32. Deibert, *Black Code*, 165.

"Patriotic hacking" is hacking activity done by citizens or groups within a country against the perceived enemies of their country. In this particular case, the group instructions on how to carry out the DDoS attack were posted in forums in order to mobilize a vast number of participants. As Singer and Friedman explain, "The advantage of using patriotic hackers is that a government can utilize the synchronization and large-scale effort it wants without being officially involved, giving it just enough cover to claim plausible deniability."[33] In fact, it is nearly impossible to know for sure when a patriotic hacker group is behind an attack. There is always the possibility that a third party might be involved, attempting to stoke the flames between two countries by framing one country or its supporters. There could be other possibilities as well, because of the attribution problem that identities can never be known with certainty online. Singer and Friedman quote a former Justice Department official who dealt with cybersecurity, saying, "I have seen too many situations where government officials claimed a high degree of confidence as to the source, intent, and scope of an attack, and it turned out they were wrong on every aspect of it. That is, they were often wrong, but never in doubt."[34] The wide number of potential actors in cyber conflict, from nation-states to patriotic hackers to terrorists, makes any simple attribution impossible. This serves to make the plausible deniability of nations involving patriotic hackers all the more plausible. This is one reason why allegations of Russian hacking surrounding the 2016 United States election are difficult to prove conclusively through exclusively online means. For instance, the cyber security company hired by the Democratic National Committee to investigate the hacking allegations had identified digital fingerprints linked to Russian intelligence agencies, but such fingerprints cannot be considered absolute proof.[35]

Patriotic hackers are not only found in Russia, to be sure. Canadian political scientist and security expert Ronald J. Deibert points out that the Iranian Cyber Army targeted supporters of the Green Movement

---

33. Singer and Friedman, *Cybersecurity and Cyberwar*, 111.

34. Ibid., 150.

35. See Corera, "Can U.S. Election Hack," for instance. Investigations continue and so more evidence may be uncovered. At the time of this writing numerous reports outline the ways that Russian entities worked to influence the election through the manipulation of online content. There is considerably less publicly available evidence of direct tampering with the election via hacking. See CNN, "2016 Presidential Campaign."

in 2009. It has since conducted successful attacks on Twitter, Voice of America, and Baidu, the Chinese search engine, with tacit approval from the Iranian government. We will turn shortly to some American and Chinese patriotic hackers. A long litany of other examples from other parts of the world could be recited. While hardly a military attack, one of the better known examples of patriotic hacking relates to the movie *The Interview*. Upset by what was felt to be a negative depiction of North Korea in the movie, the Sony websites were hacked and defaced, presumably by patriotic hackers, although there is no way to tell what level of support, if any, this action might have received from the North Korean government. This initially caused Sony to drop the release of the movie, but due to public backlash the movie was given a limited release.

While patriotic hackers can give their country a great deal of support in cyber activities, there is a downside. As Singer and Friedman note, "they may not have the level of control that governments, especially authoritarian ones, desire."[36] A variety of embarrassing episodes have occurred. For example, during the 2008 Beijing Olympics some Chinese hacking groups made available tutorials for launching a DDoS attack on the CNN website, with whom they were aggravated due to the news channel's reports on riots in Tibet. Then in 2010 patriotic hacker groups in China and Iran became engaged in a series of escalating attacks on one another, despite the fact that the two countries have an alliance with each other.

While patriotic hackers are often drawn from youth-oriented groups like Nashi, they may come from wider circles. Particularly of note is the potential connection with organized cyber criminals. For instance, there is a convergence between the platforms, tools, and computers used in the 2008 Georgia attacks with those used by the Russian Business Network, a large cybercriminal organization. Thus some observers suspect that deals are sometimes struck between nations and cybercriminals, where the criminal groups are given some leeway to operate in return for giving aid as patriotic hackers.[37] It is important, meanwhile, to distinguish between patriotic hackers and hacktivists, whom we will encounter in detail in a later chapter. Hacktivists and other online activists may engage in political issues, but do so for their own reasons rather than at the direction of a government or in support of a government's interests. Indeed, as we

---

36. Singer and Friedman, *Cybersecurity and Cyberwar*, 113.
37. Ibid., 112.

shall see in later chapters, governments have rarely looked kindly upon hacktivists.

Ethical Issues of Cyberwar

As we move into the era of cyberwar, there are a variety of areas of ethical concern that are only beginning to be addressed. A key aspect is the secrecy involved. Because of this, there is little public discussion of what are acceptable forms of cyber operations for the military to be involved in. This leads to a more general concern of the blurring of the lines between the role of the military, police, intelligence, and commercial interests.

In 2010, the United States military created Cyber Command, with cyberspace formally recognized as the "fifth domain" of war, joining land, sea, air, and space.[38] It joins all of the components of the military that are involved in cyber issues together in one organization. The command has nearly 60,000 people working for it, and its headquarters is at Fort Meade, Maryland. This location is significant, as it is next door to the National Security Agency (NSA). The NSA is a once obscure intelligence agency that has become well known in recent years because of its prowess in cyber surveillance. Indeed, Cyber Command and the NSA are not just neighbors. When Cyber Command was created, both organizations were simultaneously headed by General Keith Alexander. Thus from the beginning of the Cyber Command's work, it was integrated into the clandestine world of intelligence, rather than separating the roles of military work and espionage.

Indeed, there seems to be an extreme commitment to secrecy in regard to cyberwar. In fact, General Michael Hayden, former CIA and NSA director, has said, "This may come as a surprise, given my background at the NSA and CIA and so on, but I think that this information [about the American guidelines to cyber operations] is horribly over-classified. The roots of American cyberpower are in the American intelligence community, and we frankly are quite accustomed to working in a world that's classified. I'm afraid that that culture has bled over into how we treat all cyber questions."[39] With such secrecy in place, only those directly involved are able to engage in discussion of the ethics, which leaves out nonmilitary or intelligence figures who may have a broader range of

---

38. Zettner, *Countdown to Zero Day*, 215.
39. Carroll, "Cone of Silence." Quoted in ibid., 386–87.

viewpoints. For our concerns, this particularly includes the elimination of religious engagement in the questions of the ethics of cyber operations, but more generally to any civilian input.[40]

Another area of concern with cyberwar is the balance between offensive and defensive technologies. Singer and Friedman report that US Air Force budget plans show 2.4 times as much allocated to cyber offense compared to cyber defense. They note that this lopsided approach is cause for concern, because "experts worry about the inherently seductive nature of cyber offense and the impact it might have on the military."[41] This is troubling, they add, not just because investment in defense is more likely to bring stability while offense can inspire an attack mentality, but also because this has already been happening. Indeed, a document dated October 2012 and released by Edward Snowden demonstrated that President Obama had issued an order directing officials to draw up a list of overseas targets for potential US cyberattacks.[42]

Likewise, Ronald J. Deibert notes that there is great appeal to the use of cyberweapons because they are considered bloodless. That is, they can attack centrifuges or engage in other such acts of sabotage rather than directly killing anyone. Yet, he cautions, such use of technological weapons "mask[s] the violence that invariably accompanies the use of high-impact technological weapons, and ignores the new problems and unforeseen consequences that arise."[43] More specifically, he warns that such weapons bring with them the temptation to rely on weapons and technical might rather than diplomacy. What *can* be done technically overwhelms questions of what *should* be done.[44] In other words, possessing powerful weapons, particularly ones that can be imagined to be "harmless," create a lust to use that power and so can increase conflict rather than lessen it. Deibert further quotes James Der Derian's critique of the virtues of "virtuous wars" that rely on technology to make them "less messy." Der Derian holds, "Virtuous war is anything *but* less destructive, deadly or bloody for those on the receiving end of the big technological stick."[45] Der Derian's focus is not on cyberwar itself but rather the way that technology allows a buffer of virtuality between not only soldiers but also the media that

40. Singer and Friedman, *Cybersecurity and Cyberwar,* 137.
41. Ibid., 137.
42. Harding, *The Snowden Files,* 139.
43. Deibert, *Black Code,* 181.
44. Ibid., 182.
45. Der Derian, *Virtuous War,* xxxii, quoted in Deibert, *Black Code,* 182.

portrays them and the violence that actually occurs in war. He considers cyberwar to be less dangerous than the risk of technology causing the horrors of war to be hidden from view.[46] This may well be true, though as we have seen cyberwar cannot be completely disconnected from kinetic war. Further, cyberwar cannot be completely dismissed either, as it constitutes an aspect of the buildup of tensions that is an aspect of the loss of peace and can open the gateway to war itself. We will thus return to this question of the ethics of conflict using less than lethal force below.

Returning to the question of the balance between offensive and defensive capabilities, it is generally assumed that in the cyber realm offense has the upper hand. Offenses choose when and how to attack, while defense must be on guard against everything at all times. In particular, the hoarding of zero-day vulnerabilities by government forces means that defenses do not even know what to watch out for in terms of an attack. However, Singer and Friedman point out that it is not clear that offense actually is stronger in cyber conflicts. It takes a great deal of skill and a wide range of technical expertise to conduct a successful cyberattack. For instance, it might be possible to hack into a computer system, but you still have to know what to do once you are past security. Developing Stuxnet required having experts in physics, computer systems, and the engineering of centrifuges, among others.[47] Beyond that, it is difficult to estimate what the effect of an attack will be on a computer system. Again using Stuxnet as an example, it took a great deal of skill to develop code that was effective in making it through multiple layers but did not destabilize or shut the system down, which would have attracted attention. At any point in this chain an error by the attackers could alert defenders, allowing them to thwart the attack.

Nonetheless, as we have seen, the US budget calls for greater investment in offensive capabilities than in defensive ones, even though its offensive capabilities are already stronger than its defensive ones. In fact, according to Zetter, "In 2011, the NSA mounted 231 offensive cyber operations against other countries, according to the documents [released by Snowden], three-fourths of which focused on 'top-priority' targets like

---

46. Der Derian, *Virtuous War*, xxxiv.

47. For example, the type of centrifuge used by Iran at Natanz was studied by scientists at Oak Ridge Laboratory in Tennessee after the CIA intercepted a black market shipment of uranium enrichment components headed from Malaysia to Libya in 2003. Due to the incident a great deal of equipment was confiscated from Libya, including many Pakistan-made P-1 centrifuges, the model upon which Iran based its centrifuges that were targeted by Stuxnet. See Zetter, *Countdown to Zero Day*, 316–17.

Iran, Russia, China, and North Korea."[48] This commitment to offensive action causes Singer and Friedman to liken the current cyber offensive mind-set to the principle of *ataque a outrance,* or "attack to excess" that dominated European militaries at the beginning of the twentieth century and led to the First World War.[49] The poignancy of this analogy is that while offensive-based theory helped bring about the Great War, once the war began it became clear that the offensive advances did not in fact bring an advantage and a drawn-out war dominated by defensive tactics ensued.

Further, American strength in offense may actually be a defensive weakness. In part this is because the United States is more reliant on Internet capabilities than other countries because its military and infrastructure are so highly connected digitally.[50] This connection gives America a great deal of military power, but also means that the effect of a cyberweapon against the United States is potentially much more devastating than one against countries that have little or no cyber connection in their military or infrastructure, as is true of most of those "top-priority" countries that the NSA has launched offensive actions against.[51] Singer and Friedman argue, "The most important lesson we have learned in traditional offense-defense balances, and now in cybersecurity, is that the best defense actually is a good defense."[52] Yet the United States has greater digital territory to defend, as it were, but is nonetheless emphasizing attack rather than putting its greatest efforts behind securing its digital borders and thus keeping all who are engaged in the cyber realm safe. It has bought into the "cult of offense."

This offensive focus is not exclusively true for the United States, of course. Other countries are also involved in developing offensive capabilities. China, for instance, is often painted as the world's greatest cyber villain. The reality is, of course, much more complex. Certainly the People's

---

48. Zetter, *Countdown to Zero Day,* 217.

49. Singer and Friedman, *Cybersecurity and Cyberwar,* 153.

50. General Kevin Chilton, for instance, hold a congressional subcommittee: "We need to start thinking about cyberspace and our utility of it, not so much as a convenience, but as a military necessity, because every domain, whether it is air, land, or sea, depends on cyberspace for their operations." Chilton, Testimony, 14. In the same hearing, he also stated, "Cyberspace, another one of our key lines of operations, has emerged as a key warfighting domain, and one on which all other warfighting domains depend." Chilton, Testimony, 6.

51. Singer and Friedman, *Cybersecurity and Cyberwar,* 151.

52. Ibid., 155.

Liberation Army is building its cyber capabilities at least as quickly as Cyber Command and the NSA have been in recent years, though it is even less open about the scope of its operations than are their American counterparts. Of its various hubs, one that has particularly drawn unwanted attention is the Second Bureau of the Third Army, Unit 61398, also known as the "Comment Crew" or the "Shanghai Group" in the cybersecurity world. It was caught attempting to infiltrate the *New York Times'* computer networks. In response, the newspaper unleashed reports demonstrating that the unit was behind 141 APT attacks. Among those on the revealed target list were the Pentagon and United Nations, as well as large American corporations such as Coca-Cola. It is estimated that there are as many as forty other units in China of similar scale.[53] Thus China is indeed in possession of offensive capabilities. *The Wall Street Journal*, meanwhile, reported in 2015 on a cyberweapons arms race heating up and including dozens of countries, including India, Pakistan, the Netherlands, and Denmark. It reports that twenty-nine countries have military units dedicated to cyberweapons and fifty countries have purchased cyberweapons from private companies.[54]

Returning to China's approach to cyberwar, Singer and Friedman report that the hallmark of the Chinese military's approach to cyber operations is the concept of "informatization." This concept seeks to take advantage of the reliance of modern military forces, and particularly of the American military, on information technologies that we have noted. The Chinese approach assumes that whoever controls the cyber dimension of a war would hold the "strategic high ground." They explain that the goal of this strategy "is to degrade an enemy's decision-making, slow down its operations, and even weaken its morale."[55] The goal of cyberattacks would be to neutralize the advantage Western militaries have in advanced weaponry, exposing the weaknesses of overreliance on that technology. From this point of view, then, offensive prowess in the cyber dimension is actually a defensive position in the physical dimension if a full-fledged war were to break out.

From the above we can see why other nations, and particularly the United States, would be concerned about China's cyber capabilities. Before writing off the Chinese approach as indeed being villainous, it is

---

53. Ibid., 141.
54. Paletta et al., "Cyberwar Ignites New Arms Race."
55. Singer and Friedman, *Cybersecurity and Cyberwar,* 142.

important to note that China is not merely an aggressor. For instance, China endures the largest number of cyberattacks in the world. Somewhere between ten and nineteen million Chinese computers are estimated to be controlled by foreign computers as botnets. These facts must be tempered by the fact that as many as 95 percent of Chinese computers are estimated to be running pirated software that do not receive security upgrades and patches. Thus it is the weakness of their enforcement of intellectual property rights that account for much of the malware problem. Nonetheless, China does indeed have some basis for unease about the cyberdimension.

China reports that its military sites alone were targeted by American sources nearly 90,000 times just in 2012. While this number is debatable, Singer and Friedman point out that a large percentage of the nefarious activities on the Internet do indeed originate in or move through American computers. Moreover, the American offensive capabilities have certainly been trained on China. Documents provided by Snowden in 2013 demonstrated the level of NSA hacking of Chinese computers. One of the six "network backbones" in China, Tsinghua University in Beijing, had been hacked. So had the Hong Kong headquarters of Pacnet, operator of one of the largest fiber-optic networks in the Asia-Pacific region.[56] Thus the US has indeed been aggressive towards China. Combine this with the reality that the foundational institutions of the Internet all have roots in the United States, and one can begin to see why China would feel the need to keep up. Indeed, an article by scholars at the Chinese Academy of Military Sciences in the Communist Party-controlled *China Youth Daily* newspaper in 2011 responded to the information about Stuxnet coming to light: "Of late, an Internet tornado has swept across the world . . . massively impacting and shocking the globe. Behind all this lies the shadow of America. Faced with this warm-up for an Internet war, every nation and military can't be passive but is making preparations to fight the Internet war."[57] Given the large number of countries currently building up their cyberdimension war capabilities, this seems to be a valid concern. Cyberwar does indeed seem to be a new arena of warfare, and as such calls out for ethical consideration.

56. Ibid., 140
57. Quoted in Singer and Friedman, *Cybersecurity and Cyberwar*, 140.

Just War Theory and the Ethics of Cyberwar

Military Ethics and Just War Theory for Cyberwar

At this point, discussion over the ethics of cyberwar is in its infancy. At an academic level, it has been largely confined to discussions of military ethics. In an influential article from 2010, Randall R. Dipert argues that cyberwar constitutes a new type of warfare, and thus traditional theories of just war are insufficient to account for new dimensions of war. As we shall soon see, several theorists have responded to the article, arguing against Dipert's thesis, but it is worth first understanding the claims Dipert puts forth for the nature of cyber warfare and the uniqueness of that nature.

Dipert lists four novel features of cyberwar. First is a policy vacuum. He holds, "There are no informed, open, public or political discussions of what an ethical and wise policy for the use of such weapons would be."[58] Second is what he terms the "attribution problem." That is, simply, that it is incredibly difficult to know who an actor behind a cyberattack is with any certainty. As Dipert notes, this gives rise to a number of issues, including a shield of denial of responsibility for attacks not possible in a conventional attack. His third characteristic is that cyberattacks will generally not be lethal and may not cause permanent damage to objects. Stuxnet is a good example of this point.[59] Finally, any computer can be turned into a cyberweapon. Thus the line between a weapon and a nonweapon or indeed between military and nonmilitary is blurred. We will return to these elements.

Meanwhile, Dipert notes that in traditional Just War Theory, there is a divide between legitimate causes for going to war (*jus ad bellum*) and how a war may be fought morally (*jus in bello*). The generally, though not universally, agreed upon criteria for *jus ad bellum* are: just cause, last resort, likelihood of success, proportionality, proper authority, and right intention. His discussion focuses on *jus ad bellum*, and particularly the first of these criteria, just cause, because he sees it as the key condition for a just war. As we shall see below, Daniel Bell considers this viewpoint to be a particularly American take on just war.

---

58. Dipert, "The Ethics of Cyberwar," 385.

59. It is worth noting that Dipert's article appeared after Stuxnet was first identified but before it had been thoroughly analyzed or the extent of its work revealed; thus he does not refer to it specifically in the article.

While Dipert lists these challenges posed by cyber technologies, his larger agenda seems to be to shed the Just War tradition from military ethics. He argues that Just War Theory (or JWT), "relies upon rickety meta-ethical foundations."[60] Specifically, he argues that the tradition is grounded in natural law theory via Thomas Aquinas and Hugo Grotius, a metaphysical understanding not held by many contemporary philosophers. As we shall see in the next section, this is a problematically truncated history of Just War Theory. Nonetheless, Dipert argues, "There is a contradiction between Just War Theory and wise geopolitical thought."[61] Thus he advocates a "realistic, diachronic, universalizable, enforceable consequentialism" as an ethical framework for determining what is ethical for cyberwar, and presumably for any kind of warfare.[62] He indicates that this approach is more interested in the contributions of game theory than it is in traditional philosophies of morality.

In terms of Dipert's application of his ethical thought on cyberwarfare, he gives a few concrete proposals. Perhaps his largest concern is the attribution problem. To recall, this is the concept that it is nearly impossible to know for sure who is doing what on the Internet. Certainty about who is behind a cyberattack is difficult if not impossible to attain. Thus Dipert wonders how much evidence is necessary to morally justify a response. He suggests that this element of uncertainty makes cyberwar similar to moral questions surrounding a preemptive war. As he elucidates, "In the case of a cyberattack, the problem is uncertainty about *who* attacked us, and in the case of preemptive and preventive war, the 'who' is known, but there is uncertainty about *whether* an enemy would indeed, in the future, attack us."[63] He believes that a preemptive war is justified if it can be shown that there is a likelihood that "a high level of expected damage to us if we do not preemptively attack" would occur.[64] Thus he believes that a similar calculation is in order for cyberwar response. This is again based on game theory and consequentialist thought rather than Just War Theory.

Dipert is also concerned about the question of what qualifies as an armed attack. This is because he notes that an "armed attack" is the only

---

60. Dipert, "The Ethics of Cyberwar," 393.
61. Ibid., 402.
62. Ibid., 394.
63. Ibid., 393.
64. Ibid.

condition included in the UN Charter for which a nation may defend itself without Security Council action and thus qualify as a just cause, which he considers the essential condition for a "just war." He comments, "The paradigmatic historical form of aggression or attack is the invasion of the sovereign territory by armed, centrally commanded, enemy soldiers of another state who are prepared to use deadly force."[65] He concludes that a cyberattack does not fit this paradigmatic model, as there is no invasion of territory or action by soldiers carrying weapons. Thus he likens cyberattacks to electronic warfare such as jamming radio communications. Yet he also notes that it is conceivable that a cyberattack could damage national infrastructure or institutions significantly or possibly even kill people through "invading" essential computer systems. Thus he considers the "armed attack" requirement of Just War Theory to be insufficient for proscribing an ethically permissible response to a cyberattack.

We see here that the question of whether a computer can be considered a weapon remains open. After all, it is not the primary function of a computer to do harm to others, as a missile or a spear might, yet at the same time any computer can be conduit for a cyberattack. It is worth noting that in 2013—three years after Dipert's article appeared—the arms control organization Wassenaar Arrangement, which boasts over forty member countries, deemed software and hardware products capable of hacking and surveillance to be "dual-use" products. Export and sale of such products, which have both peaceful and military applications, are expected to be controlled carefully. This agreement is non-binding on member states, however, and does not specify how those governments can use the dual-use products themselves.[66] Essentially any computer is potentially a weapon and a surveillance tool, and so anywhere with computers and Internet connection is a potential entry into combat territory. This also demonstrates the blurring of the line between the military and espionage, not just of one nation against another but also of a government against its own people.

A third area of concern is how to judge attacks that fall short of acts of war. Dipert notes that even during wartime, cyberattacks may be nonlethal and temporary. An attack that shuts down a power grid may only do so for a short time, for example, rather than the longer term consequences of, for example, destroying a power plant. This would only be

---

65. Ibid., 396.
66. Zetter, *Countdown to Zero Day*, 114.

heightened by attacks outside the domain of war. Dipert suggests a sort of calculation be done of the potential harms done by the attack to defensive or civilian capabilities as a means of determining proportionality.

Dipert thus sees cyberwarfare as a new development that cannot be covered by Just War Theory. Therefore, he argues for a strategic approach to cyberwarfare capabilities. In particular, he holds that no limits should be placed on countries developing defensive measures for countering cyberattacks. He does note that defensive measures do run the risk of violating privacy or the civil rights of the citizens of the country. He does not comment further on this, but does not seem overly concerned about the issue. Indeed, he suggests that the "Holy Grail" of cyberdefense would be to eliminate the attribution problem by eliminating anonymity online. Yet he admits, "Such a solution would run afoul of the relative anonymity and privacy that Internet access seems to offer, and to which users (in the West) have become accustomed."[67] Nonetheless he argues for lessening the anonymity by instituting "certain identification of every user and every message."[68] In fact he further suggests developing a more secure portion of the Internet, though he does not seem to recognize the depth of challenges involved in making this suggestion viable that Singer and Friedman raise.[69] Indeed, at the heart of Dipert's proposals is a blurring of military, law enforcement, and espionage. His proposals would, in short, militarize the Internet. This, I suggest, has already happened through the advent of cyberweapons and massive data mining by governments, but Dipert's suggestions would bring this militarization to a greater and more overt level.

Meanwhile, Dipert understands offensive capabilities to be necessary in order to retaliate if and when the defenses fail. The goal of the offensive capability is to act as a deterrent to others attempting an attack, for fear of counterattack. In other words, he is advocating a "Cyber Cold War" where nations have sufficient cyberweaponry to discourage most cyberattacks from others. While similar to the Cold War containment approach, Dipert also suggests that the difference in his vision of a Cyber Cold War is that more nations and nongovernmental actors would be involved. Essential to his vision is his consequentialist approach that holds that the most moral approach is for everyone to be sufficiently armed

---

67. Dipert, "The Ethics of Cyberwar," 404.
68. Ibid.
69. See Singer and Friedman's discussion of the challenges inherent in building a more secure version of the Internet in *Cybersecurity and Cyberwar*, 166–69.

with offensive and defensive capabilities so that the potential cost of a cyberattack is not worth the potential rewards.

Such a plan is fraught with faults. In particular, it fails to recognize the disparity of resources between nations and multiple purposes of the Iinternet. For instance, tech development is essential to the overall development of poor nations. Yet in a world of escalating cyberwar they would need the same defenses as wealthier nations. Thus a cyber arms race increases the burden of development on those who are already behind economically. More than that, to reduce a dimension of life, as I contend that the cyberdimension is, to its military function is to colonize that dimension of life. The dimension of spirit is denied in such militarization of cyberspace. Its potential for creativity, common good, and relational flourishing is negated. Dipert's argument views cyberspace purely as national infrastructure belonging to the nation-state that thus has strategic military value. Further, Dipert also fails to recognize Deibert's concerns about the seductive nature of offensive weapons that we have already discussed. The more offensive capability you have, the more pull there is to use it, thus hastening the spiral of violence. Combine this with Singer and Friedman's point that in an arms race, the more states compete to build up their capabilities, the less safe they feel, thus again increasing the spiral of the build-up, and we find that the call to a cyber arms race suffers from severely limited vision.[70]

While Dipert is ready to dispense with Just War Theory, others are quick to defend the tradition's adequacy for cyberwarfare. Indeed, several scholars have responded to Dipert's article with defenses of the JWT. Matthew Beard, for example, rejects Dipert's claims that JWT cannot account for issues of cyberwar. He argues, for example, that "armed attack is not the key condition of aggression, it is the breach of territorial integrity and/or political sovereignty that constitutes aggression in international law and [Michael] Walzer's JWT."[71] In other words, Beard holds that it is the harm suffered and not the means of inflicting it that is key in determining aggression, contra Dipert's assertion. Beard goes on to hold that defining aggression via harm done allows JWT to address cyberwar issues. For instance he notes that Russian "blockade" of Estonian cyberspace lasted for about three hours and thirty minutes. Thus he suggests that from a JWT perspective such a short time span did not do

---

70. Ibid., 157.
71. Beard, "Cyberwar and Just War Theory," 5.

enough harm to warrant being considered an act of war. Beard further deals with the question of the apparent lack of physicality in cyberattacks. In response to the example of a hypothetical cyberattack to disrupt a nation's financial markets, he replies, "the obvious response is to point to the long term consequences of such an attack: confusion, panic, fear, people's investments lost, diminished faith in markets, unemployment, etc., and point to the obvious 'physical' harms these generate. It is likely that less blood will be shed, but the overall extent quality of harm may in fact be much greater than in some minor conventional wars."[72] Thus again, the justness of cyberattacks should be judged by their effect on other dimensions of life, in Beard's opinion.

Meanwhile, Beard also holds that "JWT is not ill-equipped or inadequate in dealing with the Attribution Problem *from a theoretical standpoint.*"[73] This is because, he notes, uncertainty is not a new concept for JWT. Beard points out that Michael Walzer, whose book *Just and Unjust Wars* is often considered the classic argument for Just War Theory in contemporary international relations, for example, deals with the issue of uncertainty in his discussion of nuclear weapons. In fact, if we consider Walzer's discussion of nuclear weapons, we find that he makes the argument that: "Nuclear weapons explode the theory of just war." He goes on to assert that they are the first human technological innovation to exceed human moral imagination. Yet, he continues, "there are other notions ... having to do with aggression and the right of self-defense, that seem to require exactly that threat [of nuclear weapons]. So we move uneasily beyond the limits of justice for the sake of justice (and of peace)."[74] Thus he sees nuclear weapons as a dilemma: they are in fact unjust but, once one country has them, for now the best way to ensure that the injustice of nuclear war is not unleashed is to have the deterrence of other countries also possessing nuclear weapons. Thus it would seem for him that Just War Theory's rejection of nuclear war requires the existence of nuclear weapons in the contemporary situation, even if this is recognized as "fall[ing] for the moment under the standard of necessity" and not as a long-term stable solution.[75] Beard would seem to be following this line of reasoning in regarding cyberwar. He recognizes that the difficulty of

72. Ibid., 8.
73. Ibid., 6.
74. Walzer, *Just and Unjust Wars*, 282.
75. Ibid., 283.

attribution in cyberattacks is problematic, but argues that it is possible to deal with these issues from within a JWT perspective, and thus the tradition need not be jettisoned. He does not attempt a conclusion of how the issue is to be dealt with, but is rather concerned with defending the possibility of discussion on the issue within the Just War framework.

Beard is not alone is drawing parallels between nuclear weapons and cyberwar. It is certainly a tempting connection to make. Nuclear weapons were a powerful new destructive technology from a recent previous generation where the technology for attack raced ahead of the ethical discussions of how to regard the ethical implications of the weaponry.[76] Indeed, we have just seen Walzer's attestation that nuclear weapons exceed the familiar moral framework of humanity.

At the same time, Singer and Friedman argue that it would be a mistake to draw the parallels too closely. Specifically they point to the attribution problem as a key distinction between the two.[77] Yet there are other differences as well. For instance, they point out that in regard to nuclear weapons, speed of response is essential in order to show the other side that you could respond quickly to their attack, thus assuring mutual destruction. In cyberwar, all strikes are essentially instantaneous, and yet the true advantage is in surprise. Thus a counterattack might not occur immediately, but rather be saved for a more opportune moment. Indeed, in response to the allegations of Russian hacking in the 2016 election, Obama declared in an interview with NPR, "I think there is no doubt that when any foreign government tries to impact the integrity of our elections . . . we need to take action. And we will—at a time and place of our own choosing. Some of it may be explicit and publicized; some of it may not be."[78] The invisibility and unexpectedness of a cyberattack are its hallmarks.

A second difference that we see alluded to in Obama's statement is that the type of response may be different. That is, as Walzer points out the only equivalent deterrent to nuclear missiles are nuclear missiles. In the cyber realm, however, there are many types of cyberweapons that might be used. DDoS attacks might be more obvious and make a clearer

---

76. Singer and Friedman, *Cybersecurity and Cyberwar*, 138

77. Ibid., 145.

78. Detrow, "Obama on Russian Hacking." It is worth noting that in February 2018, NSA director and US Cyber Command chief Admiral Mike Rogers informed the Senate armed services committee that he had not been instructed to counter Russian cyber activities against United States elections. Siddiqui, "Trump 'has not Ordered.'"

statement, while subtle Stuxnet-style stealth attack may be more offensively effective over the long run. The concern, therefore, is not a nuclear Armageddon, but rather a continuous state of cyber sniping, sneak attacks, and counterattacks.

Relatedly, the result of cyberwar is unlikely to be the kind of massive destruction imagined in the event of a nuclear war. While cyberwar may indeed be capable of wreaking havoc, a more likely reality is a constant level of agitation. The greater likelihood of destruction would come from a decision to respond to a cyberattack via kinetic means. Indeed, the 2013 US Defense Science Board report advocated for a cyber response force that could respond to cyberattacks not just with other cyberattacks but also through conventional means, including the use of nuclear weapons. While this proposal was not turned into policy, there were reports in 2018 that the Pentagon was considering changes that could allow a nuclear response to a massive cyberattack such as one on essential infrastructures.[79] This issue becomes even more difficult as cyberattacks and nuclear weapons become more intertwined. For instance, many countries have identified the 2017 malware known as "WannaCry" as coming from North Korea, and most likely more specifically from the patriotic hacker group known as Lazarus. It is suspected that Lazarus used the attack to steal money to support North Korean development of nuclear weapons.[80] It is conceivable, then, that some might argue that the cyberattack was sufficiently serious to justify a nuclear strike in response, though thankfully such a move has not been made nor would it follow current Pentagon guidelines.

In terms of destructive capacity, however, cyberwar in itself is not in the same category as nuclear weapons. Rather, the threat that comes from cyberwar is heightened levels of aggression and antagonism between nations due to constant lower-level harassment, as well as paranoia from never knowing with certainty whether one is under attack or not. The psychological component in cyberwar is thus particularly distinctive. The danger that comes from it is an increased likelihood of other, more overtly destructive forms of war.

Nonetheless there is a parallel between nuclear weapons and cyber weapons in that each can inspire an arms race. As we have seen, such a race has in fact already begun. An arms race means that resources that

---

79. Starr and Cohen, "Pentagon Considers."
80. Watkins, "White House Officially Blames."

could be devoted to the benefit of society are instead being devoted to military purposes. There are accusations, for instance, that an Indian Sukhoi-30 fighter aircraft that went down near the China border in 2017 was the result of interference with on-board computer systems.[81] At the same time India itself has been accused of using a zero-day exploit of InPage software against users in Pakistan.[82] Whether or not these allegations are true, these countries have significant social needs but are caught in the cycle of the cyber arms race. Indeed, Singer and Friedman note that arms races reinforce that pressure to develop offensive weapons that we have already encountered, due to a fear of being left behind. This of course creates a vicious circle of perpetuating the arms race and hardening the offensive inclinations of the military.[83] As we shall see below, this kind of offensive mania is an aspect of war that in the Christian tradition Augustine warns against.

To return to Beard's argument, then, he wishes to argue that despite the attribution problem, Just War Theory still has relevance to cyberwar issues. Specifically, he argues that following Just War Theory, the response to a cyberattack, especially a one-time attack, would be limited to stopping the threat and rectifying the damage done by the attack. He further explains, "Neither of these goals seem to justify a counter-attack, and certainly do not justify a conventional attack (which Dipert allows for). If an excessive cyber-response or conventional attack were pursued, the cause would no longer be justified."[84] Anything more than defensive and restorative measures, for Beard, would be disproportional and thus unjust. He continues, "Given this, military responses to cyberattacks are largely limited to defensive technologies: ways of preventing attacks and quickly ending them if they occur."[85] At the same time, he holds that a cyber response to a conventional attack is always justified because it is a response that limits bloodshed. Thus Beard focuses on cyberwar as a means of minimizing loss of life, if used justly.

Overall, it would seem that Dipert's desire to discard Just War Theory stems more from philosophical commitments to a game theory

---

81. Nalapat, "Sukhoi."

82. Raza, "MOIB warns."

83. Though they also note that with the speed of the Internet, the circle cycles at a much faster pace than it was for the nuclear arms race. See Singer and Friedman, *Cybersecurity and Cyberwar*, 161.

84. Beard, "Cyberwar and Just War," 9.

85. Ibid.

approach to military ethics than it does from problems caused by cyberwar issues themselves. By the same token, Beard's commitment to the Just War Tradition similarly stem more from his philosophical commitments. This should be no surprise, as philosophical commitments are by nature foundational to ethical approaches. Yet it is worth noticing that their philosophical commitments lead both theorists to frame the question in terms of what is legal or permissible for nations to do in regards to cyberwar. There is of course great importance to this discussion, but it need not be the only way of framing the question of cyberwar. Indeed, the pressing question for our purposes is how the new developments of cyber weapons might influence Christian theological reflection on involvement in and reaction to cyberwar. Thus let us turn now to specifically Christian theological discussions of just war.

The Christian Just War Tradition

While there has so far been little attention to cyberwar issues in Christian theology, Christianity does of course have a long history of contemplating the issue of war, particularly through the Just War Tradition. Indeed, while the idea of a just war is not a Christian invention—it can be traced back at least to Aristotle—Christian influence on the tradition is quite deep. As we have seen, Dipert points to its roots in Aquinas. Yet the discussion we have seen so far centers purely on international law. Is there any theological contribution to be made to this discussion?

The contemporary Christian proposal in support of the Just War Tradition that I find most persuasive comes from Daniel M. Bell, Jr.; thus I will trace his understanding of the tradition in considering how cyberwarfare might be engaged from a Christian theological viewpoint. The heart of Bell's proposal is that the Christian version of Just War Theory ought not be about international laws or public policies. Rather, the tradition's concern is about faithful discipleship in following Jesus' teaching in ever-changing contexts. As such he distinguishes between what he calls just war as a public policy checklist, or Just War (PPC), and just war as a form of Christian discipleship, or Just War (CD).[86]

For Bell, Just War (PPC) is an institutional approach centered on how modern nation-states should relate to each other through international laws. Thus its concerns do not grow out of a Christian vision of life,

---

86. Bell, Jr., *Just War as Christian Discipleship*, 72.

but rather out of engagement with the question of what is permissible for nations to do to one another, specifically when in conflict with one another. Thus for Just War (PPC) a focus on a checklist of requirements for a just war acts as an important public policy guide. It is more interested in what is legally acceptable than what is morally best. Bell explains, "Whether a people or nation typically and usually care about justice and their neighbors is largely irrelevant to the use of the checklist. All that matters is that in going to war one is able to check off the criteria."[87] Its focus is purely on rules of military engagement between countries, not a larger vision of what a good and vibrant life is. I would add that there is great value to having secular discussions of what laws should govern war, even if it is a separate question from what the specifically Christian understanding of ethics in regard to war are.

Following Bell's terms, the theorists we have covered so far that are engaging the issue of whether Just War Theory (PPC) is still a viable approach to international law in light of cyberweapons. As I have noted, all of the theorists that we have encountered discussing cyberwar consider Just War as a framework for considering what is legal or permissible in the international community. They also focus on the specific criteria of Just War theory in considering whether cyberwar can be considered just or not, and under which circumstances some or all of the criteria may be ignored. It is Just War Theory (PPC) that Dipert argues is obsolete and the others defend. I suggest that that discussion is distinct from our inquiry here into the theological significance of cyberwar on the Christian Just War tradition.

In contrast to Just War (PPC), Just War (CD) has markedly different aims and intentions. Bell explains that this approach "is an expression of the character of the Christian community; an outgrowth of its fundamental confessions, convictions, and practices; and an extension of its consistent, day-to-day life and work on behalf of justice and love of neighbor (even enemies) in the time and realm of war."[88] That is, Just War (CD) attempts to give guidelines to being loving towards enemies and seeking justice in a world where there are true threats to justice. He further explains that this approach makes sense only through participation and practice in the Christian community.

---

87. Ibid., 74.
88. Ibid.

In terms of the sources of ethical norms for Just War (CD), Bell contends that while Just War (PPC) takes the criteria proposed by Christian thinkers but does not see these criteria through the light of the faith behind them, Just War (CD) is more concerned about the Christian goal of discipleship that lies behind the stated criteria that has grown up over the years of discussion of Just War Theory. More specifically, the driving question of Just War (CD) is not what conditions countries may ethically give as a basis for going to war but rather how the church can faithfully follow Christ in seeking justice.

War as following Christ and seeking justice may sound surprising, but Bell finds these ideas at the center of the development of the tradition of just war. In particular, he points to Augustine. Augustine did not develop a systematic theory of just war. Rather, his reflections on the subject are interspersed into discussions of a variety of other topics throughout the corpus of his writings. One of the places that Augustine particularly deals with the issue of war is in his "Reply to Faustus the Manichean." Augustine's argument is that while it is true that the kingdom of heaven is a reign of peace, historical conditions change. While in the first few centuries of Christian history the church proclaimed a pacifist ethic, Augustine suggests that this was not an eternal rule. In the time of the patriarchs and prophets, God did indeed allow the temporal kingdoms of the faithful to wage war. Thus he argues that since there are now in his time Christian emperors, it is possible that God may call on those emperors to wage war at times as part of the duty of the temporal kingdom. Different times of history require different responses from people of faith. Augustine therefore understands Jesus' injunction to turn the left cheek in response to someone striking your right spiritually, as a matter of inward disposition.[89]

Indeed, Augustine insists that rationale and authority are essential components in whether or not to go to war. He holds, "When war is undertaken in obedience to God, who would rebuke, or humble, or crush the pride of man, it must be allowed to be a righteous war."[90] Ultimately, as Bell notes of Augustine's thought, all life and death belong to God. Therefore, God alone should have authority over who is to die, and therefore Christians should not engage in killing. There are, however, two cases where God shares this authority with humanity. One is that

---

89. Augustine, "Reply to Faustus the Manichean," 65.
90. Ibid., 65.

God has delegated some of the authority over life and death to those who govern. Thus waging a just war or putting a criminal to death are not in violation of the commandment. The other case is when God gives a command to kill; in particular in this case he is referring to biblical instances where God commands war or killing.

Elsewhere, Augustine advises, "when you are arming for the battle, [recall] that even your bodily strength is a gift of God; for, considering this, you will not employ the gift of God against God."[91] The goal of war is peace. He continues, "Peace should be the object of your desire; war should be waged only as a necessity, and waged only that God may by it deliver men from the necessity and preserve them in peace. For peace is not sought in order to the kindling of war, but war is waged in order that peace may be obtained."[92] War may be a political necessity but its objective must be peace that allows human flourishing.

Above all, a just war for Augustine is one that is done in order to turn sinners from their wicked ways. Christians are not to engage in war for revenge or power, certainly, but even further they are not to engage in war for self-defense. Indeed, Augustine says that the real evil in war is not in death or destruction. Returning to his "Reply to Faustus the Manichean," we read, "the real evils in war are love of violence, revengeful cruelty, fierce and implacable enmity, wild resistance, and the lust of power, and such like."[93] When the proper inward disposition is lost, these evils creep in during wartime. But if war is done so that the enemy is turned from sin, the action is rooted in love. As Bell frames Augustine's point here, "killing and death are possibilities, but they are not what a just war aims at. Rather, the aim of a just war is that the unjust enemy will turn from their wicked ways, make amends, and rejoin the community of peace and justice."[94]

Drawing on Augustine's sense of the Christian stance on war being an ongoing engagement with God's interaction with human history, Bell suggests that this dialogue must still continue. He therefore notes that there is no comprehensive doctrine or theory of just war in Christian dogma. Rather, he prefers to call it a tradition. Specifically, he sees it as "a living tradition that more closely resembles an ongoing conversation

---

91. Augustine, "To Count Boniface," 62.
92. Ibid., 62–63.
93. Augustine, "Reply to Faustus the Manichean," 64.
94. Bell, Jr., *Just War as Christian Discipleship*, 31.

about what it means to love and seek justice for our neighbors in war."[95] Because it is a living tradition, the precise criteria themselves are not absolute. They are open for debate. The goal of outlining criteria is to give a picture of what it means to love your enemies, even when you are at war with them. As such, the criteria themselves may be somewhat fluid as contexts and styles of warfare change. What does not change is the commitment to love and justice.

Along with Augustine, Bell lists Thomas Aquinas, Francisco di Vitoria, and Hugo Grotius among the key figures in the development of the dialogue on just war. We have seen already that JWT (PPC) tend to cite Aquinas and Grotius as the founders of the Just War Tradition. Yet these men were theologians building on the Augustinian tradition.

By the medieval period, the criteria of legitimate authority, just cause, and right intention had been gleaned from Augustine's writings. Bell notes that Aquinas's thought was not especially unique, but rather was largely typical of these medieval adaptations of Augustine's thought. Much of Aquinas's influence comes from his overall stature as a theologian. That said, Bell notes two contours of Aquinas's thought of particular significance. One is that to Augustine's sense that the goal of war must be peace Aquinas adds that it also must be to bring about the common good. That is, along with correcting the sinner, war must also protect the community from the damage done by sinners. This idea is perhaps latent in Augustine's thought, but Aquinas was more directly influenced by Aristotle on this point.[96] The second point of distinction by Aquinas is on the matter of self-defense. The earlier theologians had prohibited lethal self-defense. Aquinas does not disagree, but nuances the point by adding that one may not *intend* to kill another in self-defense. This means that if one accidentally kills an attacker while defending oneself, no crime or sin has been committed. This position has given rise to what is known as the "principle of double effect," where there may be a difference between the intentional effects of an action and the unintended effects. This principle eventually took on great importance in church discussions of just war.[97]

After Aquinas, Francisco de Vitoria, writing in the early sixteenth century, was the next theologian of particular import in the just war conversation. He systematized much of the theological teachings on just

---

95. Ibid., 71.
96. Ibid., 47.
97. Ibid., 47–48.

war, organizing them into what became known as *jus ad bellum* and *jus in bello*, as we have seen Dipert mention. Vitoria brings in a number of other developments into the understanding of war. For our purposes, one of the important ones is that along with Scripture and tradition, he appeals to the customary laws that peoples and nations have developed, thus sowing the seed for the eventual development of Just War Theory in international law apart from Christian theology. Vitoria also notes that it can at least appear that both sides in a war have just cause. That is, based on the information available to each side, each might think its cause is just and so can go to war with a clear conscience. For Vitoria, it is not that each has a just cause, but lack of information causes at least one side to erroneously think that its cause is just. He feels this is all the more reason to moderate waging war.[98] We see in Vitoria, then, a movement towards Just War thinking as a melding of theology and political/practical wisdom. We do not yet have the divide into Bell's two types of Just War thinking, but the elements that lead to that division have been introduced.

The seeds of distinction begin to bear fruit in the thought of Hugo Grotius a century later. In the wake of the Reformation, the ability of Christianity to speak to European society as a whole was significantly lessened. Into this gap, Grotius attempted to reformulate the Just War Tradition in more universal terms that did not depend on Christian theology. He was not working from a secular standpoint, but rather took an apologetic approach of attempting to demonstrate that the Christian vision had relevance to all, even those outside the Christian tradition. Thus he uses a natural law foundation, as Dipert has mentioned, to ground the criteria that the Christian tradition had developed. Bell suggests that for Grotius, the natural law foundation was an ethical minimum, while following the gospel called for a higher moral standard.[99] It is, however, this moral minimum for which he is remembered because it forms the basis for modern international law and the discussions of Just War (PPC) that we have seen being debated in the context of cyberwar.

Yet as we review this history, a few important distinctions between these discussions and the details of cyberwar must be noted. One is the idea of a legitimate authority. The whole history reviewed here assumes a prince or government that has been given the authority to wage war. Yet as we have seen, in cyber war we can never be sure of who is acting. Is it a

---

98. Ibid., 50.
99. Ibid., 56.

nation-state behind an attack, or patriotic hackers, or perhaps even cyber criminals? The tradition has not needed to deal with this issue. What counts as a legitimate authority in cyberwar?[100] Beyond that, recall that for Augustine the importance of the legitimate authority is that it has had responsibility for deciding on life and death delegated to it by God. Yet as we have seen, the majority of cyberattacks are non-lethal. While the Just War (PPC) debates have discussed a legal framework for considering less than lethal force, does the Christian tradition have anything to say about nonlethal conflict? After all, if the concern of Just War (CD) is peace and human flourishing, the possibility of death is not the only force that may be destructive to those goals. Indeed both in this short survey of the development of Christian Just War thinking and in Bell's book more generally, an equation between war and killing is prevalent, while as we have seen cyberwar would likely be largely "bloodless." A third limitation that we see in this history is Vitoria's distinction of ethics before war and ethics in war, which we have also seen Dipert note. When it comes to cyberwar, can there really be such a distinction? Because the most powerful cyberweapons are stealth, the distinction between in war and out of war are blurred.

Limitations and Debates in Christian Just War Theory

There is a debate, Bell notes, amongst Just War theorists over whether just war has a presumption for justice or a presumption against war. He notes that the origins of this debate stem from the 1983 statement by the US Catholic bishops entitled *The Challenge of Peace*. This document claims that just war and pacifism share a presumption against violence and war. In response, some have claimed that just war does not have this presumption against war but rather seeks justice and works against injustice. For Bell, this debate is problematic because Christianity should have more than a presumption for justice. He insists, "Christianity does not hold a presumption for justice. Rather, Christianity's commitment to justice is

---

100. Bell devotes a chapter to the issue of legitimate authority. He advocates for the church acting as a "node of authority" interacting with other legitimate nodes, such as governments. Thus he argues for a political engagement by the church on matters of war. This would seem to leave such quasi-military groups as being outside the bounds of a legitimate authority, but he does not directly address the issue. See Bell, Jr., *Just War as Christian Discipleship*, 101–25.

absolute and unwavering."[101] He feels that the concept of presumption suggests that in some cases it is possible to override a commitment to justice, a position that he rejects. Rather, he argues that the Christian commitment to justice must be total. "The only thing that changes with regard to that commitment is not its strength or constancy but how it is lived out in a given situation," he explains. "To put this in terms of the just war tradition, there are times when the church's pursuit of justice is rightly embodied in war, and there are times when the pursuit of justice takes forms other than war."[102] Thus just war is not seen by Bell, following Augustine, as a departure from Jesus' vision, but rather is a contextualization of it.

Bell's explanation of the value of the Just War tradition is based in a virtue ethic approach. That is, he understands Christian discipleship to be a call to inhabit the good.[103] Thus what he is seeking is for the church to be formed into a people who are shaped to engage in war in a just manner. He explains that, "[JWT (CD)'s] ethical focus in on the character and virtues or habits that should distinguish the Christian life in war as well as in peace."[104] Thus the criteria for just war are "a kind of shorthand for a way of life," rather than an absolute set of rules. What is important is not keeping track of which criteria are met—or arguing about which one is most important or when they can be broken—but rather being a person who seeks to love even enemies whether at war or not.

Because of the virtue approach, Bell dismisses the idea that just war is a noble but unattainable idea. Thus he counters the frequent charge that there has never been a just war. He replies: "the proper response to the call to just war is not 'Has it been done before?,'" but "How then should we order our lives so that we might respond to the call faithfully?"[105] For Bell, the virtues of a just war people include patience, courage, wisdom, and justice. The point here again is not that there is a checklist of virtues required, but rather that the Christian community be a community that instills a strength of character that includes love, service, and concern for justice for others at all times. It is not simply a personal piety, then, but rather an ethic that arises out of a community. Indeed, Bell argues that

101. Ibid., 87.
102. Ibid., 88.
103. Ibid., 35.
104. Ibid., 79.
105. Ibid., 64.

this community extends beyond the church: "The nature and character of a people's political institutions are central to the ability to faithfully inhabit the just war discipline."[106] Again, such an approach seems to assume an influence that may indeed have been available in Christendom, but is at most debatable today, and simply does not reflect reality for the church in much of the world.

Nonetheless, Bell calls on the community of the church to cultivate disciples who consider seriously the call of justice in deciding whether to go to war and in determining how to wage war morally. He argues that the way war is fought can be shaped by an active Just War ethic among the Christian community. He points out historically that in medieval times when the Just War Tradition had its greatest influence in Europe, war was approached differently than it is today. For example, "The Peace of God" was a rule designed to limit the harm done to noncombatants by designating not only persons such as clergy, merchants, and farmers, but also their land and property as protected from soldiers.

Above all, Bell is saying that war is a human invention and not an inevitable component of reality. As such, humans have some control over how war is conducted. The question for the church, then, is how to insist on justice and the good of all creation in a world filled with war. It is this question, for Bell, that should be drawn from Aquinas's discussion of just war, rather than the natural law metaphysics that Dipert rejects. The specifics of Bell's proposal of what a Christian community that fosters a Just War ethic looks like are beyond the scope of this chapter; what is key is Bell's commitment that war can be shaped into different forms through Christian fostering of an ethic of engaging in war only for the sake of justice. Specifically, the question for us is, given that the Internet is a human construction, whether there are ways to shape cyberwar so that it seeks justice. This is especially true given the diffusion of power, the attribution problems, and the reality of patriotic hacking that are elements of cyberwar so that the idea of a "legitimate authority" would seem inadequate to cyberspace.

In considering Bell's arguments, while on the one hand finding them appealing, I cannot help but wonder if Bell is overly idealizing war. Even in a limited war, death and destruction is no less real for those on whom it befalls, whether or not it is as widespread as it could have been. War will, further, always have innocent victims, as Der Derian argues. These

---

106. Ibid., 239.

casualties include all too often the psyche of those who fight. I also have my doubts of whether humans can maintain an adversarial relation with others and yet keep themselves free of hate. Likewise, I have doubts that it is possible to resist the temptation to use powerful weapons we develop to gain advantage over others, thus falling prey to Augustine's warning against the true evils of war. These ruminations, however, extend beyond our question of the relationship of Just War to cyberwar.

Despite these reservations, I find helpful Bell's reframing the question of just war towards one of how to organize Christian life so that if we find ourselves in a situation of war we are able to seek justice as much as it is possible. Even so, I am unconvinced that such a goal is attainable. Put more technically, a truly just war may not be strictly impossible, but it is indeed "im-possible" in the Derridean sense. That is, a just war may not be a formal impossibility, but it is not possible within the given structures of our world. The powers of the world will seek to enhance their own power rather than consider justice or peace as primary goals. After all, even Augustine's argument for just war depends on the presence of a Christian emperor who is willing to pursue war only through faithfully seeking to follow God's command, not a modern nation-state employing strategic use of game theory.

Indeed, the premise for a Just War Theory would seem to be a sufficiently strong social voice for the church. While this may indeed be possible in some contexts, such contexts are few and far between. In much of the world, where Christians are a minority religion, it is unlikely that the church has sufficient political influence to shape public policy towards more just considerations in engaging in war. What value might Just War (CD) have in such a context? Might it be time to reverse Augustine's move and say that the historical situation has returned to a time when Christians must be pacifist? What would such a move look like in terms of cyberwar?

Despite my concerns about Bell's proposal, I find his vision of Just War Theory as a call away from total war towards more limited engagement to be beneficial. Yet does this understanding of the Just War Tradition speak to the realities of cyberwar, which takes total war to an extreme conclusion? Can the Just War Tradition speak in a context where the battlefield is ever-present and that encourages constant nonlethal aggression?

Cyberweapons and a Christian Theology of the Cyberdimension

In considering cyberweapons, what might they tell us theologically? That is, first what might the Christian tradition of Just War say to us about cyberwar, but beyond that how might this be related to our inquiry into the cyber realm as a dimension interpenetrated by the dimension of spirit? Let us turn first to the Just War Tradition, and particularly Dipert's contention that cyberwar renders Just War Theory obsolete.

In terms of criteria for war, we can recall the classic list of: legitimate authority, just cause, right intent, last resort, reasonable chance of success, discrimination or noncombatant immunity, and proportionality. As we have seen, the attribution problem in cyberspace makes a determination of what is a legitimate authority problematic. In terms of just cause and right intent, we have the challenge of the offensive focus currently dominating cyber technologies. That is, the focus on offensive capabilities brings temptation towards an arms race, which is ultimately a search for power. Recall that this is specifically one of the things Augustine warns against in the conduct of war. Likewise, we have mentioned that offensive capability might cause governments to forego diplomacy and instead seek a cyber response to issues. Meanwhile, by making the battlefield potentially everywhere, cyberweapons potentially erase noncombatant immunity. Because the exact effects of a virus are difficult to predict, proportionality is difficult to judge. Reasonable chance of success, then, is the only criteria that offensive cyberweapons might comfortably meet. To this we may add that the withholding of zero days for offensive use violates the common good, which Aquinas included in his account of Just War.

Given this disparity between offensive cyberweapons and Just War criteria, it is possible to see Dipert's point that Just War criteria do not account for cyberwar. Conversely, it would seem to me that it would be at least as logical to conclude that cyberweapons do not meet the Just War criteria because they are in fact immoral. They simply cannot meet the criteria of a Just War, and so they should not be used. Only defensive cyber measures are acceptable. We would then find ourselves in the position that Walzer holds about nuclear weapons. They are immoral but they exist; therefore how do we regulate to ensure that they are not used? In terms of cyberweapons, however, this is a more difficult task because of the secret nature of their use.

Yet even if cyberwar and cyberweapons are deemed immoral, what would count? As we have seen, the basis for discussion of war within the Christian tradition has come from Augustine's argument that life and death belong to God. Most of the discussions center around understanding war as causing death, including much of Bell's discussion. Yet cyberattacks that kill would be an outlier. Most attacks would be nonlethal. Would this put them outside the concerns of Just War? It would seem that something along the lines of Aquinas's appeal to the common good or a sense of human flourishing would be needed to account for the state of constant nonlethal conflict that seems to be the most likely manifestation of cyberwar. Indeed the primary danger of cyberconflict is not death or even destruction but the cultivation of increasing structural violence within the cyberdimension. Given this reality, Dipert may be right from a policy view that the checklist approach to Just War Theory may not be sufficient to account for cyberwar.

This line of thinking, however, follows JWT (PPC) reasoning. What might JWT (CD) have to say? Let us recall that Bell's basic premise here is that the Christian call to seek justice may at times require war, but such situations must be limited. Thus JWT (CD) works against total war. The challenge of cyberwar here is that its nature is to expand total war to its furthest limits. By utilizing the Internet, it takes war into a realm that pervades human life. Can there be a form of peace fostered by cyberspace? Frühbauer struggles with this question in asking whether there can be an ideal of cyber *peace* that is more than rhetoric. He concludes, "The demand for CyberPeace can . . . create sensitivity and critical awareness for the problematic of CyberWar. . . . The ultimate goal of developments of information and communication technology must not be its militarization, but can only be the civilization of the information society."[107] Yet in terms of concrete proposals for what this kind of peace might look like, Frühbauer offers suggestions of international treaties and laws, but little more than sensitivity to the issue in terms of individuals or communities such as the church.

A key aspect of the challenge for the church in seeking justice in war, let alone promoting peace in cyberspace, is the invisibility of cyberwar. Most cyberwar activities are done clandestinely. Such a move to secrecy makes it impossible for the Christian community to stand up for peace and display the virtues of a community that desires peace and justice.

---

107. Frühbauer, "'Cyberwars,'" in Borgman et al., eds., *Cyberspace*, 57.

How can we insist upon the just conduct of a war that we do not know is occurring? If war is done in secret, how can we insist that it be done to turn our neighbor from sin? Moreover, if the cyberdimension is also infused with the dimension of spirit, then militarizing the cyberdimension will have a distorting effect on the manifestation of spirit. Recall here that the dimension of spirit focuses on the quest for being and meaning to correspond through the process of actualizing possibility and overcoming ambiguity.

Yet if cyberwar is ethically problematic, what option do we have but to participate? In traditional war, Christians could decide that war is not ethical and insist on pacifism. Yet in cyberwar conscientious objection is difficult. Indeed, to do so would entail following the Amish in a rejection of electrical technology, given that even power generation and sewage treatment are enveloped into the cyber realm. If the church is to make a commitment to engage the world, it means that it will be entangled in the cyberdimension. It is entangled in the ambiguity of the Internet as it is. Indeed, this moves us to the broader theological questions. If the cyber realm is indeed a dimension of life, what does it mean that this dimension is being converted into a battlefield? That is, it is not cyberweapons per se that are the greatest problem, but rather the defining of cyberspace as a military realm that is the difficulty. Certainly the inorganic, organic, and even spiritual realms do indeed have aspects of war within them. This is the reality of sin or estrangement that the dimensions of our lives are not fully of peace but instead also contain an element of violence. The challenge in the cyberdimension is its potential to become a fully militarized zone. Lurking behind every interaction is the possibility of a cyberweapon being included underneath our other transactions. As we shall see in the next chapters, as this militarizing tendency is combined with authoritarian surveillance and the commodification of complete commercialization, a dimension of life that has the potential to bring about greater connection and freedom is being transformed into a space of enslavement to consumption and violence. Such enslavement in the cyberdimension would bring with it similar consequences in the other dimensions of life. The dimensions cannot be disconnected. For the dimension of spirit to be intertwined within the cyberdimension, a vision of unambiguous essence of life in cyberspace is needed, to go alongside the metaphors of spiritual presence, the kingdom of God, and everlasting life. To get at this metaphor, we must look to the intertwined ambiguities of the cyberdimension that interlock with its militarization.

Chapter 3

Big Data, Data Mining, and the Reduction to Calculable Identity

During a panel discussion at the Consumer Electronics Show in January 2014, Ford Motor Company's Global VP of Marketing and Sales stated something both intensely frightening and in retrospect quite obvious. In discussing data privacy, he declared, "We know everyone who breaks the law, we know when you're doing it. We have GPS in your car, so we know what you're doing." He quickly added, "By the way, we don't supply that data to anyone."[1] The statement was quickly retracted, with the statement that Ford does not collect data about customers' use of their cars without approval and consent. Nevertheless, the initial statement points to the amount of data that can be collected about our behaviors. Any car with GPS included leaves a continuing record of where it is located, how fast it is going, and other details about its activities. The executive's initial comments suggest that this data is being stored and surveilled in some manner.

If Ford has the capability to record this kind of data, it would hardly be the only group doing so. Security expert and writer Bruce Schneier, in his book *Data and Goliath*, points out that data is the by-product of every activity a computer does. He explains, "Connect to the Internet, and the data you produce multiplies: records of websites you visit, ads you click on, words you type. Your computer, the sites you visit, and the computers in the network each produce data."[2] In fact, he goes on to say, nearly every activity we engage in produces data. This is perhaps most clear through

---

1. Edwards, "Ford Exec."
2. Schneier, *Data and Goliath*, 13.

cell phones. They constantly calculate their location in relation to the nearest cell towers, so if you carry one with you there is a data trail of your location. Calls or messages using the phone create data about who you contact, and the various apps that a smartphone contains each create data about how they are used. Even home appliances such as ovens or refrigerators can be computerized and create data on their functioning. Anything that engages a computer creates data, and through the Internet that data is transmittable.

Of course, computers have been around for some time creating data. The difference in recent years comes in the ability to store and analyze the data. Schneier holds that, "By 2010, we as a species were creating more data per day than we did from the beginning of time until 2003. By 2015, 76 exabytes of data will travel across the Internet every year."[3] Because the cost of data storage has plummeted, it is possible to retain an unfathomable amount of this data. He notes that the cost of cloud storage of data in 2015 was 90 percent less than it was in 2011. This drop in price has allowed the amount of data stored to increase. The NSA's Utah Data Center in Bluffdale, he tells us, is the third largest data center in the world, and while the exact details are classified, experts believe it capable of storing twelve exabytes of data. Google, meanwhile, has the capacity globally to store fifteen exabytes.

Given that the cyberdimension, then, is a dimension dominated by data—indeed not just data but of storable and observable data—what role does the dimension of spirit play within cyberspace? More specifically, what kind of manifestation of spirit is possible in a realm most frequently associated with a binary reality of ones and zeros? What does a data-driven view of reality do to conceptions of identity, particularly given the increasing tendency towards pervasive surveillance that has come to be associated with cyberspace? In this chapter, we will turn our attention to the growth of big data as working hand in hand with the militarization of cyberspace that we encountered in the previous chapter. We will then consider theories of surveillance, bringing them into discussion with theological reflections on the self and what it means to be human and infused with spirit.

---

3. Ibid., 18. An exabyte is a billion billion bites, or about five hundred billion pages of text.

What Happens to All the Data?

The fact that so much data is now generated and stored is not as important as the questions of who has access to it and how is it used. The security issue with data is that governments and corporations analyze and retain the data that is generated about us. Much of the data is generated without our consent, and it is used to draw conclusions about us that impact our lives. The analyzing of mass quantities of data is known as data mining. It is a practice that has become incredibly widespread in recent years to the point that it is a critical component in understanding the tensions within the cyberdimension. This data mining, which can be considered a form of surveillance, when combined with the militarization of cyberspace produces a unique form of ever-shifting power flows and challenges conceptions of both the corporeality of the physical dimensions and the emergence of the spirit dimension.

A key concept in this type of surveillance is what is known as "metadata." Metadata is information about how you interface with cyberspace rather than the details of what you do in cyberspace. That is, it is not the content of our online interactions, such as the message in an email we send or a transcript of a telephone conversation. Rather, it is the information about where we were when we sent the email or made the call, who we sent it to, and how long the conversation lasted. Schneier points out, "Telephone metadata alone reveals a lot about us. . . . Phone metadata reveals what and who we're interested in and what's important to us, no matter how private."[4] While in theory metadata is anonymous, it is not difficult to identify a great deal about a person solely through metadata.

The details come with even greater clarity when web search metadata is also included.[5] As Schneier explains, "We don't lie to our search engine. We're more intimate with it than with our friends, lovers, or family members. We always tell it exactly what we're thinking about, in words as clear as possible."[6] Google, for instance, keeps a complete record of every search a person has ever made while logged on to the site. Thus it has a better memory of what has interested us than we do ourselves. Here

---

4. Ibid., 20.

5. There is debate whether web searches count as data or metadata, but the NSA considers it metadata because search terms are embedded in URLs. Until June 1, 2015, the Patriot Act allowed American monitoring on American's metadata. See Breslow, "With or Without the Patriot Act."

6. Schneier, *Data and Goliath*, 22.

we begin to see our understanding of being a subject becomes of interest in the cyberdimension. If our memory is a construction of the current iteration of the ever-emerging process that we consider the self to hold a connection with previous manifestations of our self, then memory serves to help enable self-construction. Some memories are given priority while others are minimized as we continually reinvent ourselves in relation to our situation.[7] Yet in the realm of data collection, every random thought and question that is stored is equally part of a construction of us made and analyzed by governments and corporations.

Building on this point, Digital Humanities scholar N. Katherine Hayless differentiates between database and narrative worldviews. "Whereas database reflects the computer's ontology and operates with optimum efficiency in set-theoretic operations based on formal logic, narrative is an ancient linguistic technology almost as old as the human species," she contends.[8] As such, narrative was central to human evolutionary cognitive development. While databases can sort and correlate data, they cannot on their own devise the categories for sorting or how to collect the data. Further, they cannot account for indeterminate data or account for "complex syncopations" of chronology. In short, Hayless argues, narrative is a form of thinking attuned for meaning while databases are a form of thinking attending to information.[9] Thus she argues that narrative is essential to human life in a manner that cannot be replaced by databases, even as narratives in the digital era will be more and more infused by data.[10] These themes are ones that will recur as we continue.

Returning to the collection of data, telephones and web searches are far from the only source of metadata. Online purchases, social media posts, email subjects, and contact lists are all considered metadata. Metadata for a single individual can tell a great deal about that person, perhaps even more than data, because it reveals webs of relationships, interests, and movements. This becomes even more true, however, when you have detailed metadata about a large mass of people.

Most of the data and metadata about us is out of our control, and indeed we are utterly unaware of much of it. As security scholar Ronald J. Deibert argues, "All of the data about us as individuals in social network

7. On this contemporary understanding of memory, see as an example Schacter and Addis, "The cognitive neuroscience of constructive memory."
8. Hayless, *How We Think*, 179.
9. Ibid., 180.
10. Ibid., 182.

communities is owned, operated, managed, and manipulated by third parties beyond our control, and those third parties are, typically, private companies. In assessing the full spectrum of major social changes related to the information revolution, the entrusting of this unimaginably huge mass of civilian data in private sector hands ranks as perhaps the most important."[11] In fact, the current economic backbone of cyberspace could be said to be the currency of personal information. In return for the use of web services such as Google or Facebook or Twitter, we consent to give them our data. We consent not only to submitting some basic personal information, but we also give away the details of our network of connections, information about what we like, what we search for on the Internet, our thoughts on politics, details of our love life, and countless other facets of who we are. All of this is recorded and used.

Some of the data is used directly to personalize cyberspace for us. For example, if you buy a book for your Kindle through Amazon, Amazon has data on when you read it, how quickly you read it, whether you finish it or not, and so forth.[12] Amazon uses the data it has about you to tailor suggestions for you of other books to buy. This is a rather straightforward use of data. Other uses are subtler. If you have a Gmail account with Google, for instance, Google will scan the words in your email messages for clues as to which advertisements to show along the side of your screen. The use of data for personalized advertising is a major use of data mining. A well-known incident comes from Target department stores. A story in the *New York Times* in 2012 reported that a man had complained to the company about it sending coupons for baby-related items to his teenage daughter. He later discovered that Target had been correct; his daughter was pregnant. Target was able to identify this from her buying patterns.[13] More recently an article in the newspaper *The Australian* suggested that Facebook targeted real-time current emotional state in its advertising, though Facebook has called the report misleading.[14]

All of this data produced and saved is known as "big data," while the tactics for analyzing it is known as "data mining." The vast bytes of data accumulated through the cyberdimension are mined in a variety of ways. Much of the use of the data is quite different from the reason it

---

11. Deibert, *Black Code*, 52.
12. Schneier, *Data and Goliath*, 28.
13. Duhigg, "How Companies Learn Your Secrets."
14. Levin, "Facebook told advertisers."

was accumulated in the first place. Data mining is a means of producing secondary value for the data that is being stored. As Schneier points out, the underlying premise for big data is "save everything you can, and someday you'll be able to figure out some use for it all."[15] Data mining makes inferences about people based on the data collected about them. Schneier goes on to explain that some inferences are obvious, such as by knowing which websites a person visits you can intuit what hobbies they have. Yet, Schneier continues, "Some inferences are more subtle. A list of someone's grocery purchases might imply her ethnicity. Or her age and gender, and possibly religion."[16] These inferences are frequently incorrect, but can often be spot on. It is these inferences that companies use to target personalized advertising to us, yet this targeted message can also feel invasive. Thus he suggests that a key tension with big data is that data we are willing to share can lead to details about us that we do not wish to share.

While corporations love data for its marketing potential, governments like it for other reasons. Big data promises unprecedented levels of intelligence on the activities of people. On the one hand this offers a tantalizing opportunity to identify and eliminate safety and security risks for those concerned with public security. On the other hand, it also offers incredible temptations for the abuse of power and marginalizing protests to the status quo. Particularly though the ability to merge multiple data sets, governments are able to engage in massive unchecked surveillance through the cyberdimension. Security expert David Lyon declares of the government use of metadata, "The future of the internet is clearly up for grabs in the sense that its democratic potential and promise of open communication fall under what is perceived as the dark shadow of surveillance."[17] All data mining is a form of surveillance, Schneier contends.[18] It is a means of monitoring a person and predicting their actions. It is a means of calculating the future of the individual and whole populations. The ability to calculate likely futures grants the power to control and manipulate an all-too-often irresistible prize for those in power.

Surveillance, of course, is hardly a new phenomenon. Governments have a long history of surveillance, collecting large amounts of data about

---

15. Schneier, *Data and Goliath*, 33.
16. Ibid., 34.
17. Lyon, ed., *Surveillance After Snowden*, 68.
18. The US government does not consider collecting metadata to be surveillance.

people. Whether in the Soviet Union or McCarthy-era America or in countless other times and places, government agencies have kept track of phone calls, personal connections, magazine subscriptions, and countless other details as a way of developing an inferred portrait of a person's thinking and likely behavior. For Schneier, the difference with big data and data mining today is that the surveillance can be done retroactively. Traditional surveillance begins at the moment that a subject is identified as someone to monitor and continues from that point forward until the surveillance ends. In our new big data era, seemingly everything on everybody is continually being collected and saved just in case it someday proves useful. Thus it is now possible to decide that someone is to be the subject of surveillance and, instead of beginning the surveillance with the present moment, start with mining the data about that person over the previous several years. Thus not only does Google having a complete list of all of our searches point to a new sense of subjectivity in the cyberdimension, it also has a unique sense of time. We will see a variety of aspects of this new sense of time, but in terms of surveillance it manifests itself in the ability to move backwards in time. Let us recall that for Tillich an aspect of a unique dimension is a unique manifestation of time.

The power in mass surveillance is more than simply being able to review a historical record of big data, however. The perhaps even more pernicious effects come from the ability of data mining to merge multiple streams of data together. A research project at Carnegie Mellon University demonstrated the power of correlating a variety of massive databases. Using a camera in a public place, they were able to capture photographs of passersby. They could then identify them using facial recognition software and Facebook's publicly tagged photos and correlate that identity with other available data. They were able to do all of this quickly enough to display personal information about the people walking by in real time while they were on camera. As Schneier notes, such technology could already conceivably be made available as a smartphone app.[19]

Such data analysis is of great commercial interest, to be sure. Indeed a whole industry of data brokering and analysis has grown up around the commercial potential of knowing more and more details about people. Initiate Systems, Acxiom, Epsilon, and ExactData are a few companies that work to make sense of the available data and then sell their findings. It is possible to buy from these companies lists of people fitting any

---

19. Schneier, *Data and Goliath*, 41. See also Carnegie Mellon University webpage, "More Than Facial Recognition."

number of descriptions: gamblers, people with depression, hikers, people interested in Toyota trucks, and so on. The limits are few. The data broker Teletrack sold lists of people who had applied for payday loans or similar nontraditional forms of credit, so that companies wanting to target people likely to take bad financial deals would have a list of potential marks. Meanwhile in 2012 Equifax sold a discount loan company a list of people who were late on mortgage payments. These two actions were fined by the FTC because they revealed financial information, but that is one of the few limits on these brokers.[20]

Indeed, this sale of personal information is the economic foundation of the Internet. Large Internet companies such as Google, Facebook, and Amazon act as information middlemen. They command a huge share of Internet traffic and so collect an immense amount of personal data that they can then sell to the data brokers. This sale of data is their primary source of income. As Schneier contends, "Our relationship with many of the Internet companies we rely on is not a traditional company-customer relationship. That's primarily because we're not customers. We're products those companies sell to their *real* customers.... We are tenant farmers for these companies, working on their land by producing data that they in turn sell for profit."[21] He goes on to say that in return for giving them our personal data about our Internet searches or shopping wish lists and so forth, they store our files and emails and allow us to access them from wherever in the world we happen to be (thereby giving them our travel habits). They make the Internet easy to navigate for us in return for our data and our loyalty. After all, once you have a Gmail account and an Android device, it is not easy to switch to an iPhone and iPad, or to an Amazon Kindle, and so forth. In other words, for Schneier, we can think of these companies as our new feudal lords to whom we have given over control of our access to cyberspace in return for convenience of use.

In a similar vein, French Marxist philosopher Bernard Stiegler argues that post-industrial society, which he dubs "hyper-industrial," has brought about a transformation in the nature of the proletariat. Beyond Marx's understanding of the proletariat as workers, Stiegler contends that since the 1960s the nature of the proletariat has been changed to being consumers, thus transforming the middle class into proletariat as well. He argues, "The submission of existence to standardized behavioral

20. Schneier, *Data and Goliath*, 53.
21. Ibid., 58.

models of consumption follows the process of proletarianization that had begun in the nineteenth century with the standardization of modes of production. The consumer is the new proletarian figure, and the proletariat, very far from disappearing, is a condition from which it has become nearly impossible to escape."[22] That is, he argues that capitalism has changed from focused primarily on control of production to also controlling consumption and inculcating a desire to continually consume new products as the means of bringing about an individual sense of identity. Ironically, however, this mass inculcation of desire for individuality is in fact a means of homogenizing and controlling a society by forming them into perpetual consumers. Indeed, he argues that it is the quest for technological novelty that particularly locks people into being a herd (or, perhaps better, a swarm, to anticipate Tatiana Bazzichelli's term that we will encounter in the next chapter) of voracious consumers. Building on Stiegler's and Schneier's arguments, I would suggest that the data mining revolution has opened a new stage of proletarianization in the cyberdimension. There is a combination of proletariat as producers and proletariat as consumers. In tapping into a thirst for massive consumption of digital media through information technologies, the large Internet companies have turned those with a digital footprint into their workforce of data producers.

For Schneier, the problem with this model of being data producers for the Internet companies is that much of our public life is conducted in a situation where private companies are in control and set the rules with no means for us to negotiate limits on how they use the data that they collect about us. It is not practical to opt out of using them, he notes: "These are the tools of modern life. They're necessary to a career and social life."[23] To give up giving away our data would be to reject the majority of human civilization.

The sale of mined data, meanwhile, is not limited to companies aiming for targeted marketing. Through the revelations of whistle-blowers such as Edward Snowden it has become well-known that governments collect incredible amounts of data through digital surveillance. We will consider digital whistle-blowing more fully in chapter 5. We will also consider government data mining in greater detail shortly. First, however, let us note that the line between government and private company

---

22. Stiegler, *The Decadence of Industrial Democracies*, 35. His discussion in 104–5 is also addresses these ideas.

23. Schneier, *Data and Goliath*, 60–61.

data brokers is quite blurry. The United States is not alone in digital surveillance, to be sure, but is notable for a variety of reasons. For one, because of whistle-blowers we know more about United States' capabilities than about many other countries. But also, the US intelligence budget is larger than the rest of the world combined, so it operates on a larger scale. In addition, much of the globe's Internet traffic passes through the United States' borders, and most of the largest tech companies are based in the United States and thus subject to its laws. However, in 2013 the *Washington Post* reported that 70 percent of that enormous intelligence budget goes to private firms.[24] Many of these firms are run by former senior figures within the intelligence community.

We have already noted in the previous chapter the sale of zero-day finds. This is but one form of selling cyber technologies to governments. Many large IT companies are engaged in designing cyberweapons and surveillance capabilities for governments around the world. Tools such as FinFisher, produced by Gamma Group, can be bought by governments to allow them to set up surveillance on computers and smartphones. Nokia and Siemens produced hacking tools that allowed the government of Bahrain to produce transcripts of private email and chat sessions of dissidents, which they showed to the dissidents in 2011. These are but a few of the many known examples.[25] As we have seen from the previous chapter, such cyber-oriented weapons mark a militarization of cyberspace. When we add this military-corporate convergence to the data sharing between telecommunications companies and government surveillance agencies, we see that a power alliance is being formed that disintegrates the distinctions between corporate, military, and espionage. A cyber-military-industrial-corporate complex is formed. As Lyons notes, the concept that public and private agencies "inhabit different spheres, with different mandates, is currently unravelling."[26] Because these lines have become so blurred, it is difficult to pin down at any given point who exactly is watching whom. The NSA may, for instance, subcontract with a company like Booz Allen Hamilton to comb data provided by Verizon, as indeed was the case with Edward Snowden. Even without all of the clandestine surveillance strategies, there are also straightforward government requests for information from companies. Facebook reports

24. O'Harrow, "The Outsourcing of U.S. intelligence."
25. Schneier, *Data and Goliath*, 81.
26. Lyon, ed., *Surveillance After Snowden*, 31.

that globally government requests for information on users increased 27 percent in the first half of 2016 compared to the second half of 2015. The Malaysian government, for instance, in the first half of 2016 requested information on thirty-five Facebook users and accounts, almost double from the previous half year. Facebook gave the government 68.42 percent of the data requested.[27] On the one hand this demonstrates that not everything is immediately handed over just because it is requested, but at the same time the more data a company has on a person the more that can potentially be revealed.[28]

Algorithmic Power

Key to the ability to correlate the information that can be discovered in big data is the use of algorithms. Algorithms are computer programs designed to make sense of massive amounts of data and identify patterns within it. In a strict sense, algorithms are a set of procedures for finding solutions to a given problem. They are technically sophisticated software whose workings can be difficult to understand for the non-technically trained. We will not delve into this technical side, however. Rather, the relevance here is that even though they are little understood, they play a large role in making data usable. As Lyon explains, "They are part of a complex—an assemblage would be a suitable technical term—that works *with* their users to produce outcomes."[29] Lyon suggests the image of a triad of actors in big data: government agencies, private companies, and ordinary users. Algorithms are the codes that hold these groups together. Put simply, a government agency like the NSA gathers data itself and draws from data collected by communications companies. This data is generated by Internet users engaged in online activity. Algorithms are employed by the government agencies and private companies to identify patterns within the data that give some sort of insight into what meaning might be held within the data. What kind of data is correlated and how it is used is determined by the questions being asked by the designers of the algorithm.

27. "Putrajaya Ramps Up Request."

28. As *The Malay Mail Online* reports, there have been numerous cases in Malaysia of individuals being arrested for posting allegedly offensive critiques of the police and monarchy on Facebook. Ibid.

29. Lyon, ed., *Surveillance After Snowden*, 72.

Digital Media scholar Taylor Owen relates an anecdote of attending a training session for an intelligence analytics software program called Palantir. It is designed for military, security, and policing operations. Owen describes training sessions where the trainee uploads datasets such as a list of known insurgents, intelligence reports, satellite surveillance, city maps, and so forth. The software was able to analyze these various unrelated bits of information and correlate them. He notes that in the final exercise, separate sets of data were able to link the movements of a suspected insurgent with the movements of a known bomb maker, thus predicting a meeting between the two. "In 'real life,'" Owen suggests, "the next step would be a military operation: the launch of a drone strike, the deployment of a Special Forces team."[30] The analysis of big data uncovers a great deal of information, whether used for military, security, or commercial purposes.

Owen, however, reports a variety of reasons he felt uncomfortable with this demonstration. For example, he notes that the data entered can contain mistakes such as typos. Of even greater concern, however, is the ways that unconscious bias enters into analyzing big data. "Palantir's algorithms—the conclusions and recommendations that make its system 'useful'—carry the biases and errors of the people who wrote them."[31] Of the military exercise, he points out that the "suspected insurgent" may have been mentioned in multiple intelligence reports, one identifying him as a possible threat but others giving nuanced reports. "When the suspected insurgent is then cross-referenced with a known bombmaker," Owen explains, "you can bet which analysis was prioritized."[32] The point here is that each piece of information is recorded in the Palantir database as a unique piece of data. The nuance and context of the information is lost in this database approach to information. The algorithms that draw on this data are shaped by the concerns of those who programmed it to give an analysis based on certain presumptions; in this case that the intelligence report that perceives the situation to pose the highest risk will carry the greatest weight, even if its appraisal is the least nuanced. This is a security mind-set, giving the greatest attention to the highest possible threat assessment rather than being concerned with questions of

---

30. Owen, *Disruptive Power*, 169.
31. Ibid.
32. Ibid., 170.

likelihood.[33] Put into Hayless's terms, an algorithm uses a database mode of thought rather than a narrative one. The database thinking cannot on its own interpret indeterminate data to produce meaning but rather relies on human-supplied narrative thinking, and in this case it is the biases of a security narrative.

Algorithms make choices of which pieces of information to prioritize by using criteria programmed into them. These programs are written by humans with particular worldviews and biases. The goal of an algorithm in many aspects of life is to recognize patterns and assess risk to what it considers to be behavior outside of the "norm" of these patterns. Owen explains, "The calibration of this norm can either be a human decision or a computational one, but in the end these norms are built into algorithms."[34] Algorithms do not only track the movements of possible insurgents, they also determine which advertisements show up while we surf the web, our credit ratings, the coupons we receive at the supermarket, how easily we pass through airport security, and the likeliness of us being pulled over by police while we are driving. Owen contends that as automation technologies, and technologies like facial recognition and quantum computing, are developed and refined the process of calibrating the norm moves further from human involvement. This means the assumptions that slip into the programming take on greater significance.

Owen particularly warns about the ways that tools designed for battlefield usage are being employed in domestic situations. He points in the United States context to border issues but also police usage of big data technologies. He notes that the United States Customs and Border Patrol can legally enter anyone's property—including electronics such as laptops or cell phones—without a warrant while within twenty-five miles of the US-Mexico border. "What does it mean," he asks, "when the state extends military technologies and tactics beyond the battlefield? Put another way, what do computational power and surveillance-based weaponry do to the line between war and peace?"[35] We see here a sense

---

33. The name Palantir itself seems rather ominous. In *The Lord of the Rings* the "palanti" is the name for a set of stones connected to one another allowing communication over long distances. "Palantir" is the singular form. Yet when Sauraman uses one to keep a watch on the activities of Sauran, Sauran uses the connection to convince Sauraman of the hopelessness of resistance, thus using his fear to convert him into an ally of darkness. This would seem a rather bleak but perhaps accurate understanding of the psychological effect of engaging in surveillance.

34. Owen, *Disruptive Power*, 175.

35. Ibid., 179.

of how all of the world can become a cyber-battlefield, as we discussed in the previous chapter, as well as the blurring of distinctions between military and police. He concludes that making cyberspace into both a threat and a weapon allows it to be considered by the state as an object of war.[36] Even more frighteningly, this is occurring not just on international and national levels, but local levels as well, as more and more local police forces are utilizing security algorithms for their police work. The battlefield is thus extended into the streets of American cities. This is particularly worrisome given what theologian Kelly Brown Douglas terms the "Stand Your Ground culture," which includes the "construction of the black body as a guilty body" as a foundational assumption.[37] Such assumptions cannot help but influence the parameters of algorithms that in turn shape policing decision-making.

Central to any discussion of algorithms, then, is the question of how the "norm" is determined. What characteristics should define normal, and who decides the definition? The use of algorithms is empowering the software to make those decisions. Yet as I have suggested, the implicit biases of the programmers enters into the software. Thus issues of race, gender, and class become more and more encoded into the enforced definition of normal. Shoshana Amielle Magnet explores the ways in which this occurs. For instance, in considering facial recognition technology, she holds: "As these scientists label the images according to their understanding of their own biological race and gender identities, preconceptions about gender and race are codified into the biometric scanners from the beginning."[38] These prejudices have a wide range of outcomes. It is not simply about identifying terrorists. Algorithms are involved in identifying who gets a loan or qualifies for a credit card, which advertisements you see, and whether you qualify for insurance, to name a few examples. Because they are digital, algorithms work under the guise of objectivity. This veneer of being free from bias can act to cover discriminatory presuppositions. For instance, Schneier reports that there are instances of American Express reducing people's credit limits due to the type of places they tend to shop. This can be considered a form of "weblining."

The term *weblining* is drawn from "redlining," which was used in the 1960s to refer to the bank practice of racial discrimination against

36. Ibid., 184.
37. Douglas, *Stand Your Ground*, 47.
38. Magnet, *When Biometrics Fail*, 46. Quoted in Dubrofsky and Magnet, eds., *Feminist Surveillance Studies*, xv.

prospective homebuyers. Weblining could potentially be a more pervasive problem. For example, in 2000 Wells Fargo bank included a "community calculator" on a website promoting home mortgages. The calculator collected the ZIP code of potential customers and steered them to other neighborhoods with a similar racial mixture. Thus customers likely to be white were steered towards predominantly white neighborhoods, while ones likely to be African-American were steered to predominantly African-American ones. A 2014 White House report on the use of big data concluded, "big data analytics have the potential to eclipse long-standing civil rights protections in how personal information is used in housing, credit, employment, health, education, and the marketplace."[39] Thus, far from being "objective" or "neutral," algorithms' definition of normality not only has a penchant for maintaining the status quo, but can in fact exacerbate unjust trends and cycles. Indeed, one might say that algorithms have no sense of the possibilities of the future and what could be, but rather look back into the past and attempt to replicate and codify its injustices as an unquestionable norm.

Most discussions of data mining worry about personally identifying information and the loss of privacy that could potentially occur. Yet Lyon, who directs the Surveillance Studies Centre at Queen's University in Canada, contends that while this is a valid concern, it overly narrows the concerns raised by surveillance through data mining. "Surveillance also operates," he writes, "in ways that affect whole groups in the population—like people in poverty, or Muslim Germans, or North Africans in France. This process is often referred to as social sorting, targeting primarily population groups before individuals."[40] This is the issue we find in weblining, but that is far from the only example. Social sorting in the cyberdimension grows out of a long history of racial and gendered violence that has become encoded into cyberspace, as some scholars of surveillance have noted.

Surveillance Theory

Working in engagement with the field of surveillance studies, feminist theorist Andrea Smith argues that a focus on the modern state's use of

---

39. US Executive Office of the President, "Big data." Quoted in Schneier, *Data and Goliath*, 109.

40. Lyon, ed., *Surveillance After Snowden*, 25–26.

surveillance actually clouds ours view of surveillance technologies. Instead, she insists, we ought to begin with the ways that sexual surveillance worked as a central strategy of colonial forces for managing indigenous peoples. She thus argues for an anticolonial feminist analysis of surveillance that complicates the dominant Foucauldian frameworks for understanding surveillance. Before delving into Smith's argument, then, let us first detour to the use of Michel Foucault's discussion of panopticonic power and its critics in contemporary surveillance theory.

In noting the centrality of the definition of normal in discussing algorithms, many analysts have made the connection to the work of Foucault. Indeed, Jeremy Bentham's eighteenth-century concept of the panopticon as understood through Foucault's reinterpretation of it is the leading discourse within surveillance studies. As surveillance theorist Kevin D. Haggerty notes, "It is a profound understatement to say that the panopticon dominates the study of surveillance."[41] Bentham's proposal was for a prison architecture that allowed a handful of guards to keep watch on a large number of inmates. A central tower for the guards would be encircled by isolated cells for the prisoners. The guards in the tower would be unseen, but the inmates could be constantly monitored. For Bentham, this approach, coupled with explicitly articulated behavioral norms, would cure a wide range of social ills by transforming the inmates' behavior. In Foucault's analysis, however, he notes the dynamics of power in creating these behavioral norms. The panoptic formula, to Foucault, becomes the primary means for management of populations through an enforced definition of normality. We see here the relevance of this framework for considering algorithms. From the panopticon viewpoint, an algorithm has the power to enforce an understanding of behavioral norms on a society under surveillance. What the algorithm considers normal is shaped, perhaps subconsciously, by those entrusted to create the algorithm. Once programmed, the algorithm can then enforce those norms by identifying anyone violating them as being potentially problematic. The members of the society, knowing that they may be watched, then self-censor themselves into following the norms encoded within the algorithm.

Yet Haggerty, writing a decade ago, suggested that surveillance studies was at the beginning of a paradigm shift in its understanding of the nature of surveillance. He noted that a number of scholars have begun

---

41. Haggerty, "Tear Down the Walls," 25.

arguing that the image of the panopticon obscures a variety of aspects of contemporary surveillance. He asserts, "The panoptic model masks as much as it reveals, foregrounding processes which are of decreasing relevance, while ignoring or slighting dynamics that fall outside of its framework."[42] For him, the increase in surveillance by so many different actors with so many different agendas renders obsolete the concept that surveillance is for the single coherent purpose of social control, as Foucault argues. The simple divide between the watchers and the watched has been blurred in cyberspace. Participation in social media, for instance, both renders one as being watched but also as a watcher of others. "Both watching others and exposing oneself can, at times, be pleasant entertainment activities," he holds, "and are themselves occasionally part of larger processes of identity formation."[43] This is not to deny that powerful institutions use surveillance to scrutinize groups with less power, but rather to lift up that there is an increased level of visibility that extends to all segments of a social hierarchy that creates a complex web of surveillance. He contends, "Groups are differently positioned to be able to exploit these [new] surveillance potentialities, and their abilities to do so are often structured according to traditional social cleavages."[44] Nonetheless, he continues, there is still a greater level of scrutiny on the powerful as well. This challenges Foucault's depiction of those under surveillance, as the targets depicted in *Discipline and Punish* are by and large passive. This hints at the possibilities of resistance that we shall examine in greater detail in subsequent chapters.

Haggerty also notes that in the panoptic model, only people are monitored. In the era of big data, however, monitoring goes beyond humans. Ocean temperatures, air composition, soil quality, the spread of disease, and animal tagging are but some examples of nonhuman surveillance occurring through cyberspace technology. He suggests, "these developments raise questions about how advances in the surveillance of nature might transform our conception of 'nature' or 'wildlife' and whether new abilities to visualize and document nature mark an important quantitative development in the centuries-old ambition by 'man' to secure dominion over the natural world."[45] In other words, can some-

---

42. Ibid., 25.
43. Ibid., 27.
44. Ibid., 28.
45. Ibid., 30.

thing produce a data trail and still be "wild"? Or is bringing something into the cyber realm of data collection a means of domesticating it? This brings us again to the question of the relationship between the data about something and the identity of that thing.

In an influential earlier essay, cowritten with Richard V. Ericson, Haggerty advocated understanding surveillance as a "surveillant assemblage," based on elements of the work of Gilles Deleuze and Felix Guattari. "Assemblages" are a means of discussing the multiplicity of phenomena typically considered stable and singular. The assemblage is a collection of discrete objects that function together but are actually a wide range of processes and phenomena, each of which is an assemblage of its own. The phenomena form a dynamic flow of interactivity that are temporarily held together in an assemblage. In this distinction between flows and assemblages lies the difference between forces and powers. "Forces consist of more primary and fluid phenomena," Haggerty and Ericson explain, "and it is from such phenomena that power derives as it captures and striates such flows."[46] These processes function together to freeze what had been open systems or forces into a fixed power arrangement where some are able to dominate others.

In terms of surveillance, then, Haggerty and Ericson hold that rather than the singularity and uni-directionality of the panopticon, contemporary surveillance is better understood as a flow of technologies and watchers continually coalescing into assemblages. More simply, there is no single master plan or overlord behind surveillance, but rather a series of alliances and confederations of those involved in surveillance of various types. They write, "In the face of multiple connections across myriad technologies and practices, struggles against particular manifestations of surveillance, as important as they might be, are akin to efforts to keep the ocean's tide back with a broom—a frantic focus on a particular unpalatable technology or practice while the general tide of surveillance washes over us all."[47] They find Deleuze and Guattari's metaphor of the rhizome helpful in understanding these surveillant assemblages.

Here it is worth taking a bit of an excursion into some key concepts found in Deleuze's thought, both in his individual works and those coauthored with Guattari. In particular, the images of the "assemblage" and

---

46. Haggerty and Ericson, "The Surveillant Assemblage," 608–9.
47. Ibid., 609.

the "rhizome" are central to Deleuze's thought and play a major role in the concerns of this book as well.

Deleuze considered the idea of the assemblage as perhaps his most important, and yet does not fully work it out systematically. As philosopher Manuel Delanda, to whose attempt to fill out the concept we will turn shortly, points out, Deleuze and Guattari give six different definitions of the concept, each corresponding to a different aspect of their philosophy and without obvious coherence between the definitions.[48] The details of these various definitions is beyond what we need to explore in order to engage the constructive use of the concept by Haggerty and Ericson, however. Rather, a few key points will suffice. One is that the English term *assemblage* used to translate the concept only captures part of the sense of the French *agencement;* the French refers to both the *process* of fitting together a set of components and the *ensemble that results* from that process, while the English only conveys a sense of the final product.[49]

Delanda suggests that the simplest definition of an assemblage is:

> It is a multiplicity which is made up of many heterogeneous terms and which establishes liaisons, relations between them, across ages, sexes, and reigns—different natures. Thus the assemblage's only unity is that of a co-functioning: it is a symbiosis, a "sympathy."[50]

From this definition, we can see that the assemblage is not homogenous nor is it irreversibly unified. It is a functional joining together. The assemblage can be made up of humans but can also include other forces and assemblages. Assemblages, then, nest in one another. Delanda includes "the material and symbolic artifacts that compose communities and organizations."[51] While there is no sense of emergence in this definition, Delanda insists that such a concept is necessary to understand the phenomenon of assembling assumed in it. He explains that implied in the definition is the characteristic, "that social wholes must be considered to be peripheral or to exist alongside their parts. . . . The reference is not spatial but *ontological*: the whole exists alongside the parts in the same ontological plane."[52] Therefore there is no hierarchy of being; the whole

---

48. Delanda, *Assemblage Theory*, 1.
49. Ibid., 1.
50. Deleuze and Parnet, *Dialogues II*, 69. Quoted in Delanda, *Assemblage Theory*, 1.
51. Delanda, *Assemblage Theory*, 20.
52. Ibid., 12.

exists horizontally from its parts. However, once a whole has emerged from the process of assembling, it then has a top-down influence on the components of the assemblage. Assemblages are composed of assemblages. We should take care not to confuse this nesting of assemblages with a Tillichian sense of dimensions of life. Tillich would certainly agree with the concept that the organic, inorganic, and human can function together. From a Tillichian perspective, we can affirm this horizontal functioning of assemblages. At the same time, we can add an insistence on a dimension of spirit that seeks meaning and exceeding and is the vitality of life. It is a vertical dimension, not ontologically but rather in affirming meaning as a non-ontological excess.

Another relevant aspect of assemblages that Delanda raises, developed from Deleuze and Guattari in *A Thousand Plateaus*, is their role in war. Armies are prime examples of assemblages, in that they consist of a variety of types of soldiers and technologies functioning together. Within this, however, there is a variable distinction between nomadic and sedentary forms of military. Nomadic military assemblages represent greater flexibility and are deterritorialized, while sedentary military assemblages are territorialized and rigid. For Deleuze and Guattari, the limits of the nomadic form were reached with the cannon, because the development of the cannon required the economic backing of the state apparatus.[53] Delanda, for his part, contends that rather than contrasting forms of armies the degree of nomadization or sedintarianization should be seen as a variable that shifts over time with technological innovation.[54] That is, Delanda envisions assemblages as a mix of bottom-up emergence with the top-down causality that emerges from the creation of a whole in the process of assemblage. Once the assemblage is there it influences the ways that the constituent assemblages behave. To demonstrate this point he turns to the example of technical objects. In particular, he uses the example of a knife. A knife has among its capacities the ability to cut. Whether its function is understood to be to cut bread or cut human flesh depends on whether it is part of the "kitchen assemblage" or the "army assemblage."[55]

53. Deleuze and Guattari, *A Thousand Plateaus*, 68.

54. Delanda, *Assemblage Theory*, 69.

55. Ibid., 72–74. Delanda is arguing against Deleuze and Guattari's assertion that a technical object is "entirely undetermined" until it is related to an assemblage. Delanda holds that this denies the autonomous characteristic of components in an assemblage: a knife is sharp no matter what it is used for, even if the value of that sharpness depends

In this sense we can see the question of the nature of cyberspace being one of which assemblage it falls under. We can view military and commercial assemblages as forming a larger assemblage in cyberspace that wields cyberspace as a tool of control. It is a re-nomadization of military power backed by a newly deterritorialized form of state power that can be seen to form a limit to the innovative initiative of the sedentary form of power, just as the cannon had been the limit for the innovative power of the old nomads. Does this mean, however, that this is what cyberspace therefore is? Does use determine identity? Must cyberspace be wrested away from this powerful assemblage by a new assemblage? From Delanda we can find a reminder of the emergent capabilities of the components of the assemblage, however. More than this, though, is the question of seeing technology as more than merely a tool. If technology is a means of accessing meaning through the creation of media as media, then it is not simply undefined until some powerful assemblage chooses to wield it. Rather, it is always already multiply engaged in the production and transmission of meaning, rooted in the infrastructural possibilities present, as a means of nurturing life. That is, technology is not inherently morally neutral. Internet technologies are already embedded in infrastructures that contribute to climate change, exacerbate economic disparities, provide countless jobs, and so forth. Technology is morally ambiguous, but this is not the same thing as being inherently neutral. The issue, rather, is that a powerful assemblage can co-opt the whole of a contested field of potential meaning and reduce it to one possible matrix of meaning.

The other popular term from Deleuze that we need to unpack is the *rhizome*. The pairing of tree and rhizome is one of several that Deleuze and Guattari use in discussing assemblages. The tree/rhizome distinction has become an increasingly popular metaphor. The rhizome is distinguished from the rooted tree, which is sedentary and slow to adapt. Rhizomes, on the other hand, come from shallow, quick-spreading, and adaptive plants such as grass. Rhizomes have shallow roots that allow them to spread quickly and horizontally, without the slow process of spreading seeds and letting a tap root grow. That is, the rhizome represents the horizontal assemblage rather than the verticality and ontological distinctiveness of the tree, otherwise known as "strata." In *A Thousand Plateaus*, Deleuze and Guattari discuss the characteristics of the rhizome:

---

on the assemblages of which it is part.

"any point of a rhizome can be connected to anything other, and must be. This is very different from the tree or root, which plots a point, fixes an order."[56] Because of this intense connectivity, rhizomes are not easy to destroy. If they are broken, every remaining bit can re-form and continue. They explain, "You may make a rupture, draw a line of flight, yet there is still a danger that you will re-encounter organizations that restratify everything, formations that restore power to a signifier, attributions that reconstitute a subject—anything you like, from Oedipal resurgences to fascist concretions."[57] Rhizomes can thus be formed in helpful or harmful ways. Indeed, they continue, "Good and bad are only products of an active and temporary selection, which must be renewed."[58] This reminder helps with the concern to hold on to the ambiguity of assemblages; rhizomes are not automatically liberative.

The rhizome metaphor has seen a spreading popularity within recent theological works. Typically these works frame the rhizome positively. Postmodern Christian theorist Carl Raschke, for instance, elucidates Deleuze's contrast between arboreal and rhizomic means of spreading: "Rhizomic growth is global rather than local; it is basically invisible and can manifest in different ways in different places."[59] Raschke uses this image for global Christianity, suggesting that it can spread globally but take on a variety of different forms. Critical of Western assumptions that Christianity is or should be the same in all parts of the world, he instead contends that the gospel is a rhizomic and relational power that transforms cultures in unique ways. In this sense the rhizome is a counter-assemblage power. At the same time, he holds that the image of the rhizome helps us avoid binary and oppositional frameworks. Interestingly he compares the Deleuzian rhizome with the Internet as a decentralized relational structure.[60] Of course, as we have seen the actual Internet is not quite as horizontal as is popularly imaged. The rhizome on its own is insufficient to displace the ability of assemblages to concentrate flows into a static coalition of power. Thus while I find the image of the rhizome helpful, I do not see it as inherently positive or liberative. It is a framework that can allow for true multiplicity, but it does not guarantee

56. Deleuze and Guattari, *A Thousand Plateaus*, 7.
57. Ibid., 9.
58. Ibid., 10.
59. Raschke, *GloboChrist*, 41.
60. Ibid., 122.

it. This is a position hinted at by Glissant's engagement with Deleuze, to which we will turn in later chapters, but which I wish to bring out with greater urgency.[61] Again, this darker potential of the rhizome is recognized by Deleuze and Guattari, but seems to be underplayed when the concept extends into other fields.

My concern for the destructive rhizome is echoed in Andrew Culp's recent book, *The Dark Deleuze*. "Enough with rhizomes," he declares. "Although they were a suggestive image of thought thirty-five years ago, our present is dominated by the Cold War technology of the Internet that was made as a rhizomatic network for surviving nuclear war."[62] He continues that rhizomes only know how to advance, not to strategically mobilize. Thus he contends, "We know better than to think that a rhizome is enough to save us. Even something as rhizomatic as the Internet is still governed by a set of decentralized protocols that helps it maintain consistency,"[63] a point underscored and enlarged by our consideration of infrastructure in the first chapter. Given this, Culp constructively calls for a retrieval of the value of the unfolding of disconnection against the rhizomatic in-folding of connection. That is, he sees the logic of the rhizome as inherently problematic because it is a greedy force of accumulation and colonization rather than a liberative process against forces of control, though he does not follow up on his critique of cyberspace. I might add here that I find Culp's conception of the Internet to be too caught in a conception of a tool that becomes destructive through its use rather than a dimension of existence plagued by ambiguity, even as I agree with his larger premise of critiquing a too-easy acceptance of the rhizome image. For my purposes, I wish to suggest that assemblages are not mindless rhizomes, even as they are not hierarchically arranged single-minded forces. Assemblages contain the capacity for a momentum of thought that can be guided, if not fully directed, and the forces of surveillant power have more successfully directed the momentum of cyberspace than the liberative forces within the cyberdimension.

Haggerty likewise has been criticized for overemphasizing the positive potential of surveillance technologies and not taking resistance seriously enough.[64] It is worth remembering that the article with Ericson

61. Žižek, *Organs Without Bodies*, 172.
62. Culp, *The Dark Deleuze*, 37.
63. Ibid., 38.
64. See especially Kirstie Ball, about whom we shall discuss shortly.

quoted above was written in 2000, and the solo essay is from 2006. The sheer volume of data produced and the scale of known surveillance in the post-Snowden world would have been unfathomable in the pre-9/11 world of that first article and indeed even at the time of the second. In this sense the panopticon image may in fact be more helpful than they thought at the time, as states have indeed been shown to be continuing to play a central role in surveillance. However, as we have seen, it is still true that they are not alone. Businesses, patriotic hackers, and others are also engaged in types of surveillance. Yet it would seem foolish at this point to underestimate the vertical reach of state surveillance power, especially as countries such as Russia move towards greater control of cyberspace.

Returning to Smith, then, she argues that the panopticon framework has led surveillance studies to overly focus on sight. In particular, she notes Lyon's definition of surveillance studies as being "about seeing things and, more particularly, about seeing people."[65] Yet Smith argues that this is incomplete. Specifically, the intense gaze of the state on some people does indeed make those people hyper-visible, but it also simultaneously renders others invisible. "The colonial gaze that surveils native communities to monitor, measure, and account for their 'dysfunctional' behaviors," she contends, "conceals from view the settler colonial state that creates these conditions in the first place."[66] In particular, Smith focuses on the ways that directing gaze at indigenous communities provided a rationale for colonizing the spaces that they inhabited. Thus for example, the idea of *terra nullis*—not seeing indigenous people as rightfully inhabiting the land on which they live—functioned as a legal justification for expropriating these lands. Thus she contends that surveillance strategies always include disappearing from view "that which delegitimizes the state itself."[67] Indeed, as we shall see, this may be an aspect of what has brought forth such government zeal in tracing and prosecuting hacktivists and whistle-blowers.

Non-heteropatriarchal structures, Smith contends, are threats to the colonial state because they offer alternative models to the colonial structure. The union of white supremacy and colonialism rests on a binary worldview of clear racial and gender differentiation. Alternative structures thus had to be crushed in order to justify imposing colonialism.

65. Lyon, ed., *Surveillance Studies*, 1. Quoted in Dubrofsky and Magnet, eds., *Feminist Surveillance Studies*, 25.

66. Smith, "Not-Seeing," 25–26.

67. Ibid., 26.

Therefore any cultural practice that could be seen as blurring the distinction between (dominant) masculine identity and (submissive) feminine identity had to be dismissed and destroyed. Thus she asserts, "the more gender-egalitarian nature of some indigenous societies became anthropologically marked as the sign of their unevolved, premodern status."[68] Gender violence and the subjugation of any practices that could be seen as queering the line between genders was therefore a "central strategy of settler colonialism and white supremacy."[69] Thus surveillance functioned to police and "civilize" the colonized by not only seeing what was deemed normal but also by not seeing that which challenged this normalcy.

Drawing from this background of surveillance as both seeing and not seeing, we can better understand the problem posed by algorithms defining what is normal. Much of the concern with big data is that everybody is targeted by it. Everyone leaves a data trail and so can be seen at any time. Yet there is also the reality that most of the time most people will not be seen. As Lyon assures us, "[F]or many of us, most of the time, metadata may well be inconsequential, even beneficial."[70] In other words, if we fit the profile of normal, we are not seen by surveillance—and thus allowed to continue being seen as socially acceptable. Yet, he continues, "The kinds of algorithms used, the piecing together of fragments of unconnected data, often based on stereotypical assumptions about people from particular backgrounds, may create apparently incriminating profiles that are readily seized upon by those taught to think that citizens-in-general may be masquerading as terrorists."[71] Thus he suggests that cultural biases may cause innocent people to be seen and identified as threats to security.

Yet if we follow Smith, there is more to it than this. The nature of surveillance is to establish an authoritarian patriarchalism in society. It identifies alternative worldviews in order to make them disappear because they are threats to the status quo. Historically, we can see this in examples such as the FBI surveillance of Martin Luther King, Jr. More recently, the NSA and FBI have set their sights on a variety of political activists. Prominent Muslim Americans, Occupy movement activists, the antiwar movement Code Pink, Veterans for Peace, and even music

68. Ibid., 27.
69. Ibid., 26.
70. Lyon, ed., *Surveillance After Snowden*, 75.
71. Ibid., 75.

festivals have been targeted for surveillance in recent years.[72] For Smith, this is a broader issue than self-censorship in response to the gaze of the panopticon. Rather, these movements are brought into the gaze in order to disappear them from view lest they challenge the authoritarian logic of surveillance itself. Adding Haggerty's appeal to rhizomatic thought to this, we can understand the power assemblage to include not just the state, but also other actors sharing common interests. In particular we have the assemblage of military-industrial-cyber-commerical complex that we considered in the previous chapter. This assemblage works to conceal voices that would delegitimize its power.

Going further, Stiegler would include the production of American audio-visual media as a strategic means for creating a swarm mentality that will not challenge the legitimacy and power of American capitalism. He contends:

> America developed an industrial politics projecting the image of the *American 'we,'* which was also a commercial politics projecting the image of the *I* as a *consumer*.... More than its money or its military might, American power consists in the force of Hollywood images and of the computer programs which it has *conceived*—in its industrial capacity to *produce new symbols* around which models of life are formed.[73]

He further argues that the success of individuals, peoples, and other nations depends upon the degree to which they conform to these symbols. Combining this point with the insights of the surveillance studies scholars, we can understand the American military-political-media-cyber-commercial-industrial surveillant power assemblage not only to project an image of what is normal but to see those who conform to this image, thus using its symbol-production power to shape all peoples into a calculable crowd of consumers. At the same time this seeing and projecting also conceals those who differ or would challenge these same symbols of normality. Such a situation cultivates a predictable and docile humanity with no space for change. As Schneier notes, progress requires imperfect policing. There must be some space for breaking and challenging some laws so that alternative viewpoints can be heard. Using the example of American debates on lifting laws forbidding cannabis use or same-sex relationships, he holds, "There has to be a period where they are still

---

72. See Schneier, *Data and Goliath*, 103–4.
73. Stiegler, *The Decadence of Industrial Democracies*, 23. Author's italics.

illegal yet increasingly tolerated, so that people can look around and say, 'You know, that wasn't so bad.'"[74] Elasticity in social practice is essential to social transformation because elasticity allows for the new and surprising; it allows the calculable to be exceeded. The goal of data mining, however, is to reduce the ineffable to that which can be counted and thus controlled.

Data and Subjectivity

As has been hinted at already, a significant issue in the move to big data is the understanding of subjectivity that it produces. While the more popularly discussed issue of subjectivity and cyberspace is the attribution problem—that is, that it is impossible to know for sure who is actually sitting behind the computer—I suggest this is not the major issue that emerges from our discussion thus far in this chapter. Rather, there are two other noteworthy strands. One is that data mining produces a picture of a person as the sum of all of their thoughts and actions—or more precisely their Google searches, web page visits, and trackable purchases. Here the subject becomes the total sum of this data. There is no way to properly assign weight to the various pieces of data. Further, the subject becomes a constant accumulation rather than a dynamic and shifting reality that sheds aspects of the self over time as well as adds to it. The identity of the individual is something that is accumulated rather than something that emerges or evolves. The other major strand comes from approaches to cybersecurity. Specifically, one's body becomes the marker of the true self. As scholar Kirstie Ball notes that through biometric security, "The body itself has emerged as a legitimate surveillance target because of the immense level of detail and 'truth' about the person it is thought to provide."[75] Ball finds this sense of the body as a definitive source of truth to be reductive, and sees the rhizomatic understanding of surveillance to be a helpfully corrective concept. At the same time, she criticizes Haggerty and Ericson for not taking resistance seriously enough and, further, fears that their position does not sufficiently take into account the hybridity of cyborgian subjectivity, following Donna Haraway.[76]

---

74. Schneier, *Data and Goliath*, 97–98.
75. Ball, "Organization, Surveillance, and the Body," 297.
76. Ibid., 300.

Ball notes that it is not so much the body or even subjectivity in which surveillance has interest, but rather data. The body is informationized as a set of data that is not identical to the person, but is not separate either. Here she is following Haggerty and Ericson, who understand the body as a key component of surveillance. They explain that the body is first abstracted away from its concrete flesh and turned into a data flow that then can be reassembled in various configurations. They call this a "data double"; a de-corporealized virtual stand-in for the human. These data doubles are what businesses are after in their data mining. Yet the body under surveillance is also affected by the accumulation of data. Surveillance happens through the interfacing of bodies and technology, and as we have seen from Smith, surveillance makes judgments about which bodies are acceptable. As a personal anecdote, I can recall the creepy sensation the first time I used an e-tablet that gave me a message that it could no longer detect my eyes and so was going into sleep mode.

As we have noted Haggerty pointing out, the engagement in social media, for example, leads to identity formation. By engaging in mutual surveillance we create an image of ourselves and our world. For Haggerty and Ericson, the data doubles of us are constructed by the myriad technologies that collect data about us, working as assemblages of surveillance that come together around our fleshly bodies.[77] For them, this data double is a potentially positive enrichment of the self that extends beyond the limits of the flesh. Yet this seems a naïvely optimistic view of the data double. On the one hand it would seem to encourage gnostic fantasies of a self that is freed from the confines of the body, reminiscent of Barlow. Even more, on the other hand, it ignores the ways in which commercial interests, for instance, can work to manipulate our identity through reducing us to this data double and then cultivate our consumerist desires based on this calculable reduction of our identity. That is, rather than a data double allowing us to exceed our fleshly self, the goal of data mining is to reduce us to our data double.

Following feminist discussions of subjectivity, Ball notes, "The challenge is to capture the import/proximity of the body in sociological analysis, without lapsing into essentialisms, and to examine how bodies become signified and significant in relation to other bodies, contexts, and strategies."[78] Ball does not seek to solve these ongoing debates within fem-

---

77. Haggerty and Ericson, "The Surveillant Assemblage," 613.
78. Ball, "Organization, Surveillance, and the Body," 303.

inist thought on this issue, but rather seeks to incorporate the concerns of surveillance within the discussions. She holds, "The core issue for any embodied sociology of surveillance must remain as being primarily concerned with whose body information is appropriated, how it is encoded, how encoded information is reapplied, how effectively this fixes, and how it is resisted."[79] To this end, she calls for a cyborg understanding of body and data as intertwined and hybridized. "Cyborg identity is . . . constructed as a resistant multiplicity, a partial identity, and a contradictory standpoint," Ball contends.[80] This follows Haraway's sense that the interaction of human and machine can be liberative for women in that it can deconstruct binaries of gender identity. In a similar vein Veronika Schlor takes up the cyborg trope as a way of discussing digital bodies as a kind of extension of the physical body attached by "a kind of umbilical cord."[81] She sees this extension as a means of insisting on a body's right to otherness rather than a tight tying together of women's identities with their bodies. Here we see the issue of identity that comes into play with biometric security that sees the body as the measure of the true self. At the same time neither Ball nor Schlor are arguing for a dismissal of the body as a real aspect of the self. Bodies do matter. Here Peters's embodied definition of technology is helpful in seeing the body as a locus of infinite meaning and data that must be mediated via myriad technologies, some embodied and innate and others externalized. Identity cannot be reduced to data, nor can it be reduced to a body; each is incomplete. Indeed identity exceeds even the combination of the two.

The tendency in cybersecurity to understand the body as true self also factors into our discussion of the inherent biases of algorithms. All too frequently algorithms take data about bodies, such as listed racial or gender identities, to make inferences about identities, and thereby making calculations about possible actions and activities. In this bodies are seen as encapsulating the totality of identity, disregarding the unique individuation that exceeds the body. Such an understanding of the body as the true self is thus problematic because it renders identity as definitively definable and calculable.

Thus both of these strands of subjectivity lack a sense of transcendence or otherness within the subject as the site of infinite surprise and

---

79. Ibid., 311.
80. Ibid., 310
81. Schlor, "Cyborgs," 65.

creativity. Philosopher Richard Kearney calls this intangible more to the person the *persona* or *prosopon*, drawing from Latin and Greek terms, respectively. He describes his concept of the *prosopon* as the "eschatological aura of 'possibility' exuded by a person."[82] He understands this exceeding as an otherness to the *persona* that is moving towards open and surprising potentialities over which we have no power to control or define. For him it is precisely in this space in which the person exceeds the calculable that is the "capacity in each of us to receive and respond to the divine invitation."[83] It is our human openness to the divine opening of new possibilities that arise beyond the calculable.

Stiegler, in a similar vein, speaks of "consisting," which is not reducible to "existing." Consisting in his terminology is that which exceeds calculation. For him the problem of hyper-industrial capitalism is its reduction of all things to that which is calculable. This is particularly problematic with regards to understanding identity. While qualifying that calculation is necessary, he is critical of reducing concepts of trust and time into pure calculation. He argues that doing so, "which would be capable therefore of eliminating everything incalculable, is what *radically destroys all trust*, because it destroys all *possibility of believing*," by which he means belief in a future that holds many possibilities.[84] Pure calculation holds no space for hope in the future, for unforeseeable possibilities to rupture the current trajectory of probability. The indeterminacy that exceeds calculation is what inspires both fear and hope, and living in the tension between them allows for the development of individual identity. For Stiegler, hyper-industrial society, in its drive to control both production and consumption, reduces existence to calculation. Drawing from this insight, we can understand the data double as a calculated rendering of a person. To Stiegler, such a construction is a person without hope or trust or belief or individuality. This is the kind of person that digital capitalism aims to produce because the calculable person is the ideal consumer.[85] Such a person would *exist* without *consisting* in Stiegler's terms, or in Kearney's it would be a person without a *persona*.

82. Kearney, *The God Who May Be*, 10.
83. Ibid., 2.
84. Stiegler, *The Decadence of Industrial Democracies*, 45. Author's italics.
85. While Stiegler focuses on individuation, he does not see this as opposed to collective identity. Rather, he challenges the dualism of the individual being the opposite of the group. Instead, he holds that healthy collective identity allows for the true individuation of independent thought, while the so-called "individualistic" contemporary

In his critique of the reduction of existence to calculation, Stiegler turns rather theological. For him consisting is that which gives meaning, value, and novelty. Thus though an atheist, he concedes, "As for God, he does not exist at all, which does not prevent him from consisting, at least in certain souls."[86] That is, for him the name "God" is one way of speaking of the animating power of ideas to provoke novelty and vibrancy, which challenge the reign of the calculable, as it were.[87] Such a position is not far from what Kearney terms "anatheism."[88] Stiegler further argues:

> Because if the death of God, that is, the revelation of his inexistence, is not inevitably the nullification of the question of consistence, then we must nevertheless say that with the development of the spirit of capitalism, the becoming calculable of that which *projected,* as existences (as singularities), consistences (the ideas, knowledges and their powers), this becoming [*devenir*], without the future [*avenir*] with which it is not automatically synonymous, is that which tends to reduce these consistences to ashes: ashes of inexistent and inconsistent subsistences.[89]

Thus he argues for a difference between existence and consistence. We can add that what is problematic about big data is its reduction of consistence to existence. Also, Stiegler would further contend, the reduction of consistence to existence constitutes the destruction of the possibility of belief by its reduction to a trust in the calculable.

Stiegler's understanding of belief is focused on trust in the future rather than overtly religious belief, and yet there are important resonances

---

society is in fact a herd mentality of attempting to create individuality through the consumption of popular culture, particularly through information and media technologies. See Stiegler, *The Decadence of Industrial Democracies*, especially 17 and 110.

86. Stiegler, *The Decadence of Industrial Democracies*, 90.

87. The resonance between Stiegler's God as consisting rather than existing and John D. Caputo's assertion that God insists rather than exists is intriguing. I am not aware of direct engagement between the two on this issue, though the thought of each owes a significant debt to engagement with the thought of Jacques Derrida. The question of God in relation to the concept of consisting is a minor point for Stiegler, however, as opposed to the central focus God's insistence holds in much of Caputo's later work. It should also be noted that Stiegler's reflections were written ten years before Caputo published *The Insistence of God*.

88. Kearney explains: "I use the term *anatheism* as a 'returning to God after God': a critical hermeneutic retrieval of sacred things that have passed but still bear a radical remainder, an unrealized potentiality or promise to be more fully realized in the future." Kearney, "God After God," 7.

89. Stiegler, *The Decadence of Industrial Democracies*, 91.

between his contention and Protestant theological thought. One such connection would be with German Reformed theologian Jürgen Moltmann's discussion of the future, where he makes a now-classic distinction between *futurum* and *adventus*.[90] *Futurum* is what will be based on a linear projection of the past and present into the future: in Stiegler's terms we can understand it as the calculable future. *Adventus*, meanwhile, is that which is coming. For Moltmann, this is the Christian eschatological hope of the coming of the reign of God. Such hope animates Christian political engagement in the present. Stiegler, I suggest, would not be dismissive of this notion, though he would likely consider it but one form of what he means by consisting. His sense of belief is a more general sense of a belief that the world can be otherwise; that there is the possibility of progress towards a more just world, for instance.

A more important resonance between Stiegler and Protestant thought, I would suggest, comes in his distinction between existence and consistence in human subjectivity. German Lutheran theologian Eberhard Jüngel argues that fundamental to the Reformation was the identification of a distinction between a person's actions and that person's true humanity. Indeed, he argues that equating our actions with our identity was one of the primary concepts that Martin Luther protested against. That is, contra Aristotle, Luther holds that our actions flow from our identity. For example, Luther writes, "The work which I do does not make me into the person I am; rather the person who I am makes the work."[91] Key to this position is Luther's locating his reflection on theological anthropology within a discussion of justification rather than of creation. This locus frames human identity formation as a manifestation of the Holy Spirit. In Tillichian terms, then, we can see a Reformation sense of human identity formation as the self-transcending function of the dimension of spirit that cannot be reduced to calculable actions.

For Luther, to understand ourselves as our actions is to live under the illusion that we can make ourselves become good. This illusion is the crux of our sinful reality; in fact, Jüngel points out that understanding sin as that which makes us "bad" is a moralistic reduction of sin that misdiagnoses human nature. Rather, we are by nature embedded in a host of relationships with God and those around us. Yet our actions function to break those relationships because they are inevitably self-serving.

90. See Moltmann, *God in Creation*, 132–35, for his discussion of the distinction.
91. Luther, *Zirkulardisputation de vest nuptiali*, WA 38/I, 283. Quoted in Jüngel, *Theological Essays II*, 229.

It is only in breaking the illusion that we can become good that we are able to rest in our identity as belonging to God as God's good creation. Only in doing so can we become truly human. Being truly human entails knowing our deep embeddedness in relationships with God and with others. From this identity, actions may follow that are beneficial to others, or could be deemed good. These good actions, however, stem from accepting our theological identity first as coming from the source of being rather than as something that we create for ourselves *ex nihilo*. True humanity for Luther, then, is a matter of being possessed by God. While for Kant a person comes to freedom by attaining self-possession through moral virtuousness, for Luther freedom comes in living out of a response to the creative power of the Word of God addressed to them. That is, the divine law, which governs actions, does not have the authority to give judgment upon a person in themselves. "For our acts, whether good or evil, cannot determine our being," Jüngel explains. "Only the one who determines being and non-being determines our being."[92] Thus our humanity is constituted by our relationship with divine creativity.

For Jüngel, this Reformation insight about the nature of humanity offers a powerful critique of modern conceptions of humanity that continue to shape social practices today. In particular, he sees in Luther a response to the cycles of idolization and despair about human achievements and progress. "Truly human persons," he contends, "are those who are able to accept themselves, able to receive their being continually anew as a gift."[93] He makes a distinction between this kind of true humanity and the humanity that can be lost. Humanity that can be lost is humanity that arises from self-constitution through actions. From a Lutheran viewpoint the attempt to constitute the self through action is doomed to be sinful because it takes as its premise a fundamental separation of the autonomous ego. In Tillichian terms this would be to confuse existence with essence. Constructively, we can value this insistence that our identity cannot be reduced to actions, even while recognizing the innumerable ways that we are actively involved in our own identity formation.

Drawing on Jüngel's reading of Luther, what is valuable in this insight is the idea of understanding our identity as a gift rather than a creation. More than the specifics of his argument, what is relevant to our discussion is that there is a distinction, though not a separation, between

---

92. Jüngel, *Theological Essays II*, 236.
93. Ibid., 237–38.

our actions and our identity. Even more, our identity beyond our actions is primordial and is the locus of grace, goodness, relationality, and creativity. Our actions, meanwhile, if they are not flowing from this identity in excess of action, constitute sin itself. When our actions flow from the self-in-excess, then they become good and up-building. In Lutheran theological terms, the self-in-excess is the realm of the gospel, while the realm of independent action can be understood as being under the law. Repentance thus functions as a shift from the realm of the law to the realm of the gospel, where identity is received as a gift.

Repentance should not be construed solely as a turning away from our "bad" actions and resolving to replace them with "good" ones. Repentance, more fundamentally, is a rejection of understanding ourselves as fundamentally constituted by our actions.[94] To anticipate our later turn to Glissant's decolonial theory, we can hold that actions are the transparent aspect of ourselves but they do not constitute us. Rather, we are fundamentally constituted by our opacity; to repent is to place our trust in the opacity of the divine that indwells within us. This opacity is the gift of Otherness from which our lives might be constituted. Theologically this speaks to our relationship with God, but it also enacts a resistance to attempts to render the ineffable transparent through the process of proletarianization which seeks to render us calculable consumers and producers of data with no excess. More simply, it is resistance to the attempts of data mining to define us solely by our actions and instead rooting our identity in the infinity of Otherness.

Through repentance the opacity of our identity beyond our actions is recognized as primordial; again, this is the locus of grace, goodness, relationality, and creativity. Our actions, meanwhile, are sinful if they are not flowing from this identity in excess of action. When our actions flow from the Otherness of divine opacity within the self, then they become a poetic expression of the incalculability of life as an opaque excess. It is a poetic defiance of the defining power of the algorithm.

---

94. I do not wish to reject or downplay the importance of repentance as rejecting our harmful actions and seeking to make appropriate reparations for them. At the same time, I contend that this is only one level of repentance, and that another level of it is about the understanding of the self. The former can be seen as dealing with our harmful actions towards others while the latter as dealing with the human relationship with God. The former could also be understood as dealing with issues of guilt, while the latter is concerned with issues of shame. In terms of the discussion of repentance in relation to big data, it is the latter form of repentance with which I am engaging.

We can find a resonance, if not full consonance, between this Lutheran self-in-excess as the movement of the Holy Spirit, Kearney's self-in-excess as the *persona* that is openness to the divine, Stiegler's consistence as spirit, Tillich's self-transcendence as the dimension of spirit, and Ball's cyborg existence as resistance to reductionism. All seek to express the incalculability of life as an excess, even as they differ in how they understand that excess.[95] Vital to this search, I would add, is Peters's understanding that we not limit technology to forms of mastery but also include the arts of nurturing life as types of technology. In other words, technology and spirit need not be pitted against one another.

In terms of the phenomena of the data double, we can see in it a move towards a full identification of the self with the actions of the self. The data double self becomes an amalgamation of pure performance without excess. It is calculable existence without indefinable consistence. Such a move is a draining of spirit from technology, turning the two into binary opposing forces. The problem of surveillance is that through it our self is reduced to only the observations of others, so that the data double becomes a decontextualized construct of the observed self. The decontextualized construct is a humanity that can lose its humanity, while true humanity is constructed within the context of spirit, which I understand as divine relationality. It is the construction of the self situated within the context of the infinity of divinity. Indeed, Jüngel suggests that where modernity sees the subject as indefinable, the Reformation sees God as the indefinable. Yet I would suggest that such a distinction is an abstraction. If true humanity is recognizable through its situatedness within the divine relationality, then the trace of the infinite is present in each through that connection.

Stiegler, too, proposes that it is insufficient to follow the approach of nineteenth-century romantics in seeing industry and culture as opposing forces. That is, he is critical of framing culture as the domain of spirit that is capable of countering the reductionist tendencies of industry. We may recall from the first chapter that Tillich makes precisely this move that Stiegler critiques. Tillich understands culture as the function of self-creation in the spiritual dimension. For him, culture is the seeking of new symbols and expressions of meaning in response to the destructive

---

95. Slavoj Žižek helpfully notes that excess is not necessarily positive. He wishes to differentiate "obscene excess supplement" of capitalist reproduction from "constitutive ontological excess," which is a closer understanding to that to which I wish to point. Žižek, *The Parallax View*, 310.

forces of estranged existence that reduce the depth of meaning in life. Recall further that technology for him is a tool created by humanity in order to produce greater freedom, yet it carries with it the danger of enslaving people by draining them of their subjectivity and turning them into things themselves, whose value is found only in being useful in the production of other things. Stiegler, on the other hand, argues that in the hyper-industrial society, culture (or more precisely the control of culture) has become the "heart of development" that is used by the reigning power assemblages as a means of control. Following Stiegler here, we can say that through the cyberdimension culture has been co-opted from being a manifestation of depth and spirit into the ambiguous desubjectifying force that Tillich saw in technology. Thus Stiegler might find Tillich's analysis and warnings about technology to be helpful, even while asserting that the contemporary situation calls for a more drastic response. Specifically, Stiegler calls for "the constitution of a *new model of industrial development* as well as of cultural *practices* (and practices irreducible to mere usages)."[96] Thus he calls for culture to be a striving for depth and spirit, but rather than as an opposition to industry the two must both be rethought as spaces for the manifestation of spirit. While a stirring call, a challenge with this proposal is that Stiegler's understanding of culture is rather vague and reductive in comprehending it as singular. Meanwhile his definition of technology lacks Peters's appreciation for the embodied promotion of the values of life. Adopting this greater nuance found in Peters's thought would help Stiegler move from raising this important issue of rethinking the relationship between culture and industry to offering a clearer path forward. These are issues to which we will return in chapter 5. Nonetheless, Stiegler provides a beneficial framework for providing the impetus to look beyond simple oppositions in resisting reductive tendencies.

We may also recall from the first chapter that Tillich's understanding of technology is insufficient for the cyberdimension. Following Peters's infrastructuralist approach, Tillich's understanding of technology is too disembodied to account for the complexity of the cyber-reality. That is, technology is seen as purely external to us; it does not recognize the layer upon layer of infrastructure that allows human existence to function. For Peters, rather, technology is a durable externalized means of mediating depositories of experiences and data. Bodies meanwhile are an essential

---

96. Stiegler, *The Decadence of Industrial Democracies*, 15. Author's italics.

infrastructural component to the use of technology and the meaning mediated through its use. In this we see a connection to Ball's call for a hybridized sense of body and data. The body is a matrix of infinite meaning mediated through technology. The particular technology that is used for engaging a particular body will shape what meaning is discerned through the engagement. This is why algorithms are dangerous—they shape what they observe through their act of observing and through the lens by which they derive meaning from the data they collect. Thus thinking of the body as the true self is just as reductive as the creation of the data double as the essential self is. It is the cyberdimension's version of a body/mind dualism.

Theologically, then, this is where Jüngel's reminder of the Reformation distinction between actions and true humanity comes into play. The true self is found not in actions or in the body. Each is a means of observing the phenomenon of the self through which the matrix of meaning clustered around the "I" may be constructed. The question is how one frames the question of self-identity. I suggest, constructively drawing on Jüngel, that we begin with the primordial relation with divine creativity, or, in more traditional Lutheran terms, the response to the creative Word. Through this lens the self can be understood as more than data and more than body. The self bears an indefinable trace of the infinite which exceeds all frames of identification. We may, in fact, view this response to the creative Word as a poetic excess of existence.

Postcolonial theologian Mayra Rivera construes this exceeding in terms of Spivak's discussion of the wholly Other. "The wholly Other," Rivera writes, "cannot be assimilated within the limits of the system's structures of representation. The appropriating moves of any system of power can never reduce all reality to a function of itself. There is always an excess that the system cannot accommodate."[97] Rivera is not dealing with surveillance issues here, but rather with colonial discourses. Yet as we have seen from Smith, these colonial discourses cannot be divorced from our understanding of the dynamics of power within surveillance. In terms of our discussion of subjectivity and big data, we can understand the creation of the data double as an attempt by a system of power (specifically the military-political-cyber-industrial-commercial surveillant power assemblage) to appropriate human bodies into a controllable system. Yet we are reminded at this point that there is always an excess

---

97. Rivera, *The Touch of Transcendence*, 111.

beyond the simulacrum of subjectivity of the data double, a consisting that exceeds existing, to use Stiegler's terms.

Rivera's constructive project deals with understanding this gap as a this-worldly transcendence, where transcendence "designates a relation with a reality irreducibly different from my own reality, yet without the difference destroying this relation and without the relation destroying this difference."[98] In other words, transcendence is a call to responsibility to the Other while allowing the otherness of the Other. Theologically, Rivera holds that this turn to the Other "is the mark of the beginning of our very life in a reality underived from us. Theology names that reality God—as that which exceeds all names and with which our very existence is related."[99] In this we might hear an echo of Jüngel's contention that true humanity is found in receiving life as a gift. Yet how might this ethical sense of relationship address the totalizing attempts of the creation of the data double? What does God have to do with data mining? Put differently, returning to our Tillichian framework, how does the dimension of spirit interpenetrate the cyberdimension? Indeed I would suggest that the key point to take from the discussions of the excess of the Other is that it is pointing to the same dynamic to which Tillich points in his concept of spirit. It is the "more" that cannot be contained by data.

Big Data and Spirit

Let us recall that for Tillich the dimension of Spirit is the process of actualizing potentialities and overcoming the ambiguity of estranged existence. Let us also recall that this dimension is always only glimpsed rather than fully revealed. Any attempt to fully and certainly identify the spiritual dimension risks failing because it is by nature an ambiguous and uncertain dimension. Given this sense of the dimension of spirit, how might we tentatively identify the dimension of spirit working in the cyberdimension?

First let us identify the ambiguities that we have encountered in our consideration of big data and data mining. Perhaps first among these issues is the tension between seeing and not seeing. We have also encountered tensions between privacy and communication, as well as between

---

98. Ibid., 125.
99. Ibid., 126.

body and action. Underlying all of these tensions is the distinction between existence and consistence.

We can identify the perhaps most well-known and discussed tension within cyberspace as the pull between privacy and communication. Lyon argues that in the post-Snowden era, any notion of privacy requires a more foundational notion of the common good. Perhaps we can hear some echoes of Aquinas's formulation of the Just War tradition in this proposal. Concerns about privacy in the big data era, Lyon continues, must "care deeply about protecting the other person, not merely 'my privacy.'"[100] It must be concerned with the effects of surveillance on populations and individuals who exceed the proscribed norm or otherwise trigger social sorting profiles. In other words, privacy concerns must include a turn to the Other, in Rivera's framing.

At the same time, while privacy is considered a human right, it also has dangerous potential. After all, it is in the private sphere where women are generally most vulnerable to violence, for instance. Privacy, further, has never been granted to all. Thus some feminist thinkers have raised up the reality that not all women have been equally entitled to privacy. Many groups have had and continue to have limits placed on their privacy, to little public concern. Such groups include prisoners, people living in institutional care for disabilities, immigrants, and refugees.[101] Discussions of privacy must be nuanced to consider these dynamics. Privacy must support the creative illusiveness of spirit without ignoring the realities of injustice hidden from sight.

In terms of the dimension of spirit, then, privacy is an ambiguous concept. The ability to respond to not knowing everything about someone with hospitality rather than fear is a mark of emotional and spiritual maturity. This is a Derridean sense of hospitality. In terms of data privacy, the tension is between on the one hand both the need to utilize the tools of engaging the contemporary world, which includes email and social media, along with receiving the benefits of these technologies, such as the health benefits derived from using a FitBit, while on the other hand the way that the data double created by the use of these technologies can be used negatively to intrude on life and reduce it to a functional accumulation of data. This is perhaps the central struggle of big data and the realm where a theology of the common good is most needed. For our purposes

---

100. Lyon, *Surveillance After Snowden*, 113.

101. Dubrofsky and Magnet, eds., *Feminist Surveillance Studies*, 4.

here, let me simply suggest that such a desire for common good is a mark of the dimension of spirit.

Yet we can also see that the issue at stake is more than simply a question of privacy, it is a question of the accumulation and use of power. To have one's privacy taken away is to have one's power taken. In the cyberdimension, information is power. This of course is not only true in the cyberdimension, but in that the cyberdimension is primarily a realm of information it particularly comes to the fore there. Outside of cyberspace information takes time to gather, process, and disseminate. The limitations of physical time and space shape the flow of information. Yet in cyberspace time and distance do not exist in the same manner. Thus information can be accumulated and transferred on scales unfathomable outside of cyberspace. Thus power can be accumulated and transferred on scales unfathomable without cyberspace. In this we see both the value of Foucault's ruminations on the panopticon, in his recognition of the power that comes surveillance and at the same time we find the value of image of the surveillant assemblages or rhizome metaphor to describe the way that surveillant power is not static and concentrated, but dynamic.

It is cyberspace that allows this change in the nature of power. Recall Tillich's three aspects of a dimension: modification of time, space, causality, and substance under its predominance. Recall as well his three movements of life: self-identity, self-creation, and self-transcendence. In big data we see how cyberspace reorients these aspects. Self-identification, we may recall, is the creation of a centered sense of identity. In the cyberdimension this is manifested as the cyborg hybridization of body, data, and spirit received as a gift. This self is the site of infinite meaning mediated through technology. Self-creation, meanwhile, is growth and creativity in search of novelty. Within the cyberdimension, this happens through radical interconnectivity that allows access to vast amounts of data. Such data yields new insights and new frameworks for engaging the world. Self-transcendence, then, is the quality of excess found in the other two processes. It is consisting rather than mere existing. Data mining poses a challenge to this function.

While these new expressions of the functions of life can be seen in the cyberdimension, at the same time the forces of the old world seek to retain their old world power through the new alliance of the cyber-military-corporate-industrial complex or power assemblage. In this move to the power of surveillance, we see the tension between cyberspace as a forum of free expression and a means for imposing identified norms.

As algorithms sort through the data produced by our lives, we have little choice but to trust that they will not deem us abnormal and therefore threatening to the status quo. We may recall Lyon's warning that the types of algorithms used in concert with stereotypical assumptions can combine to identify innocent people as dangerous by those whose outlook is shaped by fear of security breaches.[102] The problem here, as we have seen, is in the reduction of the subject to their data double as the truth of their selves. At the same time, we have also encountered the tendency to see the body as the true self for the sake of maintaining privacy.

It is perhaps Smith who most clearly brings forth the issue here that matters for the dimension of spirit within the cyberdimension. For Smith, let us recall, the issue behind surveillance is not only what is seen, but also what is hidden or made invisible. This dual function is critical. Here Rivera's theological move is relevant. She is critical of theological constructions of God as "out there," separate from the world. She argues for a sense of transcendence within this world. She argues for an understanding of God as "over all" but not "above all."[103] This is significant for our consideration of data and surveillance. The image of God looking down from heaven, surveying—dare I say surveilling—all of the happenings of world, even entering each person's mind to know their intentions, is the ultimate image of the panopticon. In this formulation of the divine there is no privacy or escaping God's condemnation for violating divine norms. Indeed, this image of the omniscient and all-seeing divine may even provide a justification for unfettered surveillance. For Rivera, however, God's relation to the world is not one of surveillance but one of embrace. She writes, "Touch reveals the simultaneity of transcendence and intimacy, a divine enveloping through which God may caress creation and feel its joy and suffering."[104] God, for Rivera, is among us, transcendent in the "intimate and yet insurmountable space between our differences."[105]

Through her turn to an immanent transcendence, Rivera's understanding of divine glory speaks to Smith's concerns. She holds, "The glory of God reveals while concealing—or rather makes visible something while signaling that something else escapes that vision, that there is always

---

102. Lyon, *Surveillance After Snowden*, 75.
103. Rivera, *The Touch of Transcendence*, 136.
104. Ibid., 135–36.
105. Ibid., 137.

more that has passed by."[106] That is, the glory of God is the recognition of the depth of the Other. It reveals something of the Other while at the same time indicating the infinite depths that lie behind what can be seen of that Other. It is a glimpse that illuminates that there is an Other there for whom we have an ethical call towards, but also who exceeds what we can know or control. In this sense, the glory of God is the glimpse of the Other as exceeding their data double as well as their flesh as a measure of their true self. At the same time, this illuminating glory does not hide that which it does not show. It signals that there is more there, unlike Smith's concern about surveillance. The glory of God is not a dismissal of what is not seen, but a celebration of it.

As Rivera, drawing on Karmen MacKendrick, notes, in the Gospel of John, word, light, and flesh are interrelated. The Word is known in flesh, which allows the Word to be seen as light. Word, flesh, and light are all essential to the glory of God.[107] Looking back to the tension of seeing and not seeing in big data, then, let me suggest that the dimension of spirit known in the cyberdimension is known in the ability to see and not see. It is in the recognition that much of the world is understood through big data while also signaling that there is more that escapes vision. Some creatures are obscured and distorted. Bodies cannot be eclipsed by data but at the same time subjects exceed bodies. Information—words—are of value when not divorced from flesh but rather bring to light the depth of the touch of transcendence in the Other. Recall here my contention in the first chapter that cyberspace creates a unique kind of absent presence, and this presence helps us to see theologically Christ as the Word as sacramentally mediated. Words and bodies, brought to light but not fully revealed through the flickering pixels of our touch screens.

This again is the tension between seeing and privacy that can only be found in a robust sense of the common good. We might see here the value of Stiegler's call for the redevelopment of both culture and industry as elements of life—indeed of spirit—that consist rather than consume. That is, a sense of culture in its myriad diversity as a human celebration of meaning and depth, and industry likewise as a celebration of human creativity. In terms of the cyberdimension, such a culture and space requires an aspect of cyberspace that is communal and neither privately owned and geared for profit, nor militarized and geared to the increase of state

106. Ibid., 139.
107. Ibid., 19.

power. It requires at least a partial realization of the Barlowian vision of it as a realm of potential, even if tempered by a sober recognition of the reality of ambiguity.

Data mining without a sense of the common good is a force of disintegration, in Tillich's terms. Surveillance itself is unavoidable and ambiguous. We constantly see others and are seen by them. Yet when big data surveillance defines our identity, the tension of ambiguity is snapped. It loses not only a sense of common good but also a sense of true humanity in its glorious Otherness. Thus resistance to imbalanced surveillance is a theological imperative. Yet how can we go about effecting such resistance? It is to this question that we turn next.

Chapter 4

Disruptive Resistance

In March 2016, in the midst of the US primary elections, the hacktivist group Anonymous declared "war" on Republican presidential candidate Donald Trump. It set April 1 as the date to take down Trump's websites. Yet as the date arrived, most of Trump's websites remained active, with only minor effects of a cyberattack. Paul Szoldra, writing for the website *Business Insider*, reported that the operation had devolved into a civil war within the group. He points to two separate chatrooms on the operation, each signaling a different mission. The original OpTrump was begun by a hacker named Beemsee. Beemsee and two colleagues wrote that no actual cyberattack had been intended; rather it was a move to gain attention in order to highlight the authoritarian impulses of Trump and his supporters. Another group within Anonymous, however, claimed that a cyberattack was indeed intended and had been successful. A hacker called AnonymousLoyalist claimed that the operation had shifted to a separate channel that was more organized, though Szoldra reports that the chatroom itself was chaotic, filled with trolling comments from Trump supporters. For Szoldra this indicates a complete failure of Anonymous in its intended action.[1]

Yet in the days before the intended action, communications scholar Adam G. Klein suggested that the true goal of the operation may have already been achieved, regardless of the activities on April 1. He notes that the group published Trump's Social Security number and cell phone numbers on March 17. In response, Trump demanded the perpetrators be arrested, and the FBI and Social Security began investigations. Yet,

---

1. Szoldra, "The Anonymous 'War' on Donald Trump."

Anonymous soon revealed, this leaked information had been available on the Internet since 2013. It had not actually hacked anything; a quick Google search should have revealed this to the Trump campaign and government agencies. In its video response to the incident, Anonymous says, "Thank you Trump and Trump campaign. Thank you police, FBI, and the Secret Service for being a part of our little experiment on how we should expect the so-called New America will be."[2] For Klein, this indicates the protest basis for Anonymous's actions. He writes, "The group is making the political suggestion that rather than being viewed as *the* political outsider of this election season, Trump represents a brand of totalitarianism that will aim establishment power at whatever target he directs."[3] Thus he argues for viewing Anonymous not as juvenile pranksters but rather as subtle manipulators of power.

In this incident we encounter a variety of issues involved in assessing Anonymous specifically and hacktivism more generally. On the one hand it can be self-contradictory and have no obvious effect through its actions. On the other hand, it can be seen as a clever force for legitimate social action. In short, Anonymous is multiple and confusing. In response, many wish to simplify and reduce it to being a bunch of "punks." As Klein notes, his scholarly research "found that most journalists frame Anonymous as 'malicious pranksters' whose missions are broadly tantamount to tying the enemy's shoelaces together and running away. The next most frequent characterization used more ominous terms, painting Anonymous as a global threat much like the movie character in the Guy Fawkes mask who gleefully plotted the demise of world order."[4] In contrast, he argues that nearly all Anonymous operations have a clear social activist goal and so they should be treated as an activist group.

We have thus far seen through examining cyberwar and cyberweapons the militarization of cyberspace, and through big data the informatization of the subject and the coalescing of the military-corporate-political-media-cyber-industrial power assemblage. I have argued for the necessity of resistance to these tendencies. Yet the question of how to go about this resistance remains. This brings us to the topic of activism and civil disobedience within the cyber realm. This is an area of great controversy, perhaps the most widely discussed issue among the

---

2. Ashok, "Anonymous Hacker Group Dupes Trump."
3. Klein, "How Anonymous Hacked Donald Trump."
4. Ibid.

cybersecurity topics we will encounter. Discussions of hackers and groups such as Anonymous routinely fill television news. What might these figures point to, however, if we inspect them more closely? Can their forms of resistance be manifestations of the dimension of spirit? Even more, can any of the various forms of activism engaged in cyberspace fit with the Christian tradition of social activism? I contend that through tactics of disruption hacktivist and digital activist groups can indeed crack open a space in which the reductionist tendencies regnant in cyberspace can give way to an inbreaking of a creative spirit of resistance that may be understood as the movement of the Holy Spirit.

Activism in Cyberspace

Before we turn to theological reflection on resistance in the cyberdimension, we must have a sense of the various strands of resistance found there. An essential debate over the nature and value of activism in cyberspace is whether it should be understood in continuity with earlier forms of activism, or if activism in the online sphere is a new form of activism. This debate stems from different understandings of what cyberspace is and how it relates to broader realities. To understand these viewpoints, it is helpful to give a short history of the development of online activism.

A Brief History of Internet Activism

The early forms of Internet activism imagined the cyberdimension of protest to be parallel to physical forms of protest. There were some instances of Internet-based activism dating back at least as far as the late 1980s. In her overview of hacktivism, Dorothy Denning points to the creation of worms and viruses as an early means of delivering protest messages. She lifts up the 1989 computer worm, "Worms Against Nuclear Killers (WANK)" as typical of this early era. The worm was created by Australian antinuclear activists and aimed at the computer networks of NASA and the US Department of Energy as a means of protesting the launching of a shuttle carrying radioactive plutonium.[5] A variety of activist groups also communicated via Usenet groups in this era. Meanwhile, groups such as

---

5. Denning, "The Rise of Hacktivism."

the Electronic Frontier Foundation (EFF) worked to secure free-speech rights online.[6]

Internet activism began to arouse broader attention in relation to the Zapatista movement. In their uprising in southern Mexico the indigenous group used Internet communication to build a global network of support. The Zapatistas did not engage in any direct action, though. Rather, it was supportive groups in other countries, most notably the Electronic Disturbance Theatre (EDT), who engaged in direct online actions against anti-Zapatista institutions, especially the Mexican and United States governments, through DDoS and similar actions.[7] It was, however, the 1999 World Trade Organization protests in Seattle that truly brought online activism to widespread consciousness, especially through the British group known as *the electrohippies*.

For *the electrohippies*, online actions should support wider protest actions. During the WTO demonstrations, from November 30 through December 6, 1999, *the electrohippies* orchestrated a DDoS and email bombing attack on the conference's servers and public websites, as well as other websites related to the conference. They also created fake sites for the event that lured in participants, allowing the group to promote its agenda. Their actions resulted in the website for the conference shutting down briefly. The leaders attached their names to this action, prepared to face legal consequences as part of civil disobedience. For them, online space was a free zone for public discussion. Engaging in this action was a direct translation of street protest tactics into the online arena.

The electrohippies and other digital activist groups of the late 1990s, such as the CAE (Critical Art Ensemble) and the EDT, consciously used spatial metaphors in framing their understanding of activist tactics. The EDT was particularly fond of the "virtual sit-in," while the CAE essay "Electronic Civil Disobedience" called for activist groups to move their protest actions from the streets to online spaces. Scholar Molly Sauter contends that these groups "were interested in establishing the online space as an arena of activism socially, culturally, and legally equivalent to the physical world."[8] This is not to say that the various groups were in total agreement on the nature of the online world or the role of activism

---

6. For more on their history and initial concerns, see their website: https://www.eff.org/about/history. My thanks to Josh Drescher for pointing me to this early history.

7. Veigh, "Classifying Forms of Online Activism," 76.

8. Sauter, *The Coming Swarm*, 43.

in it, but they were united in attempting largely direct translations of physical-realm understandings of activism to digital activism.

The foundation of their frameworks stemmed from their models of understanding cyberspace. As Sauter explains, "The strict physical-world parallelism sought by digitally enabled activists such as the EDT and *the electrohippies* necessitates a physicalized view of the internet itself; the internet itself must be seen as a physical place, albeit one with special attributes."[9] She explains that the essential goal of direct action activism in the streets is to lay bare the true nature of state and corporate power structures through having a large number of people fill semi-private spaces. In doing so an unjustly strong response is elicited, thus exposing the underlying injustice of the situation. The classic parallel here is the lunch counter sit-in of the civil rights movement. The privately owned diner becomes a site of public protest through wide participation in disrupting business to the point of revealing the government and business world collusion in maintaining an unjust power differential. This logic was applied to online activism through a one-to-one ratio DDoS attack. That is, the JavaScript tool developed by the EDT in 1998 and used by *the electrohippies* in their WTO actions allowed participants to target conference websites and networks. *The electrohippies* claimed that over 450,000 people participated in action.[10] In keeping with the sit-in structure, the technological tools allowed only a one-to-one participant to signal ratio; that is, each participant could only make one *ping* on the websites, just as in a sit-in each person could only occupy the space of one person. Therefore the participation of many people was necessary for the DDoS action to be successful, just as in a street-level action.

If we recall the details of a DDoS action, we may remember that a DoS action is like making a phone call in order to tie up that phone line. With a DDoS action, meanwhile, it is like having a host of people make phone calls all at once in order to overwhelm the phone line. In being directed at a website, it would send so many requests to that site that the site crashes. This can be increased in volume through joining a botnet that can coordinate hundreds or even thousands of computers in sending a flood of pings at a particular server. While we have mentioned the malicious power of using malware to make a computer a zombie component of a botnet, in a DDoS action a program can also be used to voluntarily

9. Ibid., 45.
10. Ibid., 40.

become part of a botnet engaged in the direct action during the duration of that action. Whether a computer is voluntarily part of a botnet or if it has been covertly co-opted makes a significant difference in the ethical considerations of a DDoS action. When voluntary, it represents a choice to subsume one's individual identity into a collective action rather than a transgressive take-over of agency. While the early movements insisted upon a one-person-to-one-ping ratio, more recent movements have been more open to one person controlling a greater number of pings simultaneously.

For the EDT the terminology of considering a DDoS action as an "attack" is problematic. Such phrasing conjures images of cyberwarfare and an aggressive stance. Rather, the group understood itself to be engaging symbolic resistance. "We consider [direct actions] performance art . . . ," the group holds. "When we do a performance, our performance or our actions are considered symbolic gestures; we are trying to bring attention to a particular cause or event—we are not trying to do any criminal activity."[11] Indeed the names of the groups highlight this sense of electronic activism as theatrical gesture—Electronic Disturbance Theatre and Critical Art Ensemble, for instance. This artistic sense has been reinvoked more recently by Italian hacker, artist, and scholar Tatiana Bazzichelli, to whom we will turn later in this chapter.

Thus part of the goal of the WTO action was to establish cyberspace as a legitimate "space" for civil disobedience. In our Tillichian framework, we might say that *the electrohippies* understood cyberspace to be an outgrowth of traditional forms of technology rather than as a unique dimension. That is, issues such as space, time, and presence within the cyberdimension were understood to be extensions of their manifestations in other realms of experience. Space for dissent was literally needed, as was the participation of a large number of people in order to demonstrate that a position was worthy of notice.

The DDoS approach of the EDT and *the electrohippies* met criticism within the activist community, however. For example, the CAE's understanding of "Electronic Civil Disobedience" (ECD) felt that DDoS attacks were ineffective. They felt that ECD operations should be small and kept out of the public eye. In its 1996 essay, "Electronic Civil Disobedience," the group gives an analysis of the challenges of civil disobedience in resisting the authoritarian tendencies of institutions that it sees being

---

11. Conan, "Hacktivism."

magnified in cyberspace. They contend: "The question of resistance then becomes threefold: First, how can the notion of an avant-garde be recombined with notions of pluralism? Second, what are the strategies and tactics needed to fight a decentralized power that is constantly in a state of flux? Finally, how are the units of resistance to be organized?"[12] In response, they argue, "To fight a decentralized power requires the use of a decentralized means."[13] Therefore they advocate for a cell structure of groups of four to ten activists working from their particular location and point of view that is allowed to retain its distinctive identity while being held together with other groups not in uniformity but through a general shared resistance to authoritarianism. To move to larger movements is to confront power with power, which the group holds will ultimately fail. "After two centuries of revolution and near-revolution," the group insists, "one historical lesson continually appears—authoritarian structure cannot be smashed; it can only be resisted."[14] The accumulation of small groups of resistance is the best way to create a flexible and continual resistance. The goal of ECD is not to catch the public's attention, they felt, but rather to create a resistant power assemblage in response to the flows of information that enables the authoritarian assemblages of power. Here we see a difference between early cyber activist groups in understanding the goal of activism, but not of the nature of the cyber realm.

Another vein of criticism of these early DDoS actions came from the hacker community, and more specifically what are known as "hacktivist" groups. These groups, such as Cult of the Dead Cow and Hacktivismo, came from hacker roots, which places among its highest values personal autonomy and free speech. While groups like *the electrohippies* were generally made up of activists who sought to move their tactics to include an online component, hacktivists were computer people first who began to move into activism. As Sauter notes, hacktivist groups were "made up of hackers who became politically active through writing and distributing code and tools beginning in the 1990s."[15] The realm of information was their political world; they were not primarily interested in importing the concerns or tactics of physical world social justice activists. Rather, challenging censorship and restrictions on free speech were central to

---

12. Critical Art Ensemble, *Electronic Civil Disobedience*, 22.
13. Ibid., 23.
14. Ibid., 24.
15. Sauter, *The Coming Swarm*, 47.

their activities. This was particularly done through creating tools and programming to circumvent attempts at web censorship, mask their Internet activities, and encrypt communication. This is not to say that such movements did not cross out of cyberspace into the streets at times, however. A particularly notable example is the "FREE KEVIN" movement. Hacker Kevin Mitnick was arrested in February 1995 and charged with a variety of federal communications and computer offenses. He was held in prison for four and a half years without bail or trial, until he changed his plea from "not guilty" to "guilty" and agreed to a plea bargain. His time in prison included eight months in solitary confinement because, according to him, law enforcement claimed that he was able to start a nuclear war by whistling into a pay phone.[16] Many protests arose against Mitnick's treatment, particularly led by the 2600 hacker community, which spearheaded the "FREE KEVIN" movement. These protests included digital means such as putting the "FREE KEVIN" message on websites, but also included coordinated physical protests outside of federal courthouses across the United States.[17] Thus we can see a combination of physical and digital activism, although it still surrounded issues of online freedom.

Given these commitments, the use of DDoS tactics were often considered completely unacceptable by groups coming from a hacker background. They were criticized as a form of censorship. In considering the critique in retrospect, Sauter helpfully suggests that while it was sometimes valid, it more often failed to consider power differentials. She questions whether disruption practiced by those not in control of the power hierarchy can truly be considered censorship.[18] Here we see the difference between digital activists and "hacktivists." The groups are often conflated, but at least in the early phases of the cyberdimension actually operated under different philosophical understandings of civil disobedience. Thus Oxblood Ruffin, a member of the Cult of the Dead Cow, wrote, "One does not become a hacktivist merely by inserting an 'h' in front of the word activist or by looking backward to paradigms associated with industrial organization."[19] For early hacktivists, cyberspace represented something new that brought forth different concerns, tactics, and priorities. It was a separate sphere from the old physical world. Early

---

16. Mills, "Social Engineering 101."

17. Kroll, "Free Kevin, Kevin Freed." My thanks as well to Josh Drescher for pointing me to this history.

18. Sauter, *The Coming Swarm*, 49.

19. Ruffin, "Hacktivismo," quoted in Sauter, *The Coming Swarm*, 48.

digital activists, meanwhile, saw that the cyber sphere was an extension of the old world into a new form. At the same time, we ought not make this distinction too absolute, as the distinctions are somewhat fine and there was a certain fluidity and diversity to the movements.

A new phase of hacktivism began in 2008 when a group known as Anonymous decided to engage in a direct action known as Operation Chanology. The target was the Church of Scientology, which had attempted to force a takedown of a video of Tom Cruise criticizing the religious group. In other words, this was an offense in line with classic hacktivist concerns. Yet the operation included not only DDoS actions along with other digital actions, but also included physical-world protests. This was not the first time that an Anonymous action had included DDoS actions. They had from time to time before this included this tactic in raids against those engaged in perceived attempts at censorship. Yet at this point Anonymous was known as much for its pursuit of the "lulz." Lulz is a way of speaking of trolling or fun at the expense of others. It is derived from the abbreviation "lol," or "laugh out loud." Doing things "for the lulz" became a central aspect of Anonymous culture; often this meant hacking pranks such as altering hacked webpages in order to embarrass the owners as a means of mockery that might be lighthearted but just as often was intended to be downright cruel.[20] Operation Chanology, however, marked a significant change for Anonymous, both in a movement towards greater political engagement as well as incorporating street activism. The group had previously been "Internet-native," concerned only with matters within the cyber realm. The move beyond this, in fact, created dispute within the group, as some claimed it betrayed the ethos of the group.[21] Ultimately, however, it was only the beginning of a movement towards political engagement that has brought Anonymous to wide recognition and great controversy.

Since the first foray into political activism, Anonymous has developed a political sensibility, but it is one that frequently confuses commentators. This is largely because Anonymous's identity is, at its core, multiple. This multiplicity that constitutes Anonymous will respond to different issues at different times in different ways as different individuals are involved. However, Gabriella Coleman, who has studied Anonymous closely, claims that it is a frequently-made mistake to think that

---

20. Coleman, *Hacker, Hoaxer, Whistle-blower, Spy*, Kindle location 460.
21. Olson, *We Are Anonymous*, 93–94.

Anonymous is amorphous with no guiding structures or principles. She writes, "Far from lacking structure or flailing wildly about like a compass at the North Pole, Anonymous incorporates an abundance of relationships, structures, and moral positions."[22] It is not structureless or unprincipled; rather it overflows with relationships and values, even if this profusion causes some incongruities. In this, Anonymous may perhaps be best seen using Deleuze and Guattari's rhizome model discussed in the previous chapter. If surveillance structures are best understood as assemblages, so too is Anonymous; it is a dynamic group continually emerging, and yet with trajectories of continuity. That said, it is also true that Anonymous's principles can embody paralyzing contradictions such as the example of OpTrump with which we began the chapter. Moreover, because of the value placed on anonymity, it is possible that those with goals opposed to the general sensibility may choose to act under the name of Anonymous, whether for publicity or to undermine the movement. These issues become more pronounced as Anonymous becomes better known. Nonetheless, even with these contradictions and ambiguities the name Anonymous points to a phenomenon that, while not able to be defined precisely, still retains a continuity of identity. This multiple identity is actually coherent with CAE's earlier vision of cell groups of resistance, yet married not only to *the electrohippies'* and EDT's desire for larger scale movements that seek to raise public awareness but also the hacktivist ethos that cyberspace need not confine itself to a strict parallel with conventional civil disobedience. In this sense Anonymous is an inheritor—or even hybrid—of the many streams of hacktivism and digital activism.

It nonetheless remains true that Anonymous must be understood within the context of hacker culture.[23] This includes the search for lulz as having a prankster sensibility that can be jocular but more often includes a darker sense of trolling in order to humiliate those who have caused offense or to highlight hypocrisies and ironies.[24] It has an anarchic sensi-

---

22. Coleman, *Hacker, Hoaxer, Whistle-blower, Spy*, Kindle location 1633.

23. See Sauter, *The Coming Swarm*, 84–87, for more on the ways that Anonymous is embedded within hacker culture.

24. For instance, on January 17, 2012 an FBI task force held a conference call on investigations into Anonymous and similar groups. Anonymous was able to record the call and then on February 3 posted it on YouTube, as an attempt to both humiliate the FBI and highlight the irony of the investigated doing the investigating. While in this instance those involved were arrested, it demonstrates the sensibility of the group. See Owen, *Disruptive Power*, 6–7.

bility to it; Taylor Owen suggests that it "is an ideological manifestation of the most doctrinaire of the new technology elite. It represents the anarchistic end of a spectrum that includes everything from the belief that private-sector massive open online courses extend the benefits of higher education to more radical notions of markets unencumbered by taxes and regulation and offshore islands free from the control of the state."[25] It is anarchic in that it is non-hierarchical and massively distributed. This makes it uncontrollable and indefinable for the boundaries and categories that sustain the institutions of power that have been in control at least since World War II, if not the entire post-Westphalian creation of modern nation-states. It is based in fluid partnerships and collaborations rather than rigidly organized hierarchies. This comes from the imprint of hacker culture, which in turn is dependent on notions of cyberspace such as Barlow's. As we have seen, however, this view of cyberspace is more a vision of an ideal Internet rather than the Internet as it exists. As I mentioned in the first chapter, though, Barlow's vision is an important animating force for action within the cyberdimension, even as we must also recognize its idealized nature and reject its neglect of embodiment. A realized interdependence is indeed possible in the cyberdimension that is not as easily recognizable in other dimensions. In this sense the anarchic aspect of Anonymous calls to mind philosopher of religion John D. Caputo's framing of the metaphor of the kingdom of God as a turn to a "sacred anarchy" where hierarchies are turned upside down.

Indeed there are some interesting Christian resonances within Anonymous' rhetoric. Sauter points out that the phrase "We are legion" derives from the Gospel of Mark. In Mark 5:10, Jesus confronts a man possessed by a demon. In response to being asked its name, the demon replies, "My name is Legion; for we are many."[26] This religious reference is particularly interesting given that elsewhere Sauter contends that the typical media portrayal of hackers is as a folk devil. It certainly points to Anonymous's sense of moral ambiguity in seemingly aligning itself with the demonic. Yet we must also note that "legion" can be read as a reference to the basic unit of the Roman army, the occupying power of Jesus' time. Ched Myers, for instance, in his socio-literary reading of Mark, suggests that the demoniac is a representation of the mental colonialization or

---

25. Owen, *Disruptive Power*, 6–7.
26. NRSV translation.

repressed communal anguish under Roman occupation.[27] Drawing on Myers's interpretation, blogger John Mcateer contends, "And it is no accident that Jesus casts them into a herd of unclean animals and drives them into the sea just as the occupied Palestinians wished they could drive their Roman oppressors into the sea. Here Jesus is symbolically defeating the Romans while simultaneously showing that the real enemy is spiritual/demonic, not racial."[28] Of course it is unlikely that Anonymous is aware of this framing of the passage, as that would indicate aligning itself with the powers of oppression. Moreover, the phrase "We are legion" is also rooted in Rule Four of the Forty-seven Rules of the Internet, which is "Anonymous is legion."

Nonetheless, the potential allusion to the Markan passage opens up some interesting religious considerations of resistance and empire. Here a bit of excursus on Stephen D. Moore's postcolonial reading of Mark through the lens of this passage is warranted. Unlike Myers, who reads Mark as unequivocally anti-imperial, Moore sees Mark as ambiguous. He allows that Mark 5 can be read in a "zealot" fashion, but it is an oversimplification of the complexity of the Markan text.[29] Moore suggests that because Mark continually undercuts all authority figures except Jesus, the zealot reading raises the question of whether Mark views Jesus as the messianic counterforce to the power of the Roman Empire, "deftly switching Jesus for Caesar"[30] but otherwise leaving the system of empire in place. To investigate this possibility, Moore turns to Mark's use of the term *basileia*. He contends that within the Roman provinces, the use of *basileia* would have brought to mind the power of the Roman Empire. Moore thus sees the Markan use of *basileai* as something of a parody of empire, or what Gayatri Spivak calls *catachresis*. That is, it is a means of resistance by taking over the usage of the term and shifting its meaning. The Markan empire of God is one that must be received like a little child but for which wealth and social status constitute overwhelming obstacles to entering. Moore writes, "The present Empire of God, then, dimly conjured up in Mark, seethes with countercultural valence."[31] This sense

27. Myers, *Binding the Strong Man*, 193.
28. Mcateer, "When Jesus Himself Wanted to Explain."
29. Moore, *Empire and Apocalypse*, 31.
30. Ibid., 37.
31. Ibid., 39. Moore goes on to point out that Mark is somewhat inconsistent in its application of anti-imperial thought; he sees it as deconstructing the economics that empire relies on but not fully "relinguish[ing] its dreams of empire." Ibid., 44.

of the kingdom of God as a parody of imperial pretensions finds some resonance with the hacktivist tactics that we find in this chapter.

Anonymous further employs the tag line "Expect us," which gives a messianic sensibility of representing the justice that is to come, though again it is doubtful that such religious imagery is fully intended. Nonetheless, resonances are there. For instance, because of its multiple identity, Anonymous does not exist as such. It is more of an event; Anonymous happens through its interactions in chat rooms and in its direct actions. This eventive nature of Anonymous brings to mind the Lutheran understanding of the church as an event—it is something that happens as people gather and the Word of God is mediated to them through words and sacraments. Certainly I am not equating Anonymous with the church, as there is much about Anonymous that can be chalked up to vindictiveness, nihilism, and bullied people longing to be part of something powerful that can do its own bullying. Yet I would suggest that they are not altogether different, either. Anonymous can, at its best, be seen as a group that longs for the coming of justice as well as participates in its arrival. Indeed, to turn the connection around, Anonymous may help us constructively retrieve the Reformation understanding of the invisible or hidden church as a metaphor of the dimension of spirit within the cyberdimension, to which we will turn more fully in the final chapter.

The Power Assemblage Strikes Back

In the *Star Wars* movies, the repeated fatal flaw for the villains is their trust in the ability of overwhelming oppressive military power to subdue the galaxy. The Death Star and its successors feature in four of the movies so far released. They provide a centralized threat that the rebellious heroes can join together in resisting through finding unexpected chinks in the armor of these powerful weapons. Yet the forces of the Dark Side are much more effective when they are not so focused on this confrontational power, opting instead to build power through manipulation, subtle coercion, and duplicitous scheming. Fortunately for the heroes in the movies, the dark powers have trouble learning this lesson. Unfortunately for the cyberdimension, the power assemblages of this world do seem to understand this dynamic.

The Arab Spring, for instance, is often pointed to as the high point of cyber-aided resistance to tyrannical powers. Dissidents communicating with Facebook, Skype, and other social media were viewed as heralding new possibilities for protest in this world. The United States Department of State even developed plans and programs for training allies in the region in anonymizing and circumvention tools as part of a $57 million congressional allocation.[32] Yet today it is clear that the depth of domination of the cyberdimension was gravely underestimated. For instance, Egyptian authorities had files on activists containing transcripts of their communications, including Skype conversations that had previously been considered impenetrably encrypted.[33] Here we can recall from the previous chapter the private companies involved in selling security tools to governments. These tools are overwhelmingly sold to companies in the global South. Deibert reports, "Privacy International has identified at least thirty British companies that it believes have sold surveillance technologies to countries with shoddy human rights records—Syria, Iran, Yemen, Bahrain, et cetera—and it estimates the revenues of the global surveillance industry at $5 billion annually."[34] Products from French, American, and German companies have also been linked to autocratic governments. Using these purchased technologies, the governments were able to monitor the resistance movements closely.

Yet we have seen already numerous examples from the United States, Russia, China, and other countries of the reality that the domination of the cyberdimension by the military-cyber-commercial-industrial complex is global and seeks to entrench the current power structures, and this is enabled by the infrastructural backbone of cyberspace.[35] Owen insists, "The act of making the digital world both a threat and a weapon has allowed the state to treat it as an object of war, and has blurred the lines between belligerents and citizens."[36] In other words, just as cyberspace has been militarized as a battlefield between nations, as we saw in chapter 2, it is also militarized as a battlefield against those who challenge the validity to the current power regimes and assemblages. As Owen contends, militarization is the reaction of power assemblages to disruptive forces, and

32. Owen, *Disruptive Power*, 13.
33. Deibert, *Black Code*, 195.
34. Ibid., 211.
35. For instance, Deibert highlights a variety of these companies, particularly Narus, a Boeing subsidiary. In 2012, it promoted its cyber-surveillance and analysis software as being in use with commercial and government operations on five continents. See Deibert, *Black Code*, 191–92.
36. Owen, *Disruptive Power*, 184.

it is a global phenomenon. "The threat [of militarization of cyberspace] is ill-defined but omnipresent. The battlefield is global. . . . And the lines between domestic and the international, whether it be through the sharing of technology and data, or the overlapping of operational theaters, are increasingly blurred."³⁷ The power assemblages are responding to the threat to its power posed by the networked power of cyberspace through the only means it knows: coercive power.

Cyberspace has been weaponized against protesters in a variety of ways. There are numerous examples of "hack back" attacks against digital activists. As early as 1998, the Pentagon responded to an EDT DDoS action by sending a code that caused any computer running EDT's FloodNet program to crash. More recently, documents released by Snowden reveal that the British GCHQ program Rolling Thunder not only launched DDoS counter-strikes at Anonymous chat rooms, but also implanted malware that would enable them to determine the identity of specific users. Coleman, writing for *Wired,* contends, "Whether you agree with the activities of Anonymous or not . . . the salient point is that democratic governments now seem to be using their very tactics against them. The key difference, however, is that while those involved in Anonymous can and have faced their day in court for those tactics, the British government has not."³⁸ That is, for activists a DDoS action is a risk, while for a government agency it is an act of power. Coleman continues, "And it's this *power differential that makes all the difference.*"³⁹ For her it is an abuse of power to squash dissent. It is particularly concerning because engaging in an Anonymous chat room does not necessarily mean that the user even engaged in an operation, and yet they may be targeted. Sauter adds that while disruptive power is useful for bringing attention to causes outside of the gaze of normalcy, intelligence agencies do not need such tactics in order to be significant powers within the world (and certainly are not seeking to publicize issues). Thus, she concludes, "By using these tactics, organs of state power such as the GCHQ colonize them, making them less appealing, less useful, and less effective for dissident groups."⁴⁰ Indeed, in this militarization of cyberspace, the distinction between enemy, cyberterrorist, cybercriminal, and dissenting citizen is erased. All

37. Ibid., 180.
38. Coleman, "The Latest Snowden Revelation."
39. Ibid. Author's italics.
40. Sauter, *The Coming Swarm,* 148.

are equally viewed as threats to the power assemblage and thus must be vanquished/vanished.

Differences between Internet Activism and Other Types of Civil Disobedience

Perhaps the biggest difference between Internet activism and more traditional approaches to civil disobedience is the question of space. Being cyber-based, Internet activism need not be confined to a particular physical space. This aspect creates new possibilities but also new practical and theoretical challenges. In particular, we can recall from the first chapter that in Koepsell's materialist view the Internet does not exist everywhere but rather in the physical equipment necessary to sustain cyberspace. This equipment is owned by someone. In other words, from a legal point of view there is no common space. Everything is private property.

The issue of who "owns" Internet space is critical for the possibility of online activism. There are few truly public aspects of cyberspace. While it has become the leading public forum for the exchange of ideas, the platforms that allow for discussion are privately held. Social networks, blogging platforms, chat rooms, messaging services, and so forth are all privately owned. In the United States, for example, these spaces do not offer First Amendment free speech protections because of this private nature. As Sauter explains, "The overwhelmingly privatized nature of the internet is a challenge to the practice of activism online, on the levels of large-scale peaceable assembly, freedom of expression, and civil disobedience."[41] She goes on to point out that the result of the privatized nature of cyberspace is that free speech and private property rights are pitted against each other. This is why, we might recall, *the electrohippies* actions in 1999 had not only the specific WTO meetings in mind, but also attempted to establish the Internet as a legitimate space for direct action. They wanted the Internet to be recognized as a public park or street corner where a large group of people could gather in protest. A common space is necessary for the promotion of a common good that we saw in the last chapter is so essential.

Those early movements did not succeed in establishing the Internet as a common space where public protest can take place. Cyberspace has become more firmly entrenched as a military/commercial zone, so that

---

41. Ibid., 3.

protest actions are generally seen as trespassing and a threat to the controlling powers' interests. The attempts in the United States to eliminate Net Neutrality underscore this point. Thus in the current situation we find that the primary media for self-expression and communication is considered off-limits for direct political action. Given the necessity for resistance noted in the last chapter, this is a dangerous situation. The dimension of spirit within the cyberdimension is in danger of falling into profanization by its being colonized by military and commercial interests to the exclusion of a common space where spirit may flourish.

This lack of a public space for protest makes a stark difference from the civil rights movement. As Sauter notes, the civil rights movement has become the standard script for civil disobedience "done properly." It provides the standard media script that other protesters must follow if they wish to be treated as legitimate protesters. The image of the sit-in that the EDT and *the electrohippies* conjured does indeed mark the approach necessary to be deemed a "good" protest by the general public. She explains, "When trying to understand modern instances of civil disobedience or disruptive activism, be it Occupy, the global justice movement, or internet-based actions such as DDoS, the civil rights movement is often treated as a singular touchstone, used to determine the validity and political seriousness of the action in question."[42] Such an equation is problematic on various levels. The first is that many of the tactics employed by the civil rights movement had the goal of giving voice and visibility to a group who had neither. Much of this was done through protests and rallies in public spaces. In that time, this was the most effective way to be heard. In today's context, the Internet is the most effective means to get one's voice heard, but there is no public space from which to do it in cyberspace. For this reason alone, there is a novel element to direct action in the cyberdimension. The commercial infrastructure shapes what type of activism is possible.

The comparison of cyber-activism with the civil rights movements has larger faults than that, however. To get at these faults, let us first turn our attention to two common criticisms of Anonymous and its approach to online activism: it is cowardly and it is lazy. Both of these charges are leveled from a variety of sources. The charge of cowardliness comes from the facts that one can engage in a DDoS action anonymously and not need go anywhere different in order to participate. These elements are

---

42. Ibid., 22.

routinely brought up as distinctions from street tactics of the civil rights movement. We might recall that *the electrohippies* attached their names to their actions in order to make the parallelism with street protests clear. Anonymous, on the other hand, carries out its actions anonymously. For many this is problematic because it safeguards the participants from facing repercussions for their actions. It removes the time-honored tradition of being arrested for civil disobedience. The thinking goes that the threat of arrest is what makes civil disobedience a courageous act of moral outrage. Ronald Deibert formulates the critique in this way: "DDoS attacks, on the other hand, can be carried out anonymously, usually without participants accepting legal consequences, and they involve little effort or costs. They are more akin to armchair activism."[43] He goes on to conclude that DDoS actions are not justifiable forms of political action. He is not alone in this opinion. Oxblood Ruffin of the Cult of the Dead Cow charges, "By comparison to the heroes of the Civil Rights Movement DDoSing tactics are craven."[44] Internet critic Evegeny Morozov, meanwhile, calls Internet-based activism "the ideal type of activism for a lazy generation" while Malcolm Gladwell labels it "slacktivism."[45] Others dub the techniques "clicktivism." Behind all of these criticisms is the sense that Internet-based approaches are not real social protest because the space they occupy is in the cyberdimension rather than the physical realm. The cyberdimension is understood as less real than the physical realm. Above all, digital activism pales compared to the beacon of the civil rights movement.

Sauter, however, provides an impressive refutation of these critiques and offers a counter-narrative to the slacktivist critique. She holds, "Criticism that compares the developing world of online-based activism, such as DDoS actions or 'clicktavist' or 'slacktivist' actions, to the sit-ins and boycotts of the civil rights movement is essentially empty. Not only do these new movements and actions not have the same goals as the civil rights movement, they are also not organized by activists with the same level or same kind of experience, and they occupy entirely different historical moments, with respect to when they are taking place, when they are being examined, and how."[46] Above all, we can understand Sau-

---

43. Deibert, *Black Code*, 224.
44. Ruffin, "Old School Hacker," quoted in Sauter, *The Coming Swarm*, 5.
45. Gladwell, "Small Change," quoted in ibid.
46. Sauter, *The Coming Swarm*, 26.

ter's contention to be that the critics of anonymous online activism fail to understand the cyberdimension properly, though she would not use those terms. That is, we can see Sauter as offering an alternative view of space, time, and power dynamics to those available in the physical dimensions. Thus the critics are too rigidly applying the parallelism of the physical realm to the cyber. Thus we must rethink the goals and issues involved in cyber-resistance in order to understand the value of these new tactics for resistance.

The first issue is to reclaim the value of disruption as a form of resistance. For Sauter, disruption itself is full of meaning. Disruption is the interruption of meaning for others, but in doing so meaning can be communicated. She holds that, "By replacing continuity with disruption, activists attempt to create a rhetorical cavity in the digitized structure of capitalism wherein activism can take place."[47] In this sense, disruptive activities are not wanton vandalism, but rather a strategy to resist the totalization that is threatened by the power assemblages of cyberspace. If every bit of cyberspace is being monitored, collected, and controlled by corporate and state interests, then it is only in the break or disruption that another voice can speak. Indeed, Sauter, drawing on Jodi Dean's theory of communicative capitalism, contends, "The interruption can be interpreted to be the only reasonable form of response to an 'interlocutor,' such as a government or corporation, that is, by its projected nature, fundamentally nonresponsive."[48] Thus strategies of disruption are a means of resisting the monopolization of power. Sauter thus supports the use of DDoS and other digitally disruptive tactics as a legitimate means of social protest, though with some significant caveats for how to conduct them ethically.[49]

Owen has also investigated the theory of disruptive power. He notes that disruption is actually a Silicon Valley buzzword, drawing on the theory of disruptive technologies. This theory comes from Harvard Business School scholar Clay Christensen, whose work investigated how small companies are able to overtake established ones by exploiting blind spots caused by entrenched worldviews that prevent them from seeing new possibilities and new markets. This has grown into a guiding concept

47. Ibid., 28.
48. Ibid., 29.
49. She argues, for instance, DDoS actions should not be employed to have content permanently removed, interrupt essential services, and so forth. For a more complete description, see Sauter, *The Coming Swarm*, 50–51.

in technology industries. Owen notes, "The concept has also come to stand for a form of libertarianism deeply rooted in the technology sector, a sweeping ideology that goes well beyond the precept that technology can engage social problems to the belief that free market technology-entrepreneurialism should be left unhindered by the state."[50] Thus he posits that Anonymous is in essence an anarchic culmination of techno-libertarian thought that engages in disruptive rather than destructive behavior. This essentializing of Anonymous may be helpful conceptually, but at the same time is reductive in that it overlooks the multiplicity inherent in Anonymous that Coleman notes. Further, libertarianism is not essential to the use of disruption, even if the tactic is frequently associated with that ideology.

At any rate, Owen's argument is that in the same way that large companies are not nimble enough to contend with disruptive innovation, so too the institutionalized structures cannot adapt quickly to novel innovation. In cyberspace, many of the functions once filled by the state are being challenged by new technologies. He considers Anonymous and online activism more generally to be one such technological innovation. Thus he sees the power assemblages of state and corporate interests to be forming alliances specifically because the traditional power of the state is being threatened by the cyberdimension. Digital technology allows nontraditional powers the ability to influence society in a way that previously only the state could; thus states are responding through attempts to consolidate power. We have seen this most clearly in our discussions of Russian attempts to cordon off cyberspace within its borders.

If Owen is correct in his analysis, and it seems to have merit to me, then tactics that utilize disruption are indeed essential to the struggle for a balance of power in the cyberdimension. It would be overly simplistic to hold that it is a battle between the anarchic forces of digital activists and the rigid hierarchical power of cyber-military-commercial-state assemblage, but the depiction is not without some truth, either.

Sauter also argues that, while the term was not used, disruption was in fact an essential aspect of the civil rights movement. After all, at a very basic level the goal of a protest or sit-in is to disrupt business as usual in order to highlight an issue. More pointedly, she turns to Martin Luther King, Jr.'s "Letter from a Birmingham Jail." In it, King writes, "Nonviolent direct action seeks to create such a crisis and foster such a tension

---

50. Owen, *Disruptive Power*, 6.

that a community which has constantly refused to negotiate is forced to confront the issue. . . . The purpose of our direct action program is to create a situation so crisis packed that it will inevitably open the door to negotiation."[51] This guiding philosophy is quite close to that behind a DDoS action. Sauter suggests that what King calls "tension" is what she means by the word "disruption." She goes on to point out that it is much easier to praise disruption that occurred to someone else in the past than it is for disruption in the present, particularly "when it is *your* status quo being disrupted, by activists whose causes or tactics you might not fully understand or agree with."[52] Disruption is what allows for change to occur, but change is not often welcome, especially by those who are comfortable with the way things are.

Theologically it is of great interest that it is specifically this writing by King that Sauter turns to, given that the letter was addressed to Christian clergy. It was a theological epistle directed from one Christian to others. Thus King's highlighting the importance of "tension" as a tactic is not solely of sociological import. Certainly in a theological attempt to understand social activism, such as this one, its theological aspect must be taken seriously. King grounds nonviolent direct action tactics in biblical stories and church history, contending, "It was evidenced sublimely in the refusal of Shadrach, Meshach and Abednego to obey the laws of Nebuchadnezzar, on the ground that a higher moral law was at stake. It was practiced superbly by the early Christians, who were willing to face hungry lions and the excruciating pain of chopping blocks rather than submit to certain unjust laws of the Roman Empire."[53] He goes on to contend theologically that the church is to be a transformative agent for human social progress.

It is worth noting King's description of the role of creating tension or disruption in nonviolent direct action: "It seeks so to dramatize the issue that it can no longer be ignored."[54] Indeed, he further explains that direct action does not actually create tension. Rather, "We merely bring to the surface the hidden tension that is already alive. We bring it out in the open, where it can be seen and dealt with."[55] In this might we see a bit

---

51. King, "Letter from a Birmingham Jail." Also quoted in Sauter, *The Coming Swarm*, 23.

52. Sauter, *The Coming Swarm*, 24.

53. King, "Letter From a Birmingham Jail."

54. Ibid.

55. Ibid.

of a Tillichian sensibility about the ambiguity of existence?[56] At any rate, for King the goal of nonviolent direct action was to create a disruption that cracked open the structures that cast from view the mechanisms of power for long enough that they may be called into question. Here we can recall from last chapter Smith's understanding of surveillance as a hiding from view that which delegitimizes the power assemblages. King's understanding of social protest is to bring them back into view by dramatizing the issue. The word *dramatizing* has a double meaning. It can mean to magnify or exaggerate, but it also means to present as performance. In this instance hearing both meanings is helpful. The unseen flow of power—in King's case the power of racism—is made visible both by dramatizing (presenting as performance) it so that it is manifested concretely and then by dramatizing (enlarging or magnifying) this performance to the point that it cannot be ignored. We can find here a resonance with EDT and CAE in their understanding of activism as theater or art. The theological and dramatic sensibilities merge here.

Such a sense of activism generally, and digital activism/hacktivism more specifically, as the art of disruption is worth reclaiming. As mentioned earlier, Tatiana Bazzichelli has recently worked to reintroduce the concept of performance art as a means of resistance in cyberspace. It is worth noting that she has ties to the Italian hacker community dating to the 1990s.[57] She sees practices of networking as a means of resistance to hegemonic power that is "derived from intimate experience rather than power conflicts."[58] She sees in collaborative disruptive art a means of transforming business as well as art. Through her consideration of art as networked resistance, she manages to bring the various threads of digital activist, hacktivist, and more recent movements such as Anonymous together. Indeed, I suggest that her thought is a helpful contribution to Stiegler's call for a rethinking of culture and industry in a way that does not cast them as opposing force that we encountered in the previous

---

56. King was quite familiar with Tillich, having written his dissertation on the topic, "A Comparison of the Conceptions of God in the Thinking of Paul Tillich and Henry Nelson Wieman." Although critical of some aspects of Tillich's thought, he was complimentary of others. See http://kingencyclopedia.stanford.edu/encyclopedia/encyclopedia/enc_tillich_paul_1886_1965/ for more.

57. She details how the Italian hacker community has retained a politically anti-hegemony anarchist edge from the early days of hackers that has diminished in American and North European hacker communities. Bazzichelli, *Networked Disruption*, 72–74.

58. Ibid., 44.

chapter. In line with the CAE's "Electronic Civil Disobedience" strategy, Bazzichelli considers the oppositional approach to activism to be problematic. Specifically, she is critical of the strategy of starting counter-hegemony movements "from below" on behalf of the "oppressed" because it creates a clash of powers rather than undoing the oppositions. Rather, she seeks a means of lifting up multiple identities and relationalities as a deconstruction of hegemonic hierarchies and power assemblages.[59] In this there are resonances with Ball's call to lift up cyborg identity.

Social networking, in Bazzichelli's view, is best understood as a practice of communal participation and sharing. Bazzichelli problematizes the terms *multiplicity* or *the multitude*. Here she relies on Franco Berardi's contention that these terms are too neutral to shed light on reality. He prefers the terms *swarm* and *network*. Swarms are not an organized collectivity, but rather follow predetermined patterns. Thus they lack awareness and generally lack critical engagement. Networks, on the other hand, are organized through shared performances and coordinated tasks, constituting a collective plurality of beings.[60] Bazzichelli contends, "The challenge becomes to imagine how swarms might mutate into conscious collectivity, into unpredictable singularities."[61] Indeed this is the same question we raised in the last chapter: rather than being reduced to a calculable data double, how can a meaningful excess individually and collectively be expressed and accessed?

Though through cyberspace networking has become more of a mainstream activity, especially via social media, Bazzichelli insists that its roots in collaborative art practices of the 1970s–1990s must not be forgotten. In particular, she looks at examples such as the Neoist network, the Luther Blissett Project, and the mail art network as formative. The Neoist movement is particularly interesting to our consideration because it used networking to highlight the potentially critically collective nature of identity.

Examining the Neoists is helpful in comprehending Anonymous. The movement grew out of the underground culture of Portland, Oregon at the end of the 1970s. Neoists adopted the name "Monty Cantsin" in

59. We can note here again the importance that Deleuze plays in providing a philosophical background to her theorizing, as with so many of the surveillance theorists we encountered in the previous chapters.

60. Bazzichelli, *Networked Disruption*, 56–57, and quoting from Berardi and Thacker.

61. Bazzichelli, *Networked Disruption*, 57.

signing their art, as a means of protesting the individualism of art culture. The founding legend, as Bazzichelli reports, is that the name was put on a simple postcard that was sent by David Zack to performance artist Istvan Kantor. Kantor began using the name during performance activities. It is hard to assess the historicity of this account, let alone any further history of the movement, because creating paradox is central to the network's self-understanding. Members were encouraged to create fake stories and to give contradictory accounts of the movement. By 1979, however, Kantor had taken the identity of Monty Cantsin to Montreal and offered it as a pseudonym that other artists were free to borrow. A wide range of art then began to appear under this name.

The essence of Monty Cantsin, Bazzichelli argues, "is a multiple name that challenges every linear and orthodox way of thinking, raising contradictions, ambiguities and *aporias*."[62] As Stewart Home frames it, "Multiple names are connected to radical theories of play. The idea is to create an 'open situation' for which no one in particular is responsible. Some proponents of the concept also claim that it is a way to practically examine, and break down, western and philosophic notions of identity, individuality, value and truth."[63] Much like Anonymous, the collective network reflects a particular group but cannot define it. Its identity is amorphous and paradoxical. Its identity cannot be confined to the name that harbors it. These ideas follow our concerns about the reduction of identity that occurs through data mining, although the Neoist movement predates big data. To expand on this point, Marco Deseriis has introduced the concept of the "improper name" to describe the political use of collective pseudonyms. He argues that this identity that is both collective and obfuscated is designed to both protect identity and the numbers of people involved so as to provide a platform for those who would otherwise be banished from sight, that they may be seen and heard. Specifically, he contends, "One of the main functions of an improper name is to *empower a subaltern social group by providing anonymity and a medium for mutual recognition to its users.*"[64] In other words, a group that the surveillant power assemblages would identity as outside the norm can reconstitute itself within its own norms by adopting a pluri-singular identity. Transferred into the cyberdimension, this identity is further

62. Ibid., 81.

63. Home, "Multiple Names," quoted in Bazzichelli, *Networked Disruption*, 81.

64. Deseriis, "Improper Names," 3. Quoted in Bazzichelli, *Networked Disruption*, 84.

hybridized through its obfuscating attempts at data doubling through its anonymous characteristic. That is, the infrastructure of encryption allows new manifestations of pluri-singular identity in cyberspace. At the same time, Anonymous subsequently began returning the theme of anonymity to the organic dimension through the use of Guy Fawkes masks as a symbol of the pluri-singular identity of Anonymous members. That said, Bazzichelli also notes that the Neoist network eventually unraveled because of the tensions of differing intentions and question of authority, such as who has the authority to speak for a collective identity and what is the proper use of that identity. This is a danger inherent in a network that embraces paradoxical identity.

While she is focused on art, much of Bazzichelli's project is to argue for the inseparability of art and business. She is thus challenging a strong tradition in performance and disruptive art that sees commercial aspects of the "art establishment" as antithetical to true art. Bazzichelli wants to hold up disruptive business as an artistic strategy of bringing transformation within systems. She argues, "The concept of *disrupting business* . . . [is] a methodology of transformations and interventions in the network economy by the adoption of disruptive business strategies as a form of art, in which the paradox, and the recombination of orders play a central role."[65] This harkens to Stiegler's search for a renewed sense of both culture and business. Note, too, the sense of play and ironic twists within this conception of disruption. She sees in the world of social media a movement towards cooperation and wishes to work from within the business culture to expand these concepts so as to give a new vision to business. It is an inspiring concept, even as I worry that it underestimates the ability of power assemblages to co-opt strategies of resistance.

In returning to the question of art and disruption, we see that the question of the multiple identity of the improper name disrupts reductive notions of identity that are represented in the data double. More generally, in her concept of disruption, Bazzichelli argues that artistic intervention that induces confusion, disorder, and disturbance is a form of resistant disruption. Disruptive art, for her, attempts, "to provoke a dialectic of paradoxes, inversion of radical schemes of oppositional conflicts, through the direct involvement of multiple subjectivities that act playfully from within."[66] This goal is not reached, however, through

---

65. Bazzichelli, *Networked Disruption*, 63. Author's italics.
66. Ibid., 112–13.

direct protest, but rather virally from within systems. That is, rather than attempting a counter-hegemony, disruptive art seeks to work inside the system to open up new possibilities, creating what Deleuze and Guattari call "the holey space of itinerant smiths." Deleuze and Guattari use this phrase to indicate that no system can succeed in its ambition of totality; there are always holes from which all manner of subjects arise.[67]

Performance art, meanwhile, is a term that covers a wide range of movements and theories of art. Fundamentally, however, in performance art the artwork is not a physical object but rather an event or action. It is eventive art. More specifically of concern for us are the moments when the event of art is disruptive in the sense of reframing or challenging the narrative or dynamics of an unjust situation in unexpected ways that creates confusion or uncertainty in order to make visible the hidden power structures. Performance art, moreover, is an embodied artistic event. The object of art is an event of bodies in action rather than a painting or sculpture in a museum.[68]

Bazzichelli argues that Anonymous should be understood as a form of disruptive art, a descendant of the performance art of Neoism transferred into the cyberdimension. She notes the entity of Anonymous works within the reality of commercial platforms that dominate cyberspace to create changes within them. "The Anonymous 'entity' deconstructs proprietary logic by disrupting corporate contexts and branding strategies, and generating new dynamics of networking and collaborative actions," she contends. Such sly civility, to use Homi Bhaba's postcolonial framework, attempts to disrupt the "dichotomy of oppressors vs. opponents by trying to imagine new forms of participation that go beyond the creation of a compact force seeking holistic hegemony, even if presented in the plural form."[69] Participation is key here, as rather than a dichotomy of inclusion/exclusion the participation in the network allows for a multiple sense of contingent connections or temporary resistant power assemblages.

For Bazzichelli, Anonymous is a hybrid subjectivity that works within the holes of cyberspace to transform it. It is a loose collective or fluid entity rather than a group or movement. It is impossible to say for sure who is involved, or even whether any particular action comes from

67. See ibid., 137.

68. For a helpful review of ideas animating performance art, see Carletti, "The Disruptive Power."

69. Bazzichelli, *Networked Disruption,* 115.

Anonymous members or from critics who have infiltrated the group in hopes of discrediting it. It is difficult to discern what is "authentically" from Anonymous and what is not. Yet, she holds, "This also demonstrates the fact that the Anonymous entity is the disruption of authenticity in and of itself, and that the more open groups are, the more easily they are polluted." Yet such ambiguity is essential to its nature as vital and viral. It is a collection of singularities resistant to leadership and yet committed to collectivity.

Bazzichelli's consideration of Anonymous is provocative but overreaches a bit in trying to fit Anonymous into the mold of performance art. It is perhaps better to consider the performance art lineage as one element that was formative for Anonymous. Certainly the shared tactics of confusion and disorientation between Anonymous and disruptive art are intriguing. Particularly helpful is Bazzachelli's insistence on the role of art as a means of promoting the incalculable excess of meaning within cyberspace as resistance to its merging of culture and commerce. There is a change in the understanding of performance art that comes with this role, however. The role of artist as visionary creator of art is no longer helpful in a situation where the ambiguity of identity is at stake. In this vein she lifts up Simonetta Fadda's comment, "Only after, with the artistic of networking on the Internet, does the point of view become inverted: the goal is no longer to reinsert life into art, but to reinsert art into life."[70] This is again a helpful response to Stiegler's call for a new understanding of culture and industry that provide consistence. At the same time, the relationship between performance art and bodies does not have a direct parallel with Anonymous's online identity. Yet here an infrastructuralist understanding of cyberspace is helpful. The cyber is not disconnected from the physical realms but rather provides an additional dimension of activity. I think greater reflection on the relationship of the cyberdimension and the dimension of spirit is helpful for this point.

Might we see art more generally as a means of adding the dimension of spirit to the work of resistance in the cyberdimension? Tillich's sense of the religious meaning of art becomes relevant. For him, there are three components to a work of art: subject matter, form, and style. In short, the subject matter is what the artwork is about, the form is the material from which it is made, and the style the artistic approach. He explains that the subject can be anything that the human mind can receive in sensory

---

70. Bazzichelli, *Networked Disruption*, 202.

images, while the form is what gives art its ontological existence. Tillich, however, is most interested in style, contending that "every style points to a self-interpretation of man, thus answering the question of the ultimate meaning of life."[71] So the artistic style is for Tillich the religious dimension of art in that it communicates the core concerns of the artist. Thus for him different styles appear in different historical periods because different questions become ultimate. Artistic style, then, allows spirit to manifest in the subject matter and form of the artwork.

Considering art more broadly, John Dillenberger's *A Theology of Artistic Sensibilities* helpfully traces the relationship of theology and art from the early church into the 1980s. In dealing with the most recent theology, he notes Karl Rahner's 1966 essay "Poetry and the Christian," which acknowledges a special relationship between the Word and the poetic word. By the 1980s, however, Rahner had expanded his concern to a wider range of art, holding that theology and the arts belong together as aspects of humanity's transcendent nature, or what we have been calling the self-in-excess.[72] Dillenberger notes other recent theological turns to the imagination and the arts, such as David Tracy's "analogical imagination," Sally McFague's metaphorical theology, and Stephen Crites's development of narrative or story. Dillenberger sees these many different methods as an appropriate way of approaching theology in a contemporary pluralistic global setting.[73] For his own constructive contribution, he sees theology and the arts moving closer towards each other. He is particularly concerned with the visual arts not only because Protestantism has to such a large extent excluded them, but also because he senses that "language lost its powers of imagination and became that which declared, defined, set limits."[74] While he excludes poetry and drama from this tendency of language towards the calculable, he sees the reach of these forms of language to be quite limited. He feels that the dominant use of language is in propositional form and no longer inspires creative thought, but that visual means still have an ability to challenge us to open ourselves to the dimension of spirit. "Let it be said that the visual arts, like music or literature, in some sense represent a necessity of the human spirit as elemental as spirit and hunger and something so central that not

---

71. Tillich, *Theology of Culture*, 70.
72. Dillenberger, *A Theology of Artistic Sensibilities*, 226.
73. Ibid., 228.
74. Ibid., 239.

to know it deprives one of part of one's humanity."[75] Theology, he thus contends, must open itself to the arts and particularly the visual arts in order to unleash the spiritual imagination. In this sense he is arguing for theology to put the art into life. It is not a stretch to include the cyberdimension here, nor is it a stretch to include performance art within his theology of the arts.

Yet as we have seen, performance art challenges some of Tillich's notions of art. Art is seen as an event rather than an object. Thus there is no concrete form of the art, although human bodies and the space they occupy are an essential component of the art. Performance art does not exist, but rather occurs. Likewise, the subject matter that I am interested in for disruptive performance art is not limited to sensory images, but rather is a provocation to silence so that alternative voices may be heard. Nonetheless, Tillich is helpful in suggesting that the style of art corresponds to ultimate concerns of a context. In the cyberdimension, ultimate concern manifests as a quest for consistence amid the ways in which the surveillant assemblages have militarized and commercialized cyberspace, thereby reducing life to the calculable. Thus resistance and protest are essential in cracking open a space for consistence, exceeding, or ultimate concern that transcends the calculable. In this sense the style of disruptive performance art as an attempt to put art into life is indeed an act of spirit.

In fact, more than just a general act of spirit, I would argue that such disruptive performative resistance is essential to the teaching of Jesus as seen in the Gospels. That is, I am suggesting that we can view Jesus' teaching and acts of power as a form of performance art. Through his symbolic actions, I contend, he used disruptive power to reframe situations and draw out the ironies, hypocrisies, and absurdities of the power structures that he encountered. In this light we can see his enactments of the kingdom of God in the tradition of the prophets. Mcateer argues this point. He points to the unusual actions that God tells Ezekiel to perform in Ezekiel 4, Isaiah's walking naked in the city (Isa 20:1–6), Jeremiah's smashing full wine jars together (Jer 13:12–14) and Hosea's marrying a prostitute as examples. He argues, "What is especially interesting about Ezekiel's actions is that, while the scripture explains some of the symbolism to *us* the readers, nowhere does it say Ezekiel explained the actions to

---

75. Ibid., 244.

the original audience. God simply told Ezekiel to perform these actions and left it up to the Israelites to interpret them on their own."[76]

For Mcateer we should then understand Jesus' actions as symbolic interventions that bring to the surface the hidden tensions. He contends, "In a way I am arguing for an allegorical reading of Scripture. But rather than looking for a meaning behind the literal text like medieval theologians did, in pointing to Jesus's actions as performance art I am suggesting that the literal events *themselves* should be taken symbolically."[77] We can view, for instance, Jesus' asking his opponents whose picture is on the coin when they ask him about paying taxes as this sort of sly act of exposing hypocrisy.[78] Or again, his dining with tax collectors and sinners as a symbolic enactment of his parables about the kingdom of God as a banquet where the least expected are invited.

Such sentiment is very much in line with Walter Wink's understanding of Jesus as challenging the powers of this world that Wink explores in his now-classic *Engaging the Powers*. He argues, "The Powers That Be literally stand on their dignity. Nothing depotentiates them faster than deft lampooning. . . . Jesus provides here a hint of how to take on the entire system by unmasking its essential cruelty and burlesquing its pretensions to justice."[79] Wink sees Jesus' approach to nonviolent engagement to be a strategy of defusing the ability of those with power to humiliate those without.[80] He goes on to examine Jesus' teaching in Matthew 5 and Luke 6 to turn the right cheek if struck on the left and to give one's undergarments as well when one's outer garments are demanded as a pledge against a debt owed. He explains that turning the right cheek would force the opponent to abandon the backhanded slap used for admonishing inferiors as ineffective, thus robbing the oppressor of the ability to humiliate. Likewise, giving the undergarments along with the outer ones would mean walking to court naked. This sounds like a work of performance art! In both instances, the action would cause confusion and hesitation that lays bare the oppressive nature of the sys-

---

76. McAteer, "When Jesus Wanted to Explain."

77. Ibid.

78. Matt 22:15–22, Mark 12:13–17. Carrying coins with a human image on it was considered idolatrous by many in the Jewish community at that time, and so it would have been embarrassing for Pharisees to be associated with the Roman coin with the image of the head of the emperor on it.

79. Wink, *Engaging the Powers*, 179.

80. See ibid., 175–84.

tem; they are actions of disruptive protest. Wink explains, "The debtor had no hope of winning the case; the law was entirely in the creditor's favor. But the poor man has transcended this attempt to humiliate him. He has risen above shame. At the same time he has registered a stunning protest against the system that created his debt."[81] Such actions may only work once in creating the intended disruption—the specific actions are less important than the method—but in that moment the tension made invisible by the surveilling power is unveiled. In drawing on Wink's view of Christian resistance, we see a combination of King's call to disclose the hidden tensions constructed by systems of power and Bazzichelli's disruptive sense of performance art as a symbolic means of affecting this deconstruction, but also Anonymous's pursuing lulz—at least at its social justice seeking best. Such lampooning of power startles and disrupts the status quo, leading to a bit of what Caputo calls the "sacred anarchy" of the kingdom of God.

Returning to Sauter's defense of DDoS actions, a second feature that she highlights is the anti-corporate component to the actions. She notes that civil disobedience has traditionally been seen as something limited to protests against the state. Critics thus frame raids on corporate websites, for instance, as trespassing rather than civil disobedience. Yet if we recall Owen's contention that the state is in decline and so buttressing its power with corporate strength, not to mention the other ways that we have seen the power assemblages form, then it seems clear that contemporary civil disobedience cannot be confined to being directed at the state. As Sauter explains, "A refusal to adapt to the modern, accepted repertoire of contention also implies a refusal to acknowledge basic changes in how the media and governments interact with political activists, particularly in the online space. Also dismissed [by critics] are how the growing roles of corporations, multi-governmental organizations, and nongovernmental organizations have made these entities apt targets for performative, disruptive dissent."[82] Resistance against surveillant power assemblages of the cyberdimension requires recognizing and protesting corporate complicity in the reduction of consistence and meaning.

Another key component to Anonymous's disruptive tactics is a foundational belief that the state does not engage digital activism in good faith. Indeed, Anonymous generally declines to acknowledge that

---

81. Ibid., 179.
82. Sauter, *The Coming Swarm*, 27.

national governments—and particularly the United States government—have a legitimate role in Internet governance. In this sense, Anonymous retains something of a holdover spirit from the early days of the Internet. This sense of cyberspace as a unique region of a new world beyond the reach of the old powers of the state plays into the importance of anonymity for Anonymous actions.

Again, Anonymous (and, more generally, the hacker ethos) holds the right to anonymity online dearly. Yet as we have seen, this decision to undertake action anonymously has led to charges of timidity and lack of true conviction. Sauter again challenges these allegations. First, she notes that anonymity online is a more difficult task than critics seem to recognize. Our previous discussion of surveillance would support this contention. Beyond that, Sauter suggests that the debate over anonymity highlights an ambiguity in Western political thought. "Though anonymity can be granted to mainstream political activities, such as the use of the anonymous ballot," she writes, "those political minorities whose democratic participation has been hamstrung by a failure of public discourse to seriously consider a specific set of issues, or by outright disenfranchisement are denied the protection of anonymous participation."[83] It is ironic that those made invisible by colonial surveillance, recalling Smith's argument, are denied the choice of the invisibility of anonymity. Sauter goes on to argue that insistence on being identifiable means that identities are placed above content, and further that only those in a position to put themselves at risk are able to engage in protest. This results in what Hannah Arendt calls "single-minded fanaticism." The result of these two tendencies together is the ability to dismiss activists as extremist radicals that can easily be ignored by and hidden from mainstream political discussion.[84]

Against this backdrop, anonymity is more than an indication of the feebleness of activists. It is a strategic approach based on the guiding principles of Anonymous. Anonymity can be a response to the belief in the illegitimacy of state governance online and a refusal to follow traditional scripts of public disobedience. Sauter points out that while groups like *the electrohippies* and EDT courted interaction with authorities through their actions in order to produce change, Anonymous came out of a different history. Rather than 1990s optimism, Anonymous emerged

---

83. Ibid., 90.
84. Ibid., 90–91.

from the turbulence of the 2000s: state antagonism towards hackers, the Patriot Act, the post-9/11 security surveillance state. Given this historical situation, Anonymous had no reason to trust that the state and its allies had any interest in productive engagement. In this climate, as Sauter notes, an insistence on legal identity being tied to political dissent would suppress those activities.[85] To add my own hypothesis, given the swelling authoritarianism of the power assemblage in the cyberdimension, taunting the power assemblages' pretensions to complete domination through anonymous action may well be the most effective means available to expose those pretensions.

Nonetheless, Sauter maintains that mainstream political discourse has successfully pushed political dissent to the margins. That is, through critiques of digital activism and the holding up of the civil rights movement as the one pure paradigm of civil disobedience, contemporary forms of civil disobedience have been successfully painted as illegitimate and as threats. In particular, Sauter notes the way that hackers are portrayed in the media as evidence of the marginalization of the political aspects of hacker movements. She writes:

> The word "hacker" was, and is still now, used by the news media as a catchall term to apply to any type of criminal or "bad" computer activity, including those that did not break any laws. The hacker figure himself (media depictions of male hackers outnumber those of female hackers by a wide margin) became a type of "folk devil," a personification of our anxieties about technology, the technologically mediated society, and our increasingly technologically mediated selves.[86]

This caricature of the hacker depoliticizes activist actions by painting them as criminal activities. Indeed, the classic trope of the hacker as a solitary loser further marginalizes the political intent of activist actions. This is particularly noteworthy in the case of DDoS operations, given that they are by nature collective actions. In fact, even the standard media vocabulary of DDoS actions as "attacks" frames the political acts of resistance as extremist actions.[87]

Sauter characterizes DDoS tactics as a type of "impure dissent." She draws the concept from the work of Tommie Shelby. For Shelby, impure

---

85. Ibid., 104.
86. Ibid., 62–63.
87. See Sauter, *The Coming Swarm*, 7, for a discussion of this terminology.

dissent is civil disobedience that exceeds the boundaries of anticipated or accepted forms of social protest. Such dissent combines legitimate and meaningful political content with other elements, such as "profanity, epithets, negative stereotypes, or violent or pornographic images."[88] For Sauter, DDoS actions fit this description, in that they function by interrupting the flow of information within the realm of information flow. Such disruption, Sauter suggests, can be seen by some as so destructive and dangerous that the political intention of the action is drowned out.

The final plank in the critique that digital activism pales in comparison to the civil rights movement is that digital activism lacks the personal risk that physical participation in protests brings. We have already encountered one response to this charge: limiting political participation to those capable of risking everything silences those not in such a position and allows the movement to be painted as extremist. Beyond this, there is a strong argument that digital activism actually brings with it a greater level of risk. This is because governments have taken a particularly aggressive stance against digital activists.

Those who are caught taking part in digital protests are dealt with severely. Two individuals were, for instance, arrested in conjunction with Operation Chanology, both of whom pled guilty. One was sentenced to serve 366 days in federal prison and to pay $37,000 to the Church of Scientology as restitution, while the other was sentenced to one year of prison and $20,000 restitution. Meanwhile, for a 2011 action that was conducted against Koch Industries in response to the governor of Wisconsin's attempt to strip public employees of collective bargaining rights, causing the Koch Industries website to be inaccessible for approximately fifteen minutes, Eric J. Rosol pled guilty to one misdemeanor count of accessing a protected computer for taking part in the action for roughly one minute. He was ordered to pay $183,000 in restitution along with two years of probation, even though damage was valued at $5,000.[89] In the UK, meanwhile, Chris Weatherhead did not engage in any direct action. Rather, he ran the communication hub where planning for an action took place. For this he received an eighteen-month sentence.[90] The penalties for digital activism are considerably higher than for traditional forms of civil disobedience. Typical charges for physical direct action arrests, such

---

88. Ibid., 91.
89. See ibid., 141.
90. Coleman, "The Latest Snowden Revelation."

as trespassing, resisting arrest, or disorderly conduct, generally come with a maximum fine of a few hundred dollars, a far cry from the tens of thousands of dollars in the above DDoS cases.[91] Thus, far from being a low-stakes venture risking perhaps a slap on the wrist, digital activists are in fact faced with the potential of significant retribution.

While on the one hand recognizing that the dynamic and anonymous nature of digital activism poses difficulties for policy makers, Owen on the other hand raises an alarm at the ferociousness that many governments have displayed in prosecuting anything associated with Anonymous. Noting that civil disobedience has generally received lenient sentencing as it is seen as a valid form of political activity, he writes, "With digital activism, the state is seeking control in the only way it knows how: through the force of law and legal precedent. In so doing, however, it is not only radically redefining the enforcement tools at its disposal but also challenging unwritten social conventions about how to respond to civil disobedience."[92] He turns to Jürgen Habermas's statement that "the right to civil disobedience remains suspended between legitimacy and legality for good reasons. But the constitutional state which prosecutes civil disobedience as a common crime falls under the spell of an authoritarian legalism."[93] This aggressiveness in punishing digital activists and hacktivists lends credence to Smith's contention that colonial power reacts with fervent zeal to punish and push from view anything that would delegitimize colonial power. Calls for consistence, art, and Otherness in the cyberdimension expose the colonizing profanization of cyberspace through its militarization and commercialization. The power assemblages of colonial profanization thus seek to discredit and make invisible this threat to its legitimacy.

Disruption, then, is an essential tool of resistance in the cyberdimension. It cracks open the pretensions to absolute power through a combination of irony and silence. In this, as we have seen, its practice is in accord with Jesus' own teaching. It is the art of revealing what is hidden within the cyberdimension: the consistence of humanity that exceeds the calculable. In this sense disruption is a deconstruction. It is clearing away the chatter of media and data that are used to make culture devoid of meaning and a tool of control. Such deconstruction is important in

91. See Sauter, *The Coming Swarm*, 142–44, for a more detailed account of relevant US laws.

92. Owen, *Disruptive Power*, 64.

93. Habermas, "Civil Disobedience," 112. Quoted in Owen, *Disruptive Power*, 65.

the face of growing power assemblage of the cyber-military-corporate-industrial complex. Yet it is also incomplete. Disruption makes a space for deeper meanings and exceedings to occur, but what spirit emerges from this rupture? Are there ethical demands placed upon us in unleashing the event of Otherness held outside the calculable gaze?

At the same time, we must also note other limitations of disruption. It is not a tactic available to all. It requires a level of affluence in order to have computer access, sufficient technical skill, and time to invest in the cyber connections that make this sort of resistance possible. This significantly restricts the number of people able to take part in actions of digital disruption. It nonetheless has an important role in that through blocking communication for a moment it can alert the public to situations where dialogue has failed or issues have been hidden from public view. Because cyberspace has become a corporate realm rather than a democratic space, cyberactivism can work through the existent structures to open discussion.

The meaning of disruption or ironic media manipulation is also often lost to many; the majority of people will likely simply feel inconvenienced at not being able to access a downed website or fail to notice the irony an action exposes. If the goal of OpTrump, for instance, was indeed to expose Trump's authoritarian impulses, the operation may have been successful but had little effect. Meanwhile, those with slow or limited Internet access may simply assume that a disruption action is a problem with their connection. As the availability of bandwidth and secondary servers increases, meanwhile, the effectiveness of disruption tactics may decrease.

In the improper naming of collective identities we see another form of disruption. The reductive understanding of the discrete identity of each individual is challenged through the use of collective pseudonyms. As we have seen, this stems at least in part from artistic movements of the pre-Internet days. Yet through groups like Anonymous it can be taken to new levels within cyberspace as identity can be completely submerged within the network. In this sense it can be a confusing tactic that paralyzes the powers that be. As such, it is no wonder that surveillant powers wish to eliminate the opportunity to be anonymous online. At the same time, while I have focused on the potential for resistance that anonymity provides, we cannot forget the real dangers that it poses. We have seen the issues of patriotic hacking in militarizing cyberspace, for instance. We must not forget, as well, the evil perpetrated under the collective identity of the Ku Klux Klan. Thus this form of disruption is highly ambiguous. What may come of it may be transformative resistance, but it may well be truly monstrous instead.

We see, too, the ambiguity of a prank-based approach to resistance. At its best, it can be a lampooning of power in line with the methods we have seen in Jesus' teaching. Yet a resistance of humiliation can easily cross the line from lampooning power to vindictive personal assault. This is particularly true when combined with anonymous action and no clear authority. There is a constant danger of moving from disruptive to destructive in this type of resistance. Indeed, while I have lifted up Anonymous at its best as being a legitimate force of activism, it must be acknowledged that it is frequently not at its best. It is susceptible, particularly in its early form, to criticisms of destructive searches for lulz as well as for giving complete novices easy access to powerful tools that opened them to serious legal ramifications without sufficient training or warning of the potential consequences.[94] For both of these reasons, Anonymous can be rightly criticized as being reckless, ineffective, and even dangerous. Here Wink's reminder that Christian resistance cannot be separated from the command to love enemies is essential for self-critique of the appropriateness of any particular form or act of resistance.[95]

Even when done successfully, though, there remains the challenge of being continually inventive with tactics so that they do not become static or co-opted. As Wink notes, "Such tactics [as Jesus advocates] can seldom be repeated. One can imagine that within days after the incidents that Jesus sought to provoke, the Powers That Be would pass new laws: penalties for nakedness in court, flogging for carrying a pack more than a mile!"[96] More recently, we can recall that the Neoists, along with other performance art movements, included a tactic of giving conflicting stories and news. As Bazzichelli explains of another group, the Luther Blissett Project, their objective was *"to play elaborate media pranks as a form of art, always claiming responsibility and explaining what bugs they had exploited to plant a fake story."*[97] Thus the goal was not to fool people permanently, but rather to cause a moment of confusion that allowed for deeper consideration of the flow of information.

94. Thanks to Josh Drescher for raising this concern to me.
95. Wink, *Engaging the Powers*, 182.
96. Ibid.
97. Bazzichelli, *Networked Disruption*, 93. Author's italics.

Yet this approach of prank news stories exploded in 2016 as social media became full of fake news. Far from being a means of resistance, it has been co-opted as a means of destroying any credibility of journalism, as it turned out that many people were willing to believe the disinformation. Thus the subtlety of pranks may be missed, or indeed the tactics such as fake news can become a tool of manipulation by the powerful. Indeed within a year the concept of fake news was transformed into a daily tactic employed by Trump as a means of obfuscating the work of quality journalism in order to present his alternate view of reality. Its ability to subtly critique had not only ceased to be effective, but had completely backfired. By 2018 considerably more harm had been done by the tactic than successful resistance and protest, and the term had become worn of meaning.[98]

Resistance and Spirit

Seeing creativity and even aesthetics as aspects of the Holy Spirit is hardly a novel innovation within the history of Christian theology. These are clearly essential aspects of the consistence that marks the dimension of spirit generally, and so it is hardly surprising that Christian theology would name them as constituent components of the Spirit that Christian theology calls holy. We have already encountered Tillich's contention that art—and particularly visual arts—bring forth the fundamental religious question of meaning. More recently, Episcopal theologian Sam Laurent advocates a narrative understanding of the Holy Spirit.

Laurent seeks to express the elusiveness and multiplicity of the expressions of divinity within the world through the concept of storytelling. He suggests, "The Spirit whispers divine love in our ears, reveals God's love to us in time and space. In short, the Spirit tells us the story of God in and for the world. But we hear different stories. We tell different stories."[99] The Spirit, for Laurent, is the divine storyteller, telling many

---

98. The earliest draft of this chapter was written in 2015, before the term *fake news* had reached the level of widespread international debate. The incredible manipulative power of false news reporting and Internet trolling as a tool for propaganda, cyber conflict, and abuse by power assemblages has since become quite clear. As such, subsequent drafts of this section have reflected a growing sense of the ambiguity of such tactics; I now see this approach as an example of how disruptive tactics can become tactics of ensconcing powers of domination.

99. Laurent, "The Holy Spirit, the Story of God," 195.

stories on the theme of divine action and love in the world. The stories are not identical, even as they speak to this same theme. The various stories give rise to different stories of divine presence and action that humanity then tells. He continues, "Spirit as Story represents God's participation in our construction of truths, as well as God's graceful, insistent presence that invites each person into a greater fullness of life."[100] In other words, the stories of Spirit express the consistence of life and, crucially, invite us into a life of exceeding the calculable. We may recall that for Tillich the dimension of Spirit is a movement of actualizing potentiality and overcoming ambiguity. From Laurent we can add to this that the Spirit moves narratively and diversely to do this. We can further recall here Hayless's contrasting of database thinking with narrative thinking. It is the narrative that is essential to human cognition and carries with it the capacity for exploring meaning. Indeed "exceeding the calculable" is an important aspect of the theological trope of the "fullness of life." Such exceeding is not one systematically definable thing, but instead is multiple and found in the mysterious transcendence of Otherness.

Yet what of Dillenberger's contention that word-based art has lost the capacity for speaking of meaning? There is truth to his contention as well. Even narrative too easily turns into dry literal account that fails to speak of excess. Narrative must have a poetic element to it; art must be infused into the narrative. In this I particularly have in mind contemporary poet Glyn Maxwell. Maxwell is a proponent of the importance of form for poetry. Part of his reason for this is the interplay of white space with black space in the poem—the "black space" of the words and the "white space" of the unprinted spaces on the page, including word and line breaks. The white or blank space, Maxwell insists, is as vital to the poem as the black or printed space. In fact, he sees line break and the use of blank space as the divide between prose and poetry. We might see these breaks—these ruptures or disruptions even—as the space in which the opacity of the incalculable enters the written word, marking a poetic exceeding beyond the transparency of prose. Certainly there is a visual element to this and so makes poetry about more than words, but more importantly for Maxwell is that the blank space is what creates the rhythm of the poem. This, he writes, is the difference between poetry and music. "The other half of everything for the songwriters is music. For poets it's silence, the space, the whiteness."[101] The unprinted void of the page is not nothingness but

100. Ibid.
101. Maxwell, *On Poetry*, 13.

rather a disruption of the data of the words that brings focus to their sea of meaning and rhythmic shape to their limits.

Maxwell contends that this rhythm is a grappling with time, and grappling with time is grappling with the infinite. "I always have to remind myself to spell it time not Time.... But in all cases we are honouring the *other*, the element in which we thrive and fail, the entity we've tried in a thousand ways to render *human* so it can hear our words.... Poets are voices upon time."[102] Form allows for interplay with time in forging a multisensory engagement with the ineffable: "You master form you don't master time, but what have you got that gets closer? Poems must be formed in the face of time, as we are. Whatever the whiteness is to you it's *also* time.... It can be time and God, as [it is for] Gerard Manley Hopkins, where the poet's voice seems *held* in the arms of the Ineffable that bears it safely to and fro while allowing it to breathe."[103] Poetic form, in other words, makes disruption rhythmic and thus allows its beat to render the ineffable possible to engage—rendered as human, as he puts it, even though it remains opaque. The rhythm of form becomes a recognizable mode of mediation of the infinity of meaning.

The point for our discussion is that narrative on its own does not grant access to the incalculable. A poetic or performance aspect is required. A blank space of disruption is necessary to create a rhythm in which the depths of opacity might be indicated. The words of the narrative can point to the ineffable, but only in indicating that it is there, hidden beyond the stream of data. Considering the Holy Spirit as narrative, then, I would add the caveat that we are discussing poetic narrative or narrative performance, with breaks and rhythms and disruptions and flirtations with the void, and not simply prose narrative that can rigidify the divine into literality.

What stories, then, do we tell of cyberspace? Laurent suggests that the Spirit reveals God's love in time and space. In the cyberdimension, though, time and space are manifested differently. Thus the stories of divine love and of human consistence call out for a retelling to match these manifestations. The wide-eyed early stories of cyberspace, along the lines of Barlow, have lost power because their breathless enthusiasm feels quaint and naïve in the face of the dark powers moving within cyberspace; they do not adequately recognize the ambiguity of the cyberdimension

---

102. Ibid., 14.
103. Ibid., 54.

and so do not narrate a sufficient hope for overcoming it. At the same time, the cybersecurity story roots out all hope. It tells of a Hobbesian dimension where every electronic device is a weapon that can be employed against all others and cyberspace is lurking with villains out to get us from whom we must protect ourselves. Beyond even this militarized dystopia, though, the surveillance and big data movemnts tell a story of cyberspace filled with like-minded consumers offering personalized consumption in exchange for your soul—that is, allowing yourself to be reduced to your data double.

Can there be a counter-narrative, or indeed a counter-poetics? A poetic repentance of turning to the infinite? A counter-poetics that does not ignore the darkness and yet is not bereft of light? To return to a question raised in the first chapter, might the cyberdimension be a means for cracking open the encrustations of the old creation and make a space through which a new creation might be expressed? Might the cyberdimension open new stories of Spirit? New stories of hope? In these issues the tactic of disruption is crucial. The goal of digital disruption is to break up the monologue of the power assemblages who are busily telling a story of control. Disruption provides a break where a new story might be told, a silent pause in which consistence and meaning might be found or expressed.

There is a creativity to disruption itself. It requires timing and a sense of irony and an ability to subtly manipulate power. This is risky and difficult, and as we have seen, even as it sometimes works well it often goes awry. Thus on its own, it is not a sufficient tactic for resistance. Thinking back to our discussion of Jesus' use of disruption tactics, they were effective uses of confusion and reframing, but they were not his only pedagogical trick. He paired performance art with parables, stories casting a new vision of divine action. Disruption clears a space for stories and so is essential in resistance against the reductive militarization of cyberspace, but new stories must be told as well; stories of making the digitally invisible become visible while also valuing the invisibility of the mysteriously elusive exceeding of Otherness. At its best, then, disruption is still an incomplete activity. It opens a space, but what happens in that space then becomes critical. Here an art of disruption needs to be supplemented by an art of transformation. Bazzichelli's call to transform swarms into networks is helpful here.

A performance art of disruption is a valuable first step, but a broader artistic vision of digital activism is also needed. An artistic vision of hope or poetic enactment of the common good is called for to enact the transformation of the swarm. Disruption leaves an aching into which a performance poetry of the possible may speak. As L. Callid Keefe-Perry writes of theopoetics in its poststructuralist formulation, "Deconstruction may well help to break apart damaging constructs of a coercive and idolatrous god, but it is theopoetics that wades into the rubble, not to build anew, but to sing of what might have been and what might yet be, encouraging others to imagine beginning again, nearby, and listening."[104] While the focus here is on theology, I would suggest that the principle applies equally to cyberspace. Disruption challenges the Internet as it is and clears away a space, but in that space art, and particularly a narrative poetics of cyberspace, is needed to imagine what might have been and what might yet be. This moves us back towards the theological, as the cyberdimension that might be is one infused with spirit. My concern is not so much that the work of the Spirit is putting art into life so much as putting artistry into life, including the realm of life expressed in the cyberdimension.

Such stories of irreducibility are necessarily tricky. They cannot be told directly. Laurent notes, "To speak of the Spirit as the story of God made by its procession the *stories* of God invites a certain cognitive dissonance by design."[105] The seeming disharmony, he continues, is a necessary theological dwelling place in order to live in the tension of God's unity and God's multiplicity. There is an ambiguity to the multiple stories of Spirit. It is intentionally slippery, just as identifying the dimension of spirit is slippery and often ambiguous. In the same way, the artistic interruptions we have been considering in this chapter are ambiguous acts of resistance and hardly a typical image of wholesome holiness. After all, we have been discussing impure protest and improper naming. Yet it is through such ambiguous impurity that the dimension of spirit must move within the colonized and profanized cyberdimension. Straightforward stories too often miss the nuance and multiple perspectives of the reality they are expressing. They too easily become reductive, naïve, or controlling, as we have seen with the dominant stories of cyberspace. An impure element of the story introduces the necessary nuance to lift up the slipperiness of reality. One might even say that a tricky element or indeed a trickster character is necessary for expressing the subtle ambiguities of

---

104. Keefe-Perry, *Way to Water*, 107.

105. Laurent, "The Holy Spirit, the Story of God," 208.

reality. It is this trickster motif to which we shall turn next in considering what story of Spirit might be told in cyberspace. In particular we shall turn to the figure of the whistle-blower as a trickster of cyberspace.

Chapter 5

Cyber-Tricksters: Digital Whistle-Blowing

On July 2, 2013, Bolivian President Evo Morales departed from a Gas Exporting Countries Summit in Moscow for La Paz on Bolivian Air Force flight FAB-001. The flight was scheduled to refuel in Lisbon along the way. While flying through Austria, the flight crew was informed that its stop in Portugal had been canceled for "technical reasons." News also came that France and Portugal were denying entry into their airspace to the plane. Soon Spain and Italy also denied them air permits. The plane was forced to land in Vienna.

The United States government seems to have credited a piece of intelligence indicating that Edward Snowden, a whistle-blower who had been behind a series of leaked documents that had caused great international furor in the weeks leading up to this event, had boarded the airplane to seek asylum in Bolivia. Morales, a frequent critic of the United States, had indicated the day before that if he received an asylum request from Snowden it would be received favorably. Snowden, however, was not on the flight.

Journalist Luke Harding reports that Ruben Saavedra, Bolivia's defense secretary, who was also aboard the airplane, responded to questions of whether Snowden was aboard by declaring, "This is a lie, a falsehood. It was generated by the US government. It is an outrage. It is an abuse. It is a violation of the conventions and agreements of international air transportation."[1] Bolivian vice president Alvaro Garcia, meanwhile, said that Morales had been "kidnapped by imperialism,"[2] while Venezuela,

1. Harding, *The Snowden Files*, 234.
2. Shoichet, "Bolivia."

Argentina, Suriname, and Ecuador, among others, issued statements of protest.

While the United States government initially declined to comment on the event, eventually Spain's minister of foreign affairs Jose Manuel Garcia-Margallo admitted, "They told us that the information was clear, that [Snowden] was inside [the airplane]."[3] He did not clarify who "they" were, but the implication of the United States was clear, and the State Department eventually admitted to discussing the issue of flights by Snowden with other nations. As Harding puts it, "The US's cack-handed intervention demonstrated that the caricature of the US as an aggressive playground bully prepared to trample on international norms was on this occasion perfectly correct."[4] Scholar Michael Gurnow reports that the incident solidified a Latin American coalition that saw the United States and its allies as antagonistic. For instance, Argentina's President Cristina Kirchner held, "[These actions are] vestiges of a colonialism that we thought were long over. We believe this constitutes not only the humiliation of a sister nation but of all South America,"[5] while Morales held, "My only sin is that I'm indigenous and anti-imperialist, [that I question] those economic policies planned and implemented by politicians that just starve us to death."[6] Beyond this, it solidified global suspicion of the United States, which prior to this incident had been seen as having some justification in its quest to capture Snowden. By pushing its allies to block a diplomatic plane from entering their airspace, causing significant political repercussions to those countries, the United States had pushed beyond reasonable political boundaries.

What caused the United States to engage in such a naked display of dominating power? What was so offensive about Snowden that it caused the hidden power assemblages to drop any pretenses of being benign? In the preceding chapters we have considered the militarization of cyberspace, its surveillance assemblages that combine to create a military-commercial-cyber-industrial complex, and hacktivist and digital activist approaches to resistance to this power. In this chapter, we will turn to the figure of the whistle-blower as the revealer of the hidden power structures of the cyberdimension. More specifically, I will argue that

3. Gurnow, *The Edward Snowden Affair*, 133.

4. Harding, *The Snowden Files*, 235.

5. Reuters, "Latin American countries." Quoted in Gurnow, *The Edward Snowden Files*, 134.

6. Ibid.

whistle-blowers function as trickster figures that confront and confound the powers that be while weaving a story of the complexity of the cyberdimension. Before turning to this image, however, first let us take a closer look at whistle-blowing in the cyberdimension.

Digital Whistle-Blowing

Individuals feeling compelled to reveal the secret crimes of governments has a long history spanning many countries. Examples such as Spaniard Bartolome de las Casas writing about sixteenth-century slave trading in the Americas or Richard Marven and Samuel Shaw reporting on the torturing of British prisoners of war by the Continental Navy during the American Revolutionary War can be thrown about as paradigms for what is now called whistle-blowing. Yet as technology has advanced, it has allowed governments greater and greater abilities to engage in surveillance activities. At the same time, technologies have also given whistle-blowers new tools to reveal on a broader scale these same government practices. In this sense, recent technological whistle-blowing of government surveillance particularly takes us to Daniel Ellsberg.

In 1969, after thirteen years of security clearance with the United States government, Ellsberg felt that he had to let the public know about some of the practices in which the government was engaged. He released 7,000 pages of top secret documents to congress and the press. This was no easy task; journalist Andy Greenberg reports that it took nearly a year of spending nights photocopying page after page, removing the "Top Secret" markers, and taking the copies to professional copy shops to have more copies made. The total stack of papers that he copied was eight feet tall. It cost him several thousand dollars (which adjusts to over $20,000 in today's dollars). Yet it was the relatively new technology of the copy machine that allowed him to leak the amount of information that he did.[7] When completed, his leak gave the secret history of the American involvement in Vietnam, better known as the Pentagon Papers.

Just as Snowden's leaks brought an intense reaction from the State Department, Ellsberg's whistle-blowing with met with fury from the White House of his day. Greenberg reports that tapes reveal President Richard Nixon telling Secretary of State Henry Kissinger and Attorney General John Mitchell, "We've got to get [Ellsberg]. Don't worry about his

---

7. Greenberg, *This Machine Kills Secrets*, 11–13.

trial. Just get everything out. Try him in the press.... We want to destroy him in the press. Is that clear?"[8] This was followed by operatives breaking into Ellsberg's psychotherapist's office to comb through Ellsberg's records to find details that could be used against him, but there were no files there. The next plan was to slip LSD into his soup at a dinner in Miami in which he was giving a speech so that he would appear incoherent and untrustworthy. The plan was approved but did not happen because approval did not come until it was too late to arrange the logistical matters.[9] These and a variety of other heavy-handed attempts to discredit Ellsberg ended up having his case declared a mistrial, allowing him to go free. The point in noting these outrageous plans is the way that unmasking even a bit of the power schemes behind the curtain provokes rage from the power assemblages.

The development of the Internet has brought on not only extensions of surveillance power but also provided new opportunities for whistle-blowing at a scale unimaginable for Ellsberg. The biggest innovation in whistle-blowing came from the website WikiLeaks. As Greenberg notes, "WikiLeaks' key advancement in the science of spilling information has been in separating the leaker from the leaked information."[10] Digital anonymity is essential to the ability to share uncovered secrets, and to do that online requires sophisticated encryption abilities and anonymizing software such as Tor. It is a great irony—indeed an ambiguity of cyberspace—that the ability to share secrets requires the ability to keep secrets.

The driving figure behind WikiLeaks is Julian Assange. He has been the subject of numerous magazine articles, books, and film depictions. On the one hand a dynamic and driven personality, he has also been accused by many who have had a falling out with him of imperiousness, complete disregard for those out of his favor, and a sharp temper. He has a sharp mind for analysis and a long history of hacking, dating to the 1980s. In the 1990s he had run a website, called "Best of Security," that offered advice on computer security. He has also committed to making everything on the Internet available for free. For instance, Assange was involved in the creation of several free software programs as part of what became known as the open source movement.[11]

8. Ibid., 40.
9. Ibid., 41.
10. Ibid., 6.
11. Leigh and Harding, *WikiLeaks*, 45.

Assange long held aspirations to the creation of a leakers' website, registering the wikileaks.org domain in 1999. In the early 2000s he posted on his blog his theory of combating injustice:

> The more secretive or unjust an organization is, the more leaks induce fear and paranoia in its leadership and planning coterie. This must result in minimization of efficient internal communications mechanisms (an increase in cognitive 'secrecy tax') and consequent system-wide cognitive decline resulting in decreased ability to hold on to power.... Since unjust systems, by their nature, induce opponents, and in many places barely have the upper hand, mass leaking leaves them exquisitely vulnerable to those who seek to replace them with more open forms of governance. Only revealed injustice can be answered; for man [sic] to do anything intelligent he has to know what's actually going on.[12]

In short, Assange felt that an end to secrecy would lead to justice. If the populace only knew what was happening, it would demand justice. Thus the secrecy for corrupt institutions was the primary cause of injustice, in his view. This concept of a war on secrecy for the sake of justice was central to all of his thoughts and plans.

He finally commenced plans to launch WikiLeaks at the end of 2006, emailing a variety of people to solicit support. Among those contacted was Daniel Ellsberg. Ellsberg eventually became a supporter of the project, but says that he originally thought that it was overly naïve to think that such a website could work.[13] Other than a mention from Canada's CBC News, the launch of WikiLeaks was barely noticed.

WikiLeaks used Tor, PGP, and other similar cryptographic and anonymizing software to maintain security for leakers. Yet Tor also served another purpose. While it makes messages untraceable, it does not render those messages unreadable if they are not otherwise encrypted. Journalists David Leigh and Luke Harding believe that much of the early material that WikiLeaks released was drawn from unencrypted Tor communications.[14] These documents built WikiLeaks a strong reputation among human rights groups, which led to some genuine leaked documents coming to the site. At the same time, it became clear that simply posting leaked documents online did little to arouse public interest.

12. Quoted in ibid., 46–47.
13. Ibid., 47.
14. Ibid., 55.

What truly brought WikiLeaks into intensive public scrutiny was the cache of documents leaked by Chelsea (then known as Bradley) Manning. Manning allegedly replicated 91,000 files from the war in Afghanistan, 392,000 from the Iraq War, 779 files on inmates at the prison in Guantanamo, and approximately 225,000 State Department memoranda.[15] The scale of this leak compared to Ellsberg's is a matter of several magnitudes. Greenberg estimates that a leak of this size using the technology Ellsberg had available would have taken eighteen years to prepare, as compared to the one year that the Pentagon Papers took.[16]

Manning points to a decisive incident that made her decide to become a whistle-blower. The Iraqi Federal Police had detained fifteen protesters for printing "anti-Iraqi" literature. Manning, working in Army intelligence, was assigned to investigate. She found that the prisoners had written a thoughtful critique looking at possible corruption in Prime Minister Nouri al-Maliki's cabinet. She excitedly passed along this information, but her officer was uninterested and instead demanded that she find ways to help the police increase their number of detainees. Disillusioned with the lack of interest in truth or justice, she began to browse the State Department database that she had access to with her security clearance. She became even more disillusioned as she encountered candid accounts of backroom political dealings.[17] Eventually she came across a video of a group of men killed by an attack from an AH-64 Apache helicopter, shot from the helicopter's cockpit. Of the video, she writes, "At first glance, it was just a bunch of guys getting shot up by a helicopter."[18] While it was a common occurrence, this particular video was stored on the file of the Judge Advocate General, which implied there was some connection to a military justice proceeding. Manning tracked down the video date to July 2007 and the coordinates to a *New York Times* story about two journalists killed on the ground in a helicopter air strike. The military said that the journalists were with a group of insurgents in a black van who were firing on US soldiers. Yet the video showed the helicopter attacking the men without any evidence of them being insurgents. In fact, it showed the

---

15. Greenberg, *This Machine Kills Secrets*, 14.
16. Ibid., 15.
17. Ibid., 28.
18. *Wired.com* Lamo-Manning chat logs, quoted in ibid.

helicopter firing on civilians, including a family trying to help those who were injured. Two children were wounded, while their father was killed.[19]

Manning found security to be incredibly lax in the Baghdad forward operating base where she worked. The network security did not have sophisticated monitoring: analysts frequently watched video clips or listened to music and downloaded the material to CDs and DVDs. Even the locks on the doors were not working properly.[20] With her technical skill, Manning had no trouble downloading large amounts of data and burning it onto CDs marked as Lady Gaga music.

During Thanksgiving 2009, WikiLeaks published 500,000 intercepted pager messages from September 11, 2001 in order during a twenty-four-hour period. Manning was impressed not only with the content of this exercise, but that WikiLeaks had managed to obtain these messages anonymously from an NSA database. This inspired Manning to contact Assange.[21] The exact details of their communication are not known, but Manning managed to send a massive number of documents to WikiLeaks to publish. The Apache helicopter video was the first to be published, but the most important was a collection of 251,000 State Department diplomatic cables. These cables revealed a great deal. For instance, it showed that the State Department did not think highly of Tunisian president Ben Ali. This was a factor in the people's courage to oppose the dictator soon thereafter. Indeed the cables were a factor in the events of the Arab Spring, as they pulled back a layer of secrecy surrounding many of the Middle Eastern governments, thereby providing concrete reasons for protest.[22]

Along with the cables, Manning leaked documents about the war in Afghanistan, conditions at Guantanamo prison, and other important stories. Through WikiLeaks, Assange released the Apache helicopter video, but it did not create much controversy as the media did not pick up the story strongly. By this time, however, Manning had been caught and the United Sates government knew that WikiLeaks had the documents. Manning likely would not have been caught had she not essentially confessed in an online chat and her conversation partner turned her in. Nonetheless, she was being held in a prison in Kuwait and American

---

19. Ibid., 29.
20. Ibid., 37.
21. Leigh and Harding, *WikiLeaks*, 31.
22. Greenberg, *This Machine Kills Secrets*, 3.

officials were searching for Assange. Assange then arranged a deal with *The Guardian* newspaper in the UK and eventually also *The New York Times*.[23] The partnership was not entirely smooth, as Assange had a viewpoint that all information was good and should be made available, while the newspapers used the traditional journalistic approach of evaluating security concerns in deciding what to publish and what should not be published.[24] Nonetheless, they were able to work through the details and release a huge amount of information. Manning, however, was convicted of espionage and sentenced to a thirty-five-year prison sentence. In 2012 Juan Mendez, a UN special rapporteur on torture, formally accused the US government of cruel and degrading treatment of Manning, particularly for its excessive use of solitary confinement. In 2016 Manning was sentenced to solitary confinement on at least two incidents, both in response to suicide attempts.[25] Her sentence was commuted in 2017 and she was released in May of that year.[26]

Snowden

At the time he became known for his whistle-blowing, Edward Snowden was a contractor with Booz Allen, a private company contracted by the NSA to work with digital surveillance. Despite being only twenty-nine years old and having no college degree, he had an extensive resume. Before contracting with the NSA he had had other jobs within the intelligence sector, including with the CIA and the Defense Intelligence Agency. He had even gone through basic training for the Special Forces, although he broke his leg during it and so did not complete the training. Harding surmises that it was at this point that his computer skills were recognized and he was recruited into intelligence. By the time of his whistle-blowing he had top-level clearance that gave him wide-ranging access to surveillance documents.

When he was ready to make known the documents he had gathered, he flew from his home in Hawai'i to Hong Kong. There he arranged to meet with activist filmmaker Laura Poitras and journalists Glen Greenwald and Ewen MacAskill from *The Guardian* newspaper. There he spent

23. Leigh and Harding, *WikiLeaks*, 100.
24. Ibid., 112.
25. Savage, "Manning Tried Committing Suicide."
26. Pilkington, "Chelsea Manning Released."

several days with them, being filmed in interviews and taking the time to explain the technical details of some of the key documents in a manner that the journalists could understand.

Just as Manning's leaked documents were exponentially greater in quantity than Ellsberg's had been, Snowden's whistle-blowing was of greater importance than Manning's by a similar magnitude. Snowden had thousands of documents, most of which were "top secret." By contrast, only 6 percent of Manning's documents were classified as "secret"; none were "top secret."[27] What Snowden revealed combined Manning's quantity with Ellsberg's security level.

The details of Snowden's whistle-blowing story read like a spy novel, and in fact inspired an Oliver Stone film version.[28] From cryptic (and encrypted) emails summoning a select journalist and filmmaker to a hotel in Hong Kong to the global politics of extradition to slipping discreetly into Moscow to the Bolivian flight incident to ultimately being granted asylum in Russia, the summer of 2013 was one plot twist after another in the Snowden escapades. While fascinating, the complete details are beyond our focus here.[29] What is of greater interest to us is what the leaks reveal, Snowden's motivation for the leaks, and the hostility of government response to the leaks.

The Snowden documents uncover both a range of programs of surveillance and ambitions of total control. This attempt to control the Internet was done through a variety of programs revealed in the documents. Boundless Informant, for instance, gave the NSA a country-by-country map of how much information had been collected from computer and telephone networks by the NSA. It revealed some ninety-seven billion data points worldwide in March 2013, with particular concentrations in Iran, Pakistan, and Jordan.[30] It is worth noting that the NSA had lied to congress about the existence of such a tool.[31] While this amount of data is staggering, it only accounts for the NSA's own collection. PRISM, meanwhile, is a tool for collecting data through corporations. In the interview taped in his hotel room in Hong Kong where he explained some of the programs that he revealed, Snowden says of PRISM that it "is a

27. Harding, *The Snowden Files*, 146.

28. Stone's film draws on Harding's *The Snowden Files*.

29. See Harding's *The Snowden Files* and Gurnow's *The Edward Snowden Affair* for accounts of the episode.

30. Harding, *The Snowden Files*, 140.

31. Gurnow, *The Edward Snowden Affair*, 147.

demonstration of how the U.S. government co-opts U.S. corporate power to its own ends. Companies like Google, Facebook, Apple, Microsoft, they all get together with the NSA and provide the NSA direct access to the back ends of all the systems you use to communicate, to store data, to put things in the cloud, and even to just send birthday wishes and keep a record of your life."[32] The companies would deny giving the NSA this kind of access, but it was eventually revealed that the NSA had created secret backdoor entrances, through a program with the code name MUSCULAR, into the companies' servers in order to have direct access.[33] The companies claim to have unsuccessfully attempted to challenge the handing over of information to the government in secret FISA courts and were unaware of the back doors.[34] Given what we have seen in chapter 3 about the amount of data on each person that these companies have accumulated, we can see just how much information was available to the surveillance assemblages.

Tempora, which we mentioned previously, was a British GCHQ program that tapped the fiber-optic cables that pass through Britain, collected all of the data that passed through them, and stored metadata for thirty days and live data for three days. It was started in 2008 and was fully operational at the beginning of 2012, with the United States having full access.[35] This cooperation came through the participation of the "Five Eyes" group of English-speaking countries: the United States, the United Kingdom, Canada, New Zealand, and Australia. These countries had been collaborating on intelligence since the post-World War II period. This arrangement allowed sharing of all of this data. In particular, it allowed the United States to have access to data on its own citizens without directly spying on them.[36]

Another major program revealed was XKeyscore. This program catalogues terms used in search engines and allows them to be researched retroactively. Beyond that, it is able to track users in real time. That is, through this program an Internet user's online actions can be tracked

32. Quoted in Gurnow, *The Edward Snowden Affair*, 147.
33. Harding, *The Snowden Files*, 206.
34. Ibid.
35. Grunow, *The Edward Snowden Affair*, 96.
36. This is illegal but done. See Gurnow, *The Edward Snowden Affair*, 205–7. Tempora, and many of these programs, were also used for country-to-country espionage. For instance, Tempora was used by the British to spy on ally Germany. Such espionage, however, is beyond our interests here.

keystroke by keystroke as they type it, and that information is stored. This includes not just metadata but full-take data. *Der Spiegel* reported that this program was used to collect five hundred million pieces of information on German citizens, including one hundred eighty million in December 2012 alone. It later reported that Germany's domestic intelligence agency had made a "formal request" for access to the program.[37] The existence of this program refutes claims that only metadata is collected and analyzed. It also points to the fact that it is not only the United States government involved in such activities; even Germany was moving towards "relax[ing the] interpretation of the [nation's] privacy laws to provide greater opportunities of intelligence sharing," as *Der Spiegel* puts it.[38] Germany also had some of its own spying tools, such as Mira4 and VERAS, and held discussions with the NSA about programs able to detect behavior patterns based on corporate data mining practices.[39]

Fairview was a program for expanding American access to foreign intelligence through "bridging over" into foreign telecommunication systems. The United States government uses the partnerships between American telecoms and their foreign counterparts that allow for international communication to gain access to systems. Many of the hubs or "chokepoints" through which international calls are routed are located in the United States, so many non-American telecom companies must work through the United States' infrastructure. In return for access for 81 percent of international telephone calls, the United Sates pays the telecom companies hundreds of millions of dollars per year, Harding reports.[40] Gurnow, meanwhile, suggests this system "subtly implies that other nations may also be exploiting their domestic telecom and Internet firms' U.S. relations, especially interactions involving the other Four Eyes and 'friendly governments.'"[41] In response to this, Brazil called for regulations to be put into place "to impede abuses and protect the privacy" of people around the globe.[42] In addition to this bridging, it was also shown that the US had hacked the systems of Pacnet, the telecommunications giant with headquarters in Hong Kong and Singapore and data centers in China,

---

37. Grunow, *The Edward Snowden Affair*, 161–62.
38. Gude et al., "Mass Data." Quoted in ibid., 162.
39. Ibid., 208.
40. Harding, *The Snowden Files*, 203.
41. Gurnow, *The Edward Snowden Affair*, 139.
42. Ibid., 141.

Japan, South Korea, and Taiwan as well as Hong Kong and Singapore. The NSA had data mined SMS, or text messaging, data from the system by accessing backdoor entryways in various components made by American companies and sold to Pacnet. Unicom, China's second largest communications provider, meanwhile had discovered deliberate security weaknesses in its American-made Cisco routers that had allowed the United States to spy on two hundred fifty-eight million users.[43]

The overall picture from these many programs is a surveillance and power system that baffles the imagination. While many people today simply throw up their hands and say that everything on the Internet is being watched, it is worth pondering more explicitly just how much surveillance this entails. At least 75 percent of US Internet traffic, it would seem, is surveilled by the US and its allies.[44] This surveillance is not only monitored in real time, but is also stored for retroactive searches and subjected to predictive algorithms to anticipate future actions. Nearly anyone can be a target. The NSA uses a system of hops; that is, someone with a direct connection to a target is one "hop" from them, while a person connected to this second tier connection is two "hops" from the target. Investigation of people up to three hops away from a target was deemed permissible, allowing hundreds or even thousands to be under surveillance for connection to a single subject. In the wake of Snowden's revelations, there was a reduction to two hops by a presidential directive in 2014.[45] It is also important to note that this is just what was revealed by Snowden as of mid-2013. We have already discussed the sale by private security companies of algorithms such as Palantir to many national governments and local police forces, allowing them to conduct their own surveillance. It is also worth noting that violations of policies do occur as well. One document released by Snowden showed 865 NSA violations of policies restricting surveillance in the first quarter of 2012, with 89 percent of these violations involving full-take intelligence.[46]

Given this magnitude of surveillance, we see a thirst for total domination, an attempt to render each and every person on earth knowable and calculable. This claim of an attempt at total control may sound

43. Ibid., 100.

44. Gorman and Valentino-DeVries, "New Details Show Broader NSA." Gurnow notes that *The Wall Street Journal* did not reveal its primary sources behind its articles on Snowden-related disclosures.

45. Obama Presidential Policy Directive/PPD-28

46. Gurnow, *The Edward Snowden Affair*, 216.

grandiose, but then so are these surveillance programs. Indeed, the documents Snowden released showed sufficient hubris within the spy agencies to attempt such a grand plan. The theme of total control comes through in a quotation used as a slogan on one of the slides disclosed from the Tempora program, which will be discussed below. It quotes NSA director General Keith Alexander saying, "Why can't we collect all the signals all the time? Sounds like a good summer project for Menwith."[47] Meanwhile one of the British GCHQ components of the program bears the title "Mastering the Internet."[48] This certainly indicates a vertical view of cyberspace rather than a Barlowian horizontal vision.

In all of this, cyber security experts have generally given the reminder that even with the ability to pick up so much data, it can only be read if it is unencrypted. Good encryption is powerful and keeps data private; it is for this reason that many in government security industries would do away with publicly available encryption technologies if they could. Indeed, a 2017 BBC report claims that British weapons company BAE sold an advanced surveillance system called Evident to repressive regimes, and that system includes the capability to break through encryption.[49] If this is so, then one of the strongest bulwarks against unfettered surveillance has fallen.

Snowden's Motivations

While there has been considerable debate over what Snowden's motives were in becoming a whistle-blower, it is worth hearing his own summary from his interview in Hong Kong: "I don't want to live in a world where everything that I say, everything that I do, everyone I talk to, every expression of creativity or love or friendship is recorded. . . . So I think anyone who opposes that sort of world has an obligation to act in the way they can."[50] Thus in part what we see is that Snowden became distressed with the system of surveillance that he had been a part of, and decided to act from within to open up discussion. In fact, in that same interview he went on to say that he had waited and hoped that United States govern-

---

47. Ibid., 98. "Menwith" refers to Menwith Hill, the location of a US intelligence station in Britain run with British blessing.

48. Ibid.

49. "How BAE sold cyber-surveillance tools."

50. Gurnow, *The Edward Snowden Affair*, 148.

ment would pull back but when it instead expanded the surveillance he decided that he had to act. Harding reports that while Snowden became disillusioned with intelligence secrecy during the Bush administration, he was hopeful that the Obama administration would back off on some of the invasive practices put into place post-9/11. Instead, the Obama administration became more aggressive in pursuing leaks and the anonymity of journalists' sources. Disappointed with this turn of events, Snowden began to plan how to go about revealing the extent of the surveillance programs to which he had access.[51]

Snowden was aware that he would likely be charged as a criminal for theft and espionage. Yet, he said, "We have seen enough criminality on the part of government. It is hypocritical to make this allegation against me."[52] He saw his actions as a patriotic defense of the United States Constitution. He expected, nonetheless, that he was likely to spend the rest of his life imprisoned. He was quite aware of the treatment that Manning had received, as well as the aggressiveness with which figures like Bill Binney and Thomas Drake had been pursued. Binney and Drake had worked for the NSA and spoken out about wasteful spending by the agency.[53] Yet Snowden firmly believed that revealing the details of the surveillance could create a necessary public discussion of what the Internet should be and what limitations should be in place on government spying through cyberspace.[54]

Notably, Snowden did not release all of his documents at once, unfiltered, through a site like WikiLeaks. Rather, he intentionally courted journalists. He felt that Congress could not be trusted to hold a debate, and online document dumps were too careless about collateral damage, in his estimation. Instead, he had a strong sense of the importance of pacing out the revelations for maximum impact. He was actively involved with the journalists in deciding which programs should be revealed in which order.[55] He also wanted the journalists to redact portions of the documents that would compromise individuals and ongoing operations that were in the interest of public security. Unlike Assange, Snowden

51. Harding, *The Snowden Files*, 104.

52. Ibid., 109.

53. See Greenwald's account of Snowden's intention to identify himself and recognizing the likely consequences of that decision in Greenwald, *No Place to Hide*, 19, 50.

54. Harding, *The Snowden Files*, 174.

55. See, for instance, Greenwald, *No Place to Hide*, 82. Gurnow, meanwhile, includes a chronology of disclosures supplied by Snowden, 285–91.

believed that some secrecy in intelligence was necessary for safety. Yet he felt that government practices went well beyond reasonable safety measures. He left it to the newspapers to judge how best to balance secrecy and revelation.

The newspapers themselves ran into a great deal of resistance from their governments. Before each story was released, the newspapers followed journalistic protocol and contacted the government for response. In the United States this meant contacting the White House. Janine Gibson of *The Guardian's* New York office had a tense conference call that included NSA deputy director Chris Inglis and FBI deputy director Sean M. Joyce before the first of the Snowden articles ran. Harding proposes that this call was an intended show of strength to "flatter—and if necessary bully" *The Guardian* into delaying or even backing off from publishing the leaked material.[56] In the following days *The Guardian's* laptops frequently malfunctioned: presumably they were "middlemanned," a term for the NSA inserting itself into a device to obtain private data.[57] Yet in London the pressure was even greater. British law does not afford journalists the same measure of freedom that American law does. A gag order could easily be placed on the newspaper; thus the need to have copies of the documents in New York as well as London. Oliver Robbins, Britain's deputy national security advisor, voiced the government displeasure with the leaks over a three-day span from July 16–19. In another of the surreal episodes of government displays of power, on July 20 the British government demanded that the servers containing the documents be handed over. *The Guardian* refused, but ultimately agreed to destroy those computers.[58] GCHQ officials oversaw *The Guardian* staff take angle grinders and drills to the hard drives. They were then placed in a degausser to erase all data. Thus GCHQ forced the newspaper to destroy its own computers. British officials also stopped David Miranda, journalist Greenwald's partner, as he passed through Heathrow airport, detaining him for a day, in hopes of catching him carrying a flash drive with the documents on it. Thus we see again the heavy-handed response to those who present a challenge to the control of the power assemblages of cyberspace.

56. Harding, *The Snowden Files*, 129–31.

57. Ibid., 135–36.

58. Gurnow, *The Edward Snowden Affair*, 222, and Harding, *The Snowden Files*, 190–91.

Resistance and the Digital Whistle-Blower

How do we understand whistle-blowing in the era of the cyberdimension? To attend to this, let us first turn to the series of letters exchanged between philosopher Slavoj Žižek and Nadezhda Tolokonnikova, the Russian political activist, street artist, and member of the feminist punk rock and activist group Pussy Riot, while the latter was in a Russian forced labor camp. The letters engage in a range of discussions on power, economics, and resistance, and were published as *Comradely Greetings*. In one of the letters, Žižek discusses his thoughts on digital whistle-blowers, praising them. For instance, he contends, "Assange, Manning, and Snowden are exemplary cases of the new ethics that befit our era of digital control and communications. They are no longer just whistle-blowers who denounce illegal practices of private companies (banks, tobacco and oil companies) to public authorities; they denounce these public authorities themselves when they engage in the 'private use of reason.'"[59] He sees them as pulling back the curtain on the hidden works of power in a way that cannot be denied. They "render public the unfreedom" hidden underneath the experience of freedom held by many, particularly in the United States and Western Europe.[60] In this sense we could say that Žižek sees whistle-blowers as exposing the social infrastructure of the idea of democratic freedom.

Žižek's thoughts on the whistle-blowers help to enlarge his critique of late capitalism. Earlier in the exchange of letters, he expresses seeing late capitalism as uniquely difficult to resist because its "very principle is one of a constant self-revolutionizing."[61] This is possible because it has become less a hierarchical apparatus of the State and more horizontally organized and thus adaptive. This means it adjusts quickly to attempts at resistance. Yet by the end, when his reflections on Snowden come, he seems to see in the digital whistle-blowers a new tact for naming the powers behind the capitalist curtain. Thus a peak at the infrastructures underlying the assemblage of power is crucial in getting past the misdirections of continual metamorphosis.[62]

59. Žižek, "A New and Much More Risky Heroism will be Needed," 97.
60. Ibid., 98.
61. Žižek, "Is Our Position Utopian?," 50.
62. Žižek discusses late capitalism early in the correspondence and Snowden in the later letters and so I am somewhat conflating his arguments here, but I believe I do so within the spirit of Žižek's thought.

Žižek deals more fully with cyberspace in his earlier *Organs without Bodies*. In it, he suggests that anti-centralization is the key topic in discussing digitized capitalism.[63] He views cyberspace primarily as being tied to technological domination that encompasses social formation. That is, cyberspace is the exemplar for Žižek of the vicious circle of capitalist productivity of multiplying the problems that it claims to solve and thereby necessitating new answers. He holds, "The more cyberspace brings us together, enabling us to communicate in 'real time' with anyone on the globe, the more it isolates us, reducing us to individuals staring into computer screens."[64] He thus views cyberspace as promoting Gnostic visions of disembodiment designed to disintegrate community and serve capitalist interests and eliminate the possibility of resistance. In a realm where finitude is banished and decentralized multiplicity reigns, resistance is impossible: "What gets lost in this Gnostic vision is the fact that the obstacle to our fulfillment (our finitude) is a positive condition of (a limited) fulfillment: if we take away the obstacle to fulfillment, we lose fulfillment itself."[65] The struggle is necessary to make meaning possible. Thus he sees cyberspace as numbing us to resistance through a sense of personalization that shifts to counter our resistances. Yet we must note the Barlowian tendency here to see cyberspace in Platonic terms that ignores the infrastructural basis of the Internet and thus fails to think broadly enough about the cyberdimension.

Drawing on Deleuze, Žižek further questions the ability to resist by noting that from Deleuze it can be concluded "that the struggle for liberation is *not* reducible to a struggle for the 'right to narrate,' to the struggle of deprived marginal groups to freely articulate their position."[66] He notes that Deleuze addressed this in an interview, saying, "Perhaps, speech and communication are rotten. . . . To create was always something else than to communicate."[67] This complicates our discussion in the previous chapter about the Holy Spirit as narrative and the question of what narrative we have about the cyberdimension. In this the concept of disruption as a clearing of space becomes important, as does Maxwell's poetics of the blank space. The narrative or counter-narrative must have the poetic

63. Žižek, *Organs Without Bodies*, 165.
64. Ibid., 166.
65. Ibid., 167.
66. Ibid., 170.
67. Deleuze, *Pourparlers*, 237. Quoted in Žižek, *Organs Without Bodies*, 170.

rhythm of invisible excess in order to return artistry and spirit into life within the cyberdimension

Returning to Žižek's letter exchange with Tolokonnikova, meanwhile, we find that she challenges his characterization of late capitalism's horizontalization. "Late capitalism's anti-hierarchic and rhizomatic posture amounts to good advertising," she replies.[68] Rather, she points to a deeper level of infrastructural hierarchy at work. She explains, "But the logic of totalizing normality still has to continue its work in those places whose industrial bases are used to shore up everything dynamic, adaptable, and incipient in late capitalism. And here, in this other world hidden from view, the governing logic is one of absolutely rigid standards, of stability reinforced with steel."[69] She goes on to insist that the role of the radical activist is to unmask the static hierarchical structure that lies behind what is seen as the unbridled creativity of capitalism. Given that her protest often comes through her role as a musician, we can see again a connection between art and exposing structures and infrastructures. It would seem that these thoughts help set up Žižek's hopeful sense of the resistance of whistle-blowers at the end of their exchange.

Tolokonnikova also connects the work of resistance to Christian thought. For instance, she cites 2 Corinthians 11:32–33, where Paul recounts having so angered King Aretas in Damascus that Paul had to escape by being let over the walls in a basket. "This episode has for me become key," she explains, "opening as it does the possibility of resistance, of saving one's own life, of being calculating, even sly, in apostolic Christianity."[70] Beyond this, she also references the "holy fool" tradition that has particular importance in the Russian Orthodox tradition as essential to the work of resistance, a point which Žižek affirms.[71]

Tolokonnikova also points out midway through the exchange that they had fallen into a colonial pattern of discussion, considering a universal nature of capitalism. She notes, "What I mean [about having a colonial perspective] is that we haven't so far been accounting for regional differences and quirks in the operation of the economic and political mechanisms we're discussing."[72] She thus advocates for a consideration of

68. Tolokonnikova, "I Write You from a Special Economic Zone," 54.
69. Ibid.
70. Tolokonnikova, "When You Put on a Mask, You Leave Your Own Time," 88.
71. A key element of Pussy Riots protests have been the close ties between the Russian Orthodox Church hierarchy and Putin.
72. Tolokonnikova, "As I Serve My 'Deuce' in Lockdown," 63.

regional variants in any analysis of capitalism, even as she also insists that despite some anti-hierarchical trends there continues to lurk a great deal of hierarchicalism. We might hear this along the lines of our discussion of power assemblages.

In the exchanges between Tolokonnikova and Žižek we see something of an intersectionality between global economic critique, Christian thought, and issues of whistle-blowing. Yet to go further with these issues requires a more sustained analysis of culture and technology. To that end, let us next return to Bernard Stiegler, who engages in a more sustained reflection on the role of technology in contemporary society from a Marxist framework.

Technology and Proletarianization for Stiegler

Given Žižek's view of cyberspace as an extension of global capitalism in his Marxist analysis, let us return to the thought of Bernard Stiegler, who shares a Marxist framework but has been more focused on a philosophy of technology. This time let us turn to his more recent *For a New Critique of Political Economy*, written in response to the 2008 economic bubble burst.

In this work, Stiegler introduces the concept of "cognitive and affective proletarianization." This movement includes "a vast process of the loss of knowledge(s): *savoir-faire, savoir-vivre,* theoretical knowledge [*savoir theoriser*], in the absence of which all savor is lost."[73] Stiegler's definition of technology is an externalization of memory. Through technology, thoughts, ideas, and values are taken from the human mind and experience and given a durable form.[74] These aspects of consciousness are given material form through a process he calls grammatization, in a nod to Derrida's *Of Grammatology*. Material forms, however, are objects that can be controlled through sociopolitical and biopolitical power structures. Such control, meanwhile, then exerts influence on social, political, cultural, and personal processes of identity formation, thus alienating humanity from the memory initially externalized.

73. Stiegler, *For a New Critique*, 30. Author's italics.

74. We can note how Stiegler and Peters disagree in their definitions of technology. While Stiegler sees technology as memory externalized into durable form, Peters understands it to be techniques externalized into durable form. Stiegler's definition preferences the cognitive aspect of technology and its ability to control, while Peters attempts to account for embodied life-nurturing processes as well.

Stiegler argues that in the hyperindustrial phase of exteriorization of memory and knowledge, the exteriorization reaches the point where it is controlled by the structures and powers of the control society. Such control works on cognitive, cultural, and political as well as economic levels. In this sense, digital networks demonstrate how vast human knowledge and memory is while simultaneously dis-individualizing knowledge and memory. As studies have shown, humans remember less when they know they have Google to rely on.[75] Thus in cyberspace, for Stiegler, we are increasingly alienated from knowledge and memory even as more of it is available to us. By releasing unique and individually gained knowledge into cyberspace we give over the consistence of life into the calculable realm of controlled cyberspace. This, contends Stiegler, turns all who engage in cyberspace into proletariat.

Stiegler employs the term "mnemnotechnical retention" for the process of exteriorization. John Hutnyk, in his analysis of Stiegler's understanding of proletarianization, explains, "This 'tertiary' layer of retention exists as material culture into which we are born, into a world not of our own making so to speak, though as the exteriorization and spatialisation of individual time becoming collective time," so that this retention forms the original exteriorization of the mind.[76] The structures such as buildings, language, machines, and cultural practices and ideas that we are born into would qualify as mnemotechnical retention. Together they form a collective exteriority that provides a group identity from which our individual identity can be produced through the process of grammatization. It is the source of knowledge of how to live meaningfully and joyfully. New technologies of hyperindustrial society, Stiegler holds, co-opt mnemnotechnical retention mechanisms and convert them into products that we must consume. This commodification distorts the process of individuation as well as collective identities, forcing all people into the role of cultural consumer.

Thus the proletariat, Stiegler argues, is not about class identification. He insists this is a misreading of Marx. Rather, the tie between the proletariat and the working class was a matter of historical fact in the nineteenth-century context in which Marx and Engels were writing. Proletarianization concerns, rather, the alienation from *savoir-faire*. Thus in the current context, as we saw in chapter 3, the proletariat manifests itself

---

75. Bloom, "How the Web."
76. Hutnyk, "Proletarianization." 138.

as the reduction of humanity to consumers. "The problem," he contends, "is that the surplus that has by necessity been redistributed to proletarianized producers who have become consumers led, toward the end of the twentieth century, to the destruction of their libidinal energy and to its decomposition into drives—the result of what Herbert Marcuse called 'desublimation.'"[77] Proletarianization is an alienation from the knowledge of the excess of life, which gives meaning to existence. Through Maxwell, we might hear Stiegler saying that proletarianization is the loss of the blank space of life.

Constructively, Stiegler calls for the development of an economy of contribution. He draws here on Derrida's contention in *Of Grammatology* that through what he calls the "logic of the trace" it can be shown that the interior and the exterior cannot be opposed. Each is inscribed within the other. We may recall that for Stiegler technology is an externalization of memory. Through this externalization, control of the knowledge of how to live meaningfully is lost and humanity becomes alienated from consistence. The excess of consistence is inscribed within technology even as we are alienated from that technology. Technology is thus *pharmakon*, Stiegler contends: that which is both poison and remedy.[78] In technology lies the capability to reconnect with the depths of meaning of life even as it separates us from it. An economy of contribution, then, must court the integration of the external and the internal. To do this, the economic system cannot be solely driven by the financial subsystem, but must also involve subsystems of production, culture, technological research, and so forth, as partners rather than as servants.[79] Such partnership allows the process of grammatization to produce creative new individuation through the formation of what he calls "systems of care." "The economy of contribution," he thus explains, "is the stimulation of desire through the reconstitution of systems of care founded on contemporary *pharmka* and constituting a new commerce of subsistences in the service of a new existence."[80] Such an economy of contribution sounds curiously like Tillich's New Being scrubbed of its theologically-imbued symbolic naming.

---

77. Stiegler, *For a New Critique*, 40.

78. Ibid., 29.

79. See Stiegler, *For a New Critique*, 93–98, for his account of a history of economic reduction to finance.

80. Ibid., 121.

Critiques of Stiegler

Hutnyk notes that Stiegler has simultaneously narrowed and broadened Marx and Engel's notion of the proletariat in order to account for "psychotechnologies" such as television and the Internet. Hutnyk worries that lack of differentiation for region, culture, or class empties out the concept by framing everyone as proletariat. Specifically, it loses its original context as a concept designed to describe the coming of a political struggle aimed at transformation of the world through mutual recognition of the needs for development of the individual and the masses.[81] I would suggest that a fair response from Stiegler would be that the creation of everyone as a consumer is in fact the problem with hyperindustrial capitalism, and not with his work. I find this answer appealing, but at the same time would long for more than a diagnosis; I would hope from Stiegler a greater sense of a call to action, even if it is a call to act from within rather than gearing up for direct confrontation. Meanwhile, Hutnyk's critique points to a more significant limitation in Stiegler's work; his range of interlocutors is disturbingly small. He does not engage feminist, postcolonial, or other marginal or subversive voices in his analysis. Manuela Zechner and Bue Rübner Hansen are particularly critical of Stiegler on this point in their review of *For a New Critique of Political Economy*. They assert,

> Missing out on the wealth of self-generating knowledges in the experiences of women and subaltern people, Stiegler also fails to address the repression and deprivation of reproductive knowledges that have occurred with colonization, housewifization and capitalist accumulation across the globe and centuries. Whether women and the subaltern have a different point of view on contemporary "proletarianization" remains unknown: a promising story reverts to its usual protagonists.[82]

In other words, they argue that Stiegler has narrowed his analysis of the world to an oppositional transaction that ignores the insights of alternative voices that have a long experience of resisting dominant norms through passing down collective wisdom. For Zechner and Hansen, it is precisely Stiegler's narrow focus on the dynamic of production and consumption that blinds him to a consideration of quotidian life-giving tasks as a means of production of meaning in life. Thus when Stiegler calls constructively for the production of an online culture of care through an

---

81. Hutnyk, "Proletarianization," 147.
82. Zechner and Hansen, "Unchained melodies."

amplification of geek and hacker culture, they find his conception of care to ring hollow and to come across as elitist and abstract. In this we may recall Peters's insistence on understanding technology in an embodied way was precisely an attempt to honor the quotidian life-giving tasks often particularly identified as feminine existence.

For Hutnyk, Stiegler is at the same time too curmudgeonly in his approach to digital technologies and too quick to dismiss Marx's insights as outdated. He argues that Stiegler writes too apocalyptically, as if true literacy has been destroyed by television.[83] Hutnyk asks, "Can we really say the contemporary post-Google situation is more commodified than the bourgeois family already always was—with all its psychotic investments and constraints?"[84] Hutnyk's point is well taken here, in lifting up the potential for connection and relationship formation available in interactive cyber media. Stiegler seems to have lost a sense of the ambivalence of cyberspace in his critique of its economic dimensions. At the same time, Hutnyk does not sufficiently consider the depths of control of the power assemblages in cyberspace that the whistle-blowers have revealed. My concern, if not Stiegler's, extends beyond commodification. It is the covert colonization of a dimension of life, which threatens to colonize all aspects of life, thus distorting the dimension of spirit's drive to self-transcendence into profanization. In the colonizing of the cyberdimension there is thus far no available metaphor of unambiguous life in which to symbolically participate. In this, Stiegler makes an important contribution with his focus on the ways that the joyful knowledge of life is strangled through technology used as tool of control.

Stiegler's Rhythm of Individuation

In his earlier work, particularly the *Technics and Time* series, Stiegler looks to the interconnection of individuation, time, and aesthetics as the potential site of de-proletarianization. Yet the three are held together by technology, which for Stiegler is an example of *pharmakon*, or that which is at the same time poison and antidote. In giving commentary on Stiegler, Bram Ieven suggests, "Aesthetics is what makes individuation

---

83. Hutnyk, "Proletarianization," 131. He is more specifically referring to early Stiegler's work *Taking Care of Youth and the Generations* on this point, but at other points extends the charge of technological alarmism to other works as well.

84. Ibid., 132.

possible ... but equally, technology serves as the framework in which the aesthetic ground for individuation is organised, enhanced, or thwarted."[85] Aesthetics, then, is a means of reclaiming meaning in life, for Stiegler, though he has specific technical understandings of this claim which we must unpack.

We have already briefly encountered Stiegler's understanding of individuation. It is important to bear in mind that he differentiates individuation from individualization, which is an individual's person development. Individuation, on the other hand, is a process of acquiring uniqueness through interaction. It is a process that occurs not just to individuals but also to communities. This process is what makes a unique person and a unique community, rather than generic ones. It is the process of gaining specificity. This is done through interaction with the objects of mnemnotechnical retention that shape particularity. These are the physical manifestations of the collective memory of a community; these manifestations provide a basis for culture. Yet he insists that such a construal of community formation is not primarily nostalgic, but rather allows for a collectively imagined future that is structurally always open and unfulfilled. Technology as the externalized memory of a community can be a material means for passing down knowledge of what gives life meaning. One might say that these technologies of memory give rise to a communal story of what may be and thus provide an infrastructure for hope. One must wonder, though, about what kind of role a messianic expectation of the arrival of the unexpected Other, the stranger, and the immigrant can have in such a community. That is, while a diversity of cultures seem to be affirmed in this configuration, are individual communities not overly atomized and homogenized? Nonetheless, we see that for Stiegler individuation is a process that occurs over time through a framework of technology allowing the individuation to endure.

Stiegler's conception of time is rhythmic. The interaction between the individual and the community is one of attempting to synchronize with each other. "Individuation takes place," Ieven writes, "because we tune in and adjust to the rhythms of the community and yet never quite succeed in adjusting completely; we always differ, we are always slightly out of sync."[86] Such being out of sync gives something of a syncopated rhythm to the process of individuation and thus of time passing. It is in

---

85. Ieven, "The Forgetting," 77.
86. Ibid., 83.

the surprising cadences of this rhythm that uncertainty and thus newness might arise; recalling Maxwell we might see this as a poetic rhythm of disruption. Yet such uncertainty is not calculable. Thus as globalized culture presents commodified experience to all, it threatens the rhythm of individuation. Humanity becomes overly synchronized. The rhythms for dance and poetry become broken and the diversity of stories is lost.

Aesthetics, then, becomes both a process of group formation and of producing differences. It is in aesthetics where the inner life that marks the incalculable can be expressed. Stiegler holds that those engaged in the performing arts, "continue to cultivate a relationship to the *pharmakon*, in order that they may *still* pass into the noetic act, from which they draw a distinct pleasure that cannot be considered to be mere enjoyment, given that it consists in a feeling of *infinite difference*."[87] Yet the mechanization of humanity endangers this incalculability.

Stiegler's linkage of aesthetics as threatened by technology fits within a trajectory of the philosophy of technology that particularly bloomed in the mid-twentieth century. Particularly of interest in this background is American philosopher Lewis Mumford. While there is little evident direct connection between the two, there is an important resonance between their works. In considering the interconnection of art and technology, Mumford suggests that the great art of modernity has been a proclamation of the autonomous human spirit over against the machine. Yet, he laments, "those triumphs could be expressed only so long as a belief in the human person, and particularly in the inner life, the creative moment, remained dominant. . . . By the end of the nineteenth century, this evocative protest began to die away."[88] Machines, he continues, became autonomous and arbiters of truth, while humanity became servile and dissociated from spirit. That is, while technical advances provided great help to human life, at the same time overreliance on them also brought a curse along with their gift: an impoverishment of the inner life due to "overcommitment to the external, the quantitative, the measurable."[89] This history of human and machine follows a similar path to Stiegler's account as well as a similar critique of over-externalization as a reduction to the calculable.

---

87. Stiegler, *For a New Critique*, 69. Author's italics.
88. Mumford, "Art and Technics," 350.
89. Ibid., 351. Author's ellipsis.

Much like Stiegler, Mumford does not call for a renunciation of technology but rather a re-balancing. He suggests that art requires understanding life as a sacred site of potential significance. Technology, he proposes, should be seen as a means to enhance the appreciation of life. We might say that he sees the necessity of the various dimensions of life working together. He argues,

> The fact is that the organic and creative, the mechanical and automatic, are present in every manifestation of life, above all within the human organism itself. If we tend to exaggerate one phase and neglect the other, it is not because civilization inexorably develops in this fashion, but because, through a philosophic foundation of mainly false beliefs, we have allowed our balance to be upset, and have not actively regained that dynamic equilibrium in which state alone the higher functions—those that promote art, morality, freedom—can flourish.[90]

Thus he contends that in giving unlimited reign to machines, humanity has lost its ability to create significant symbols that communicate meaning within life. We might infer from him that this marks the loss of the sacred within humanity. It is certainly for him the loss of spirit. In response to this loss of spirit, he calls for a return to the aesthetic. However, he insists, "Before art on any great scale can redress the distortions of our lopsided technics, we must put ourselves in the mood and frame of mind in which art becomes possible, as either creation or re-creation; above all, we must learn to pause, to be silent, to close our eyes and wait."[91] It is in the silence, which we might call disruption, that God may speak.[92] Whether or not God speaks, Mumford continues, the discipline of silence allows for regaining control of the "tempo and rhythm of our days,"[93] which we may hear along with Stiegler's appeal to rhythm. Such a regained control of tempo manifests itself as an integration of spirit and machine: the symphony orchestra is a triumph of engineering as much as it is a triumph of art, he suggests. This sense of alienation from

---

90. Ibid., 355.

91. Ibid., 359.

92. Mumford is lifting up here the thought of nineteenth-century Catholic thinker Abbe Gratry, thus the terms are specifically Christian. Mumford suggests it can be translated into naturalistic terms as "one's hidden potentialities" rather than God. He also notes Mahatma Gandhi's use of silent mediation. Thus he is not attempting to be specifically religious but at the same time does not discount the religious.

93. Mumford, "Art and Technics," 360.

the surplus meaning of life that we find in both Stiegler and Mumford also recalls Bazzichelli's call to return art to life and Dillenberger's desire for the spiritual imagination to be unleashed. Indeed, Stiegler notes an openness to understanding hacker ethics as a struggle for abstraction.[94] However he does not push this insight further.

At the same time, for Ieven, Stiegler's technological touchstones are outdated. Ieven notes that the description of cultural synchronization better fits early days of television than digital technological realities. The personalization of social media, on-demand television, personalized streaming music, and so forth allow highly customized media experiences. Ieven qualifies this critique by noting the consumer-oriented nature of these technologies as well as the role of data mining in producing such personalization. Yet he seems to underestimate the pervasive power of data mining and particularly the ways that personalization locks us into fealty to a few corporations, as was discussed in chapter 3. Cyberspace as it is produces a chimera of individuation rather than authentic individuation. Ieven contends that we should focus on the flexibility of time in our situation where communication is a productive force of technology, rather than Stiegler's concern with synchronization. Rather than a hyper-industrial society, Ieven sees cyberspaces as reaching beyond industrialization. He sees Stiegler's understanding of time and space being functions of memory to be reductive. In this Ieven has something of a Barlow-esque horizontality to his view of cyberspace, while Stiegler is rather more hierarchical in seeing power structures of capitalism looming behind cyberspace. Yet with the revelations of the whistle-blowers as to the extent of surveillance in the cyberdimension, horizontalism ends up sounding rather idealistic rather than a reflection of our Internet as it is.

Stiegler and Whistle-Blowers

It is precisely here that Stiegler's thought intersects with our consideration of digital whistle-blowers. In the cyberdimension, the structures of mnemnotechnical retention have not only been co-opted by the power structures, but also withdrawn. As the coverage of wireless technology increases, for instance, the presence of cyberspace becomes less visible. More than that, the control of the cyber-military-commerical-industrial

---

94. See Stiegler, *For a New Critique*, 48.

complex over our access to cyberspace becomes less noticeable. We become more and more serfs within the data system, where any personalization and individuation is done within choices given by the power assemblage for the purpose of creating more effective consumers rather than a pursuit of *joie de vivre* or *savoir faire*. Whistle-blowing reveals the hidden structures of proletarianization. In this it is an authentic act of individuation that not only resists the reduction to calculability but also creates a possible alternative narrative for the cyberdimension from the one told by the power assemblage. In a sense, whistle-blowing can be an act of aesthetic resistance. This explains the ferocity with which governments have pursued whistle-blowers. Following Andrea Smith's contention that the colonizing powers disappear from view that which delegitimizes them, the whistle-blower reveals the power assemblage and thus delegitimizes its authority and so the power assemblages respond by attempting to make the whistle-blowers disappear by briefly revealing themselves as a brute force.

As with much of Stiegler's writings, I find the general concepts to be helpful, while the details are more problematic. More specifically, I find his analysis of the problems of technology and cyberspace intriguing and generally insightful. His constructive proposals, however, are narrowly constructed and better as abstract principles than as concrete proposals. In particular his discussion of aesthetics is quite abstract and rather staid, particularly given its focus on rhythm. Much like his description of care, it lacks vitality and practical wisdom. In this, Bazzichelli's call for artistic disruption is generally in line with Stiegler's sensibility but her call to eschew pitting power against power through working to disrupt systems of power from inside comes across as more nuanced and less ideological. As I have indicated, I find it to be a fleshing out of one of Stiegler's better constructive pleas; constructing new culture and new industry that do not compete with one another. I further worry whether in Stiegler's focus on technology as memory we see another example of the prioritization of the cognitive. It seems indicative of a general loss of embodiment within his theory of technology. The abstraction of his theory, combined with loss of embodiment and the lack of diversity in the voices he engages, leads me to worry that his concept of culture falls into the colonial trap of a concept of "Culture" as a single phenomenon toward which all societies move with more or less success. That is, I worry that his rhythm is hierarchical rather than truly allowing for local manifestations and insights. As such it may play into the very schemes that he wishes to resist. For these reasons, Peters's conception of technology as embodied is a more helpful concept than Stiegler's exteriorization. At the same time, Stiegler's critique of the political economy of proletarianization remains insightful. It does helpfully diagnose an important part of the ambiguity of the cyberdimension.

Trickster Figures

Returning now to whistle-blowing, Stiegler helps us to frame the value of the whistle-blower. They disclose knowledge from which people have been alienated. As such, they perform a transgressive function within the cyberdimension by making seen that which the power assemblage wishes to keep invisible. We can thus frame them as tricksters of the cyberdimension. The trickster figure has an important theological role to play in unclogging the colonization of the dimension of spirit, and ironically bringing an ambiguity that allows for symbolic participation in metaphors of unambiguous life. To unpack the image of the trickster, we now shift our focus to theologian Marion Grau.

Like Stiegler, Grau also turns to Derrida's *Of Grammatology* for inspiration, as in it Derrida references the Greek trickster god Hermes. Hermes is the slippery, tricky god of trade, thieves, deception, and various other ambiguous activities, but is above all known as the messenger of the divine. Derrida makes of this a nod to the "unstable ambivalence" of the task of communication. Indeed the word *hermeneutics*, the practice of interpretation of meaning, is derived from the name "Hermes."

Grau examines the wide range of trickster figures found across cultures around the world. As she notes, "Many trickster figures engender trouble, and trouble gender through their actions."[95] Tricksters are fluid, so that different ones from different places may exhibit different traits; even the same ones may be paradoxical or shift characteristics over time. "Even trying to grasp how trickster figures function or how to understand them is fraught," she tells us.[96] In fact, she continues, part of the allure of the trickster figure is its being puzzling, which cries out for grappling. For Grau the draw of the trickster is in its figuring of ambivalence, polyvalence, and indeterminacy and its tracing of paradox and excess. The trickster is not calculable, but rather is elusively extravagant in meaning.

95. Grau, *Refiguring*, 105.
96. Ibid., 106.

Such shifting vibrancy opens the multileveled ambiguities of the human/divine encounter in its luminous paradoxes.

Trickster figures dance on the margins of chaos and order, invoking the energies of the abyss. In this they contain the potentiality for both good and ill. Trickster narratives rarely display a neat and tidy line between good and evil, but are, rather, morally complex. At other times, trickster figures can be outright destructive. She notes that some tricksters expose vanities and illusions of a culture; others introduce a culture to new knowledge or technologies. Others may disrupt patterns and values in communal life, keeping them from becoming overly entrenched. Trickster figures expose the limits of a system and demonstrate the ways that creativity can open a space beyond that system. In doing so, they often invoke the wrath of those who rely on the system. In this, tricksters can be agents of disruption.

Theologically, Grau lifts up the call of Kidwell, Tinker, and Noley's *A Native American Theology* to add the category of trickster as an intervention into Western doctrinally-focused systematic theology. In this spirit, she highlights the prevalence of trickster figures in the body of biblical writings. Key to recognizing them is to look for the use of the "weapons of the weak" such as "speech, rhetoric, strategic dispensation of information, intrigue, and deception."[97] The biblical texts, she points out, are full of examples of these types of strategies: Joseph, Jacob, Jonah, and Jesus use them, just among the male "J"s! Trickster figures push boundaries that have been turned into idols by a community.

Grau notes that Hermes as a trickster figure fits a figure, in some cultures, of the wandering and lecherous male, as opposed to the female who stays in place to tend to the home. Yet tricksters cannot be reduced to this gender formulation. Tricksters queer boundaries, whether gendered or cultural, or between spirit and flesh. She finds biblical women to work as translators between boundaries: "biblical women who build a bridge between peoples with their bodies, through sexual encounters, and through marriage and children."[98] In particular she points to Mary as *theotokos* as the central act of translation for Christian theology. Through giving birth to a child who is the enfleshment of divinity she disturbs the boundary between the divine and the human. "Mary is a translator into Jewish flesh, the body that will become expanded as divine logos,"

97. Ibid., 113.
98. Ibid., 90.

Grau declares. "She births the Word that becomes conceivable in other tongues."[99] Thus the boundary transgressing permeates the biblical text and Christian hermeneutics not just through male but also female trickster figures.

Indeed, once we attune ourselves to the feminine trickster figures, we find that many of the female figures of the bible have trickster-like functions. Rebekah, Rahab, the Samaritan women, Ruth, and many others can be seen in this light. Grau points out that there is some debate over whether, in the book of Esther, it should be Esther or Vashti that is seen as the trickster figure. Grau is open to seeing Esther not as a collaborator but as an activist. She quotes Susan Niditch: "the Book of Esther encourages attempts to work from within the system, to become an indispensable part of it. This model personified by Esther is strongly contrasted with that of Vashti. Direct resistance fails."[100] Rather than an oppositional clash which only results in mirroring the authoritarian assumptions of the power assemblage, we see a possibility of a more subtle unveiling of the power structures and plots with the hope of creating an alternative vision from within.

In turning to Jesus, Grau also finds trickster themes. "The synoptic Jesus," she holds, "is perpetually on the move, crossing boundaries and offending people right and left, challenging convention when it has begun to run counter to the core of communal values."[101] We might hear this "run counter to the core of communal values" as "co-opting the process of grammatization," in following Stiegler. Grau sees Jesus' teaching of parables and riddles as inherently ambiguous but also as a means of establishing authority in traditional cultures. Elsewhere she lifts up the caution that any "strategic Jesus" that we might construct can also be deconstructed, and thus we must hold on to it with a certain looseness. Nonetheless, she sides with Chicano cultural theorist Chela Sandoval in identifying the trickster figure as a particularly promising trope for coalition building that gives space for a range of cultural, ethnic, and class backgrounds to interact in a common commitment of challenging oppressive systems.[102] Perhaps we can see what in the previous chapter we called the performance art of Jesus' teaching as but one form of trickster

99. Ibid.
100. Quoted in Grau, *Refiguring*, 114.
101. Grau, *Refiguring*, 116.
102. Grau, *Of Divine Economy*, 179.

tactic. More broadly, Grau sees the theme of reversals in the New Testament as a trickster theme of folly. For instance, the crucifixion can be seen as "parodic exaltation" that mocks the colonial hierarchies of Palestine and imperial Rome. The resurrection thus transforms an act of dominant power by the state in executing an insignificant colonial peasant into an act of divine salvation. Here we see Paul's "folly of the cross." Thus she argues that the very nature of the gospel is ironic and paradoxical, unable to be pinned down through cold rationalism.

Grau's focus is on theological hermeneutics. For this point of view, she argues to return Hermes to those hermeneutics. That is, she calls on theology to invoke the trickster. She notes that it is not a new theme to Christian theology, beyond the biblical figures. From the Reformation era, for instance, she points out Luther's self-identification as a jester and Erasmus's ode to folly. The Russian Orthodox tradition, meanwhile, has a robust history of holy fools that we have already seen Tolokonnikova reference. Indeed, Grau sees the ascetic tradition more generally as being ripe with potential sites of subverting expectation. These moves are ambiguous; they represent an impure dissent against prevailing systems. In this we can hear echoes of Sauter's defense of DDoS actions and other disruptive techniques of protest.

In an earlier book, *Of Divine Economy*, Grau considers the trickster figure as a counter-economic figure. Tricksters from Christian texts, she notes, have a crucial difference from hucksters and other trickster figures. "These [Christian] trickster figures suffer deeply from an oppressive, exploitative economic status quo. Its madness marks their bodies and minds, and their hysteria allows them to articulate its craziness, if in a coded, ambivalent way."[103] Rather than being crushed by systems of oppression, they find a creative resistance to it by unmasking its inhumanity. They do this, she argues, "by producing—in Derrida's terms—an excess of meaning, their figures are ex-orbitant, excessive, well . . . *différant*."[104] Thus they mark a counter-economic theology. Economic here is not limited to finance but rather embraces the range of economies of exchange. I would suggest in terms of our discussion of the surveillant power assemblages that it is precisely this kind of trickster that is needed to challenge the economies of power and promote what Stiegler calls an

---

103. Ibid., 175.
104. Ibid., 176.

economy of contribution. Indeed, it is in this sense that I would consider the whistle-blower to be a type of trickster figure.

Grau sees theology's task as folly. Its challenge is "How to render, translate, interpret the unintelligible, the infinitely untranslatable without indeed admitting to its impossibility?"[105] In other words, she is dealing with the question of how the untranslatable message of the divine might be communicated. Such translation is always an improper naming of the divine. Indeed, as we recall the pluri-singularity of resistance through the use of pseudonyms like Anonymous, might we too see this kind of improper naming in Christian Trinitarian discourse? Might the naming of God as Three-in-One be a form of resistance to any simple reductive identity? Grau echoes Homi Bhabba in contending that a stark boundary between mythos and logos is a Western abstraction. Such a distinction can be helpful when regarded as provisional distinction but damaging if taken as absolute. Grau continues that because Western thought developed a framework of the mythic as inferior to the logic of logos, "the emergence of Christian theology included an articulation of the stark contrast between Christian logos and pagan mythos, that is, despite its dependence on the structures of mythos, Christocentric interpretation positioned the Christological Logos as the core principle of the structure of history."[106] Yet such a reduction of theology to logos diminishes the richness of truth found within myth. Theology's aim cannot be reduced to the historical and logical, but rather to combine these with an expression of the excess to existence, giving voice to the ineffable and shape to the invisible consistence of life.

Thus Grau advocates a return to Christian mythmaking. Drawing on Raimundo Panikkar's reading of James 1:22, in which he advocates the exhortation to be "doers of the word" be taken in its broader literal sense of being poets/artists/makers of the Logos, Grau calls for a poetic mythologizing of divine activity in the world. Poetic mythmaking, she insists, is not pure fiction but rather can be a form of critical engagement with the world that functions from a different set of principles than logical argumentation. Myth holds up ambiguity and allows multiple interpretations. She explains, "mythos frustrates all attempts to find clean definitions and renders impossible neat summaries or final interpretations. . . . Or to put it positively, myths invite interpretation, and they

---

105. Grau, *Refiguring*, 189.
106. Ibid., 60.

do so by representing the embodiment of the transcendent in the everyday human world."[107] The narrative approach of mythos opens ways of speaking of the multidimensionality of existence, injecting the physical realms with the spiritual. In our contemporary theopoetics it must also speak of the spirit in the cyberdimension. This is essential for keeping the ambiguity of the dimension open and not falling into its digital default of a reductive either/or. To this call for theopoetic mythos as doers of the Word, let us add Laurent's call to construe the Holy Spirit as story. Mythos can thus be heard to speak to and from the dimension of spirit as an elusive discursive rendering of ambiguous excess. I do not wish to completely identify the Holy Spirit with the dimension of the spirit, but at the same time there is a close relationship between them. The mythos of spirit is an imperfect naming of the divine, which can ambiguously be known as the Holy Spirit.

This question of the imperfect communication of the divine returns us to the first chapter, and Peters's infrastructuralism. Peters reminds us that there is no unmediated story; infrastructures are always at play in communication. Peters helps us to see that too often technology is only understood as logos. That is, it is a purely rational and material concern constructed by human (read masculine) ingenuity for the purpose of controlling the unruly forces of nature. Logos and technology are thus aligned against the chaotic excesses of the world. A theology of technology must challenge such an alignment, holding that spirit also pervades the technological through the porous boundaries between mythos and logos. Infrastructural consideration is one such way to lift up the dynamic mingling. Cyberspace cannot be reduced to the logos of a series of machines that happened to be networked even as dreams of disembodied cognition in cyberspace ignores the electrical and electronic aspects of the dimension. The divine Word as logos and mythos is a mediated and imperfect communication, whether it is mediated through the air as speech, through paper as text, or through pixels in cyberspace.

This mythos of the cyberdimension arises from its aesthetic dimension of consistence. It must, I contend, offer up a vision not merely of resistance but of a vision of constructing new culture and new industry that are not opposed but rather complementary. The heavily horizontalized tale of Barlow was overly optimistic and provided cover for the power assemblages to craft a hidden vertical story of cyberspace. Whistle-blowing

107. Ibid., 166.

unveils that story so that both can be seen together in ambiguous tension. Tension dramatizes the narrative, to recall King, and drama opens space for uncertainty that counteracts calculability. The economic domination—indeed profanization—of cyberspace is subverted by the whistle-blower's story. It thus acts as a conduit of the dimension of spirit into cyberspace. Whistle-blowing thus adds a trickster element as an ingredient in the construction of a mythos of cyberspace.

Chapter 6

The Hidden Church in the Cyberdimension

In November 2016 the Indian Prime Minister Narendra Modi announced the withdrawal of 501,000 rupee bank notes from circulation. Not only would these notes no longer be produced, but their use would be banned. These notes represented 86 percent of the cash in circulation, with only a small amount of new notes released to replace them, and these particularly in the form of the high-value 2,000-rupee note. This was done under the guise of eliminating counterfeiting and other "black money" or unaccounted-for wealth in India. The idea behind this, along with being seen as an anti-corruption tactic, was a move towards electronic payment and online banking. Modi urged people to use checks, rolled out a bouquet of incentives to encourage buying online, launched a biometric e-wallet app, and even organized a lottery to reward digital transactions.[1]

Yet the introduction of this demonetization was disastrous for many Indians. The rollout caused massive queues at ATM machines. These rollout issues were "made worse by poor implementation that saw repeated changes in cash exchange and withdrawal limits, causing over 100 deaths, widespread inconvenience, and paralysing large segments of India's mostly cash-driven economy," according to journalist Debasish Roy Chowdhury.[2] The 2,000-rupee note, meanwhile, is of much too great a value to be useful for the bulk of everyday payments for many Indians because few are willing to break such large bills. Beyond this, online banking and

1. Chowdhury, "Note Ban."
2. Ibid.

payment is simply unavailable for many in India. While e-paying services such as Paytm and FreeCharge are available in cities, many villages do not have electricity or nearby banks, let alone Internet access. For these people, the demonetization has made their already formidable economic challenges potentially insurmountable. They were truly invisible in this decision. Despite not having Internet access, the movements of the cyberdimension have inflicted direct suffering upon them.

In this incident we see a number of issues that bring together threads that we have been tracing thus far. We find the cyberdimension's deep implications in the structures and infrastructures of this world, bringing about significant ramifications for a wide range of people and communities. We also find the digital divide of those with access and those without, and see how this makes some people invisible. It thus brings up the question of how to be community in its various levels of manifestation with a sense of common good in the cyberdimension era.

Thus far, as we have traced our way through the cyberdimension, we have followed the interplay of visibility and invisibility or hiddenness. In the first chapter we considered the nature of cyberspace, including views of it as a quasi-Platonic realm of forms or a Barlowian disembodied space. Yet I contended that cyberspace was more appropriately described by Peters's infrastructuralism, which he contends is, at heart, a consideration of hidden infrastructure. Further, I argued that cyberspace qualifies as a Tillichian dimension of life, where new possibilities and challenges latent in other dimensions of life may be revealed. In the second chapter, then, I considered cyberweapons and the covert warfare of the cyberdimension. Through turning everywhere into a potential yet hidden frontline of cyber-battle, I argued that the cyberdimension has been militarized and colonized. This colonization, however, is invisible. In turning to big data and digital surveillance in the third chapter, then, we encountered the ways in which algorithms simultaneously make some hypervisible while others are rendered invisible. Chapter 4, meanwhile, turned to modes of resistance and the role of art as a means of expressing the ineffable. In particular, we found the value of the poetic blank space around the words of the poem as a type of hidden opacity that indicates unseen excess. The fifth chapter, meanwhile, explored digital whistle-blowers as trickster figures who make seen what the power assemblages of cyberspace wish to keep hidden. Central to my exploration of the cyberdimension, then, is the interplay of sight and hiddenness.

In the first chapter I suggested that understanding cyberspace as a dimension means that it is interpenetrated by the other dimensions of life. Life is beset by ambiguity, and the dimension of spirit marks a yearning for an unambiguous existence. For Tillich such metaphors as Eternal Life and Spiritual Presence speak of this vision of unambiguous life. Within the cyberdimension, cybersecurity issues represent the ambiguity encountered in the cyberdimension. It is the reality of the Internet we have rather than the Internet that could be. In this chapter I wish to lift up a constructive retrieval of the Reformation concept of the hidden or invisible church as a metaphor for the unambiguous Internet that could be as an image of the interpenetration of the dimensions of spirit and cyberspace. Thus let us first turn to how this metaphor functioned in the Reformation era, and particularly in my own Lutheran tradition. Following that I turn to contemporary reflection on the church in cyberspace through the thought of Lutheran theologian Deanna Thompson. I will then bring these concepts into dialogue with postcolonial theology and decolonial thought as represented by Catherine Keller and Édouard Glissant, respectively, in order to consider how we might employ the hidden church metaphor in presenting a decolonizing vision of the cyberdimension.

Martin Luther's Hidden Church

Let us turn first, then, to Martin Luther's understanding of the church as hidden or invisible. This is a concept that evolved in his thought as he sought to find a way to speak about the event of church community rather than the institutional manifestation of the church. It was the event of community that represented to him the truth of the reality of the church, rather than the structures of the church that he considered to have fallen prey to imperial pretenses.

Clearly dividing the church as the body of Christ from the church as a visible institution was not an innovation of Luther's. Rather, it dates at least to Augustine, whose position arose against the Donatist argument that sinners could not belong to the church, and such sinners could be identified by their failure to meet ethical criteria. Augustine responded with the position that only God knows who the elect are. The historic church is not yet perfected but always in a state of becoming. As such it is made up of elect and non-elect. Only at the end of history will the true people of God be known as the true church triumphant.[3]

The Lutheran movement took these views of Augustine and sharpened them for use in the historical situation of the Reformation. Luther criticized the Roman church for losing the Augustinian sense of the invisible church and seeing the visible church as the only means of salvation. This focus on the visible church was viewed as a merging of the visible church with imperial Rome. Indeed, Luther suggests this merging was prophetically warned against in the book of Revelation through the image of the two beasts. "The one is the empire," Luther writes in a preface to the book. "The other, with the two horns [13:11] is the papacy; it has now become also a temporal kingdom, yet with the appearance of [having] the name of Christ." He then goes on to enumerate the offenses of the "imperial papacy" and the "papal empire."[4] Philip Melanchthon, meanwhile, holds of the Roman understanding of the church, "Perhaps the opponents demand that the church be defined as the supreme external monarchy of the entire world, in which the Roman pontiff must hold unlimited power, which no one is to question or censure."[5] Thus the Lutheran use of the concept of the invisible church has overtones of a resistance to the merging of the church with the trappings and ideology of empire, even though it would be too much to understand the concept as being outright anti-imperial.

Philip Melanchthon, meanwhile, gives a more formal statement of the Reformers' understanding of the church in his *Apology to the Augsburg Confession*. He writes, "Therefore in accordance with the Scriptures we maintain that the church is, properly speaking, the assembly of saints who truly believe the gospel of Christ and have the Holy Spirit. Nevertheless, we admit that in this life many hypocrites and wicked people, who are mixed in with these, participate in the outward signs."[6] Drawing on this description, twentieth-century Lutheran theologian F. E. Mayer contends, "It is foreign to Lutheran theological thinking to compare or to contrast an invisible and a visible church. To do so is a false antithesis, since the word *Church* has an entirely different connotation in each term: in the one it is the communion of saints; in the other it is a *corpus*

---

3. Mayer, "The Proper Distinction," 179.
4. Luther, "Preface to Revelation of St. John [II]," LW 35:406
5. Melanchthon, "Apology of the Augsburg Confession," in BC, 178.
6. Ibid.

mixtum, not even an *ecclesia mixta*, in fact, strictly speaking, no Church at all."[7] This is not to say that Luther does not discuss the two churches, but rather that he is consistent in understanding the true church as the communion of believers. Mayer thus notes, "For this reason Luther nowhere in his New Testament translates *ecclesia* with '*Kirche*,' but always as '*Gemeinde*.'"[8] That is, Luther's focus is on the local community as a phenomenon rather than the institutional structure known as church.

For Luther, then, it is perhaps better to speak of the church as hidden rather than invisible, Luther scholar Hans-Martin Barth argues.[9] That is, Luther's understanding of the church follows a similar *absconditus* logic as is found in his well-known concept of *deus absconditus*. In other words, for Luther God is hidden in the world. Jesus, the lowly crucified outcast, represents where humans are least likely to assume that God would be present. God's greatest acts occur in the world but are hidden from human sight because they contradict human logic. In the same way, the holy community of Christ is in the world but hidden from human ways of seeing. In debating with Erasmus of Rotterdam, Luther exclaims of attempts to prove the validity of the visible church rationally, "What, then, are we to do? The Church is hidden, the saints are unknown. What and whom are we to believe?"[10] Just as the presence of God in Jesus cannot be deduced by reason but only seen in faith, so too the true church can only be seen in faith. The church is marred by sin and corruption, but yet the work of God is hidden within that sinful edifice. Luther notes that in the book of Revelation "we see clearly what ghastly offenses and shortcomings there have been prior to our times, when Christendom is thought to have been at its best. By comparison, ours is really a golden age. Do not think that the heathen did not also take offense at this and regard the Christians as self-willed, loose, contentious people."[11] Luther refuses to see the history of the church as a triumphal history of victorious conquering of the world in the name of Christ, but rather as at best an ambiguous struggle. Yet despite this problematic history, the church also marks the gathered saints of God. Just as individual believers are both saint and sinner, so too the church is both corrupted and holy. In

---

7. Mayer, "The Proper Distinction," 185–86.
8. Ibid., 186.
9. Barth, *The Theology of Martin Luther*, 308.
10. Luther, *The Bondage of the Will*, LW 33:89.
11. Luther, "Preface to the Revelation of St. John [II]," LW 35:410.

Tillichian terms, the hidden church is the essence of the church while the visible church is the existence of the church.

Early in his thought, Luther discussed two churches, one internal and the other external. "The first, which is natural, basic, essential, and true, we shall call 'spiritual, internal Christendom.' The second, which is man-made and external, we shall call 'physical, external Christendom,'" Luther holds.[12] He hastens to add that the two cannot be separated, just as the spiritual or soul and the physical or body cannot be separated in an individual. Nonetheless, as Lutheran theologian Oswald Bayer notes, Luther soon moved away from this dualistic framing because it could too easily fall into spiritualism.[13] Yet he retains a sense that the true church can only be seen in faith; it is invisible in the world. As Barth describes Luther's thought, "The true church filled with the Holy Spirit is, as such, not visible to the naked eye. The all-too-obvious visibility of the papal church conceals precisely what the church is really about and what is invisible about it. The unity and holiness of the church cannot be discerned from external phenomena."[14] It is not, however, that there are two churches, but rather that the one true holy church is imperceptible by human reason. The hidden holy church exists in opaque excess of the visible church.

The holiness of the church, then, is withdrawn from sight. Notably it is also withdrawn from commerce. Luther continues in his preface to Revelation,

> In a word, our holiness is in heaven, where Christ is; and not in the world, before men's eyes, like goods in the market place. Therefore let there be offenses, divisions, heresies, and faults; let them do what they can! If only the word of the gospel remains pure among us, and we love and cherish it, we shall not doubt that Christ is with us, even when things are at their worst.[15]

Looking at the first part of this quote, one may be tempted to read it as spiritualizing the church as a rejection of the world. Yet the second part indicates that this is the opposite of Luther's intention. Rather than removing the true church from the earth, he is insisting that the true church remains in this world despite the ambiguities of its existence.

---

12. Luther, "On the Papacy at Rome," *LW* 39:70.
13. Bayer, *Martin Luther's Theology*, 278.
14. Barth, *The Theology of Martin Luther*, 281.
15. Luther, "Preface to the Revelation of St. John [II]," *LW* 35:411.

Even though the church is plagued by division, corruption, pettiness, and evil deeds, nonetheless there remain signs on earth of the essential nature of the church as holy and faithful to Christ. The marks of this holiness do not conform to popular notions of religiosity and so cannot be commercialized, marketed, or calculated, but they do interpenetrate the existential life of the church and provide hope and inspiration that sparks faith.

Specifically, for Luther, the marks of the invisible church within the visible church are the presence of word and sacrament. In fact, to turn back to Melanchthon for a moment, the *Augsburg Confession* defines the church as "the assembly of all believers among whom the gospel is purely preached and the holy sacraments are administered according to the gospel."[16] Thus the event of the church can be seen through the word of God being heard as gospel in the midst of the assembly.[17] This does not mean that all who are gathered in the assembly are moved by faith and are thus part of the hidden church, but rather that within the mixed group gathered together around word and sacrament the true church would manifest itself. This role of the gospel as impetus for Christ's presence and thus the manifestation of the church was central to Luther's theological vision. He succinctly puts it in the Smalcald Articles, "[The church's] holiness exists in the Word of God and true faith."[18] Meanwhile, in the Large Catechism, he contends, "For where Christ is not preached, there is no Holy Spirit to create, call, and gather the Christian church, apart from which no one can come to the Lord Christ." The word of God through Scripture, preaching, and sacrament as well as the faith inspired by these outward signs, constitute the core identifying markers of the church. As Barth explains, "The sole enduring and infallible sign of the church has always been God's word. Insofar as the word also constitutes the sacrament, the sacraments themselves are part of this infallible characteristic."[19] Other signs may also be present, though of lesser importance.[20] The word

16. Melanchthon, "Augsburg Confession (German Text)," BC, 42.

17. Luther understands the Word of God to come in the two distinct forms of law and gospel. By "gospel" he means the promise of salvation by grace as known through Christ.

18. Luther, "Smalcald Articles," BC, 325.

19. Barth, *The Theology of Martin Luther*, 283.

20. Barth notes a gradation in Luther's "On the Councils and the Church" that includes word, baptism, Eucharist, the power of the keys, ordination, prayer, praise and thanksgiving, and suffering for the sake of the cross. Elsewhere Luther mentions

of God is key because it communicates—or indeed mediates—the presence of Christ and initiates faith. Thus Luther holds, "When people hear the Word and accept it in faith, they are born invisibly. Thus the church grows, not indeed in outward appearance but invisibly."[21]

In the hearing of the gospel and in celebrating the sacraments, the invisible church becomes visible. This is not about the institution of the church, but rather about the event that occurs as the faithful gather and Christ is present in their midst. Of course those who are gathered are both saint and sinner even as Christ is present to them and so the church is both holy and sinful. Likewise, one cannot externally judge whether faith is present in the hearts of those who are gathered. Indeed Luther suggests that we should assume they are the saints and the true church, but not out of certainty but rather out of the virtue of assuming the best of one another: "I call them saints and regard them as such; I call them and believe them to be the Church of God; but I do so by the rule of love, not the rule of faith."[22] Only God knows for certain the faith in the hearts of those gathered under the name of the church. Yet despite the uncertainty, the external proclamation of Christ through word and sacrament infuses the gathered with an external sign of the presence of Christ through the Holy Spirit, thus marking the gathering as holy. Yet these signs cannot be interpreted through the use of reason, but rather are only understood in light of faith that our holiness belongs to Christ rather than ourselves.

Human reason, Luther argues, looks to the wrong signs to identify the church; it identifies the visible church with the true church. "It calls that 'the Christian Church' which is really the worst enemy of the Christian Church," he contends in his Preface to the Revelation of St. John [II]. "Similarly it calls those persons damned heretics who are really the true Christian Church."[23] Thus for him the history of Christianity is full of abuses of the visible church that obscure the true church. Yet, he continues, "Christendom will not be known by sight, but by faith. And faith has to do with things not seen. . . . A Christian is even hidden from himself;

---

creed, the Lord's Prayer, respect for authority, praise of the state of marriage, and a refusal of vengeance. Nonetheless these are peripheral signs, while word and sacrament are central. See ibid.

21. Luther, "Lectures on Isaiah," LW 17:407.

22. Luther, *The Bondage of the Will*, LW 33:88. Luther's point is that none can be proven to be saints or not to be saints. It is beyond the human capacity to judge their faith; therefore, we regard others as saints as a practice of assuming the best of others.

23. Luther, "Preface to the Revelation of St. John [II]," LW 35:410.

he does not see his holiness and virtue, but sees in himself nothing but unholiness and vice."[24] Bayer holds here that any attempt to reason as to the nature of election and holiness "gets into the realm of speculation or falls headlong into the abyss of temptation concerning predestination."[25] The eyes of reason view the world falsely; faith for Luther makes visible the invisible reality of Christ, which subverts human expectations.

The church cannot be pinned down objectively, but rather occurs. Elsewhere, Luther contrasts the papal understanding of the church as identifiable in particular concrete locations with the holy church of Christ, which is "neither here nor there" and "not built on anything temporal."[26] He concludes his critique of the structural church by arguing, "It is clear enough, I trust, that the holy Christian church cannot be demonstrated physically but can only be believed . . . it will have to remain a spiritual place standing in the Spirit, invisibly built upon the rock of Christ."[27] Humans must live with the ambiguity of not knowing what is the true church and what is not. It is for God alone to be able to make the distinction.

Edmund Schlink, in his study of the Lutheran confessions, argues that the invisible church must be understood as an eschatological expectation. He contends that the invisible church cannot be separated from the visible church, but rather the visible church is the site in which the event of the kingdom of Christ occurs. "Only because it *manifests* here, only because here Christ acts through the outward Word and sacrament," he explains, "do we know that it is *hidden* among the enemies, that it is *not yet revealed* in glory."[28] Thus in his framing the invisible church *is* the kingdom of Christ. Barth concurs with this eschatological framing, holding that the concept of "one, holy, catholic and apostolic church" is an eschatological rather than a phenomenological description. At the same time, he suggests that this eschatological goal helps to guide and shape the empirical church.[29] For both, the concept of the invisible or hidden church is an expected reality rather than a current one. For our purposes, we can find in it a metaphor to go alongside spiritual presence, the king-

24. Ibid.

25. Bayer, *Martin Luther's Theology,* 280.

26. Luther, "Some Thoughts Regarding His Companion, the Fool Murner," LW 39:220.

27. Ibid., 222.

28. Schlink, *Lutheran Confessions,* 222.

29. Barth, *The Theology of Martin Luther,* 282.

dom of God, and eternal life as means of speaking about the movement of the infinite that theology terms *Spirit* within the varying dimensions of life.

What we find, then, is that for Luther the church is not a visible structure but rather a creation of the Holy Spirit that works through preaching and sacraments to transform a gathered people into a holy community. This transformation is not directly visible in an objective sense, but is rather a matter of an inward creation of faith that links individuals with one another as members of the body of Christ. In this sense the hidden church could be described as an assemblage in the Deleuzian sense of the term. In this it is a resistance to being subsumed by the cyber-military-industrial-commercial power assemblage. Because it is understood as the body of Christ, the crucified, it would be improper to understand it as a counter-power assemblage. Rather, it engages through weakness in protesting the imperial implications of the terms set by the power assemblage. It is a protest from within, along the lines called for by Stiegler and Bazzichelli. It is a weak force of commitment to a world "otherwise"; a holiness that is not like the goods in the marketplace, to borrow Luther's phrase. As I have argued elsewhere, the cross represents the hopelessness and futility of resisting the powers of this world, but the resurrection speaks to an im-possible hope beyond this hopelessness.[30] So too the hidden church as the body of Christ speaks to the im-possible hope of resistance against the powers of this world. How, then, might we understand this hidden sense of the body of Christ in the cyberdimension?

The Virtual Body of Christ

Theologian Deanna Thompson, in her book *The Virtual Body of Christ in a Suffering World*, argues for an understanding of the body of Christ in a way that can work through ties created by online community. Key for her argument is her distinction between strong ties and weak ones. Strong ties are ones that draw on a deep well of connection and mutual vulnerability, while weak ones are more superficial connections. While noting that theologians such as Stanley Hauerwas focus on the importance of the church being a strong-tie community, Thompson suggests that social media and other online interactions foster important connections that have a fluidity of strength and that these connections are an important

---

30. In particular, see my discussion in Trozzo, *Rupturing Eschatology*, 165–73.

aspect of the church. Thus she suggests, "Through social media sites and other virtual connections, our networks expand and offer increased possibility to encounter those beyond our immediate circles who are in pain and need real presence and support."[31] These "weak ties" that hold a cloud of community around the church serve an important function, she argues, in helping the church in its task of caring for those who suffer.

Thompson prefers the term *virtual* for considering the online connections. She considers a variety of terms for the online connectivity, but settles on virtual, drawing on anthropologist Tom Boellstorff's argument that "it is in being virtual that we are human; since it is human 'nature' to experience life through the prism of culture, human being has always been virtual being."[32] Following this, Thompson would seem to see the virtual as a means of discussing the cultural frameworks with which we makes sense of the world. In this she sees the Internet as the latest technological tool to be used to enhance human capabilities. Thus the virtual is not to be understood as an alternative to the "real" world but rather as an addition or expansion of it. In this sense Thompson follows an instrumentalist view of technology as an aspect of culture similar to Tillich's. Yet as we might recall, I find this approach limited by its externalization of technology and lack of attention to infrastructural concerns. Indeed, Thompson limits her concerns to online content and interactions rather than the deeper structural and infrastructural issues. As such she is dealing with a separate set of concerns from mine. At the same time, the sensibility of cyberspace as an expansion of the experience of life is in line with my argument for understanding cyberspace as a dimension of existence.

In discussing cyberspace for the Christian community, Thompson turns to the Pauline imagery of the church as the body of Christ. On the one hand she acknowledges the trope of framing the cosmos as a body to be a common one for Paul's context. Nonetheless, she sees him as taking a familiar image and giving it a distinctive shape. He is attempting to go beyond a general sense of connection and instead lift up a sense of interconnection. More than just a general relationship to one another, Paul emphasizes that each part of the body must depend upon the other parts. Thompson notes that this would be a significant resocialization in Corinth, an assembly where "gender, class, education, familial status, or

---

31. Thompson, *The Virtual Body*, 72.
32. Boellstorff, *Coming of Age*, 5. Quoted in Thompson, *The Virtual Body*, 25.

status as a slave were just some of the factors that determined a person's standing and worth within the community."[33] She finds Paul's imagery valuable in that it simultaneously recognizes a unity of mutual dependence while also honoring diversity as essential to that unity.

A particularly noteworthy aspect of Paul's body imagery is found in 1 Corinthians 12:22–24. Here Paul holds that the weakest members of the body are indispensable and the disreputable are to be held in greater esteem. First Corinthians 12:24 then concludes, "But God has so arranged the body, giving greater honor to the inferior member."[34] For Thompson this passage highlights the countercultural aspect of Paul's message. It subverts prevailing hierarchies of the society, emphasizing the importance of the marginalized. Drawing on the work of biblical scholar Michael Gorman, she calls the vision of the weakest being the most privileged in the body of Christ a "cruciform hierarchy." For our purposes, this sense of honoring or indeed making visible the hidden parts of the body is an important aspect of the spiritual presence in the cyberdimension. As one of the great ambiguities of the cyberdimension is the way it makes the weakest invisible, Paul here thus gives us a scriptural basis for a central function of the church to be making those who are hidden become visible. In the cyberdimension this means challenging the structures that make some invisible, such as the Indians without Internet access, just as Paul is challenging those structures within the community at Corinth. At first blush this may sound different from Luther's hidden church as those who have faith. Yet we have also seen, coming from Augustine, that the true invisible church is the church that truly is the body of Christ. Thus implicitly the hidden church is the church that lifts up the hidden ones. Such an emphasis on honoring the weakest runs counter to human reason and thus can only be understood in faith.

In fact, Thompson points out not only a social challenge within Paul's body imagery, but also a political one. Paul contends that Christ is the head of the church. This comes in a context where Caesar is portrayed as the head of the body of the cosmos. "To call the community in Corinth 'the body of Christ' that proclaims Jesus as Lord, then, counters a culture that proclaims that Caesar is lord, where Caesar is seen as ruler and head of the body," Thompson holds.[35]

---

33. Thompson, *The Virtual Body*, 36.
34. NRSV translation.
35. Thompson, *The Virtual Body*, 37.

In applying this imagery of the body of Christ to cyberspace, Thompson returns to the concept of strong and weak ties. She points out that biblical scholars often conclude that Paul's ministry had more weak ties than strong ties. His frequent movement, use of coworkers like Timothy and Phoebe, and the factions and challenges to his authority that developed in congregations point to the presence of weak ties, even if his ministry also relied on strong ties with his coworkers and at least some of the congregations. Thus she suspects that Paul's ministry contained a mix of strong and weak ties. Importantly, though, she points out that even if his ministry in places such as Corinth was rooted in strong ties, much of his relationship with them was virtual. He was physically present with them for relatively short periods of time, and so when he was absent his letters formed a virtual relationship. He is virtually present not in the sense of being "almost" there, but rather as a nonphysical presence. It is something of what I have called an absent presence. It is a presence mediated by the technology of writing to create an invisible presence. Such a presence creates its own forms of connection and community. In the case of Paul's letters, it created a new role for the church that received the letter in being an interpretive community.[36]

Indeed, public letters are meant to be read communally, and thus provoke discussion as to their meaning. We might imagine the community in Corinth reading aloud Paul's passage about the body of Christ. We can imagine the disgust that some at the cultural top of the social hierarchy might have felt while hearing his words and looking over at some of the slaves or other "inferior" members who were hearing them too, and the impetus this may have provided for addressing the issues of division. We might even understand the oral performance of reading the letter aloud in the assembly as a disruptive act. Perhaps in Paul we can find a rhetorical aesthetic of disruption or resistance, where familiar metaphors are turned into theopolitical critiques of the cultural hierarchies.

In this vein of an absent present community, Thompson seeks to understand the body of Christ as virtual. It is everywhere but also nowhere. She appreciatively points to theologian Guillermo Hansen's construction of the body of Christ as "neither an institution nor a society in the strict sense of the term. It is really the expression of a swarm without a center, for Christ is mediated by a decentered and decentering network

---

36. Ibid., 42.

of charismata."[37] While in previous chapters I have questioned the word *swarm* and have advocated a move from swarm to a conscious collective, we can still appreciate the sense of what Hansen is arguing here. In the assembly of the church, Christ is both withdrawn and present. Christ becomes an animating force that enlivens a decentralized and diverse assemblage gathered under the name of Christ. Thompson, for her part, takes Hansen's image but argues that it needs to be extended to include digital and social media networks. In her expanded vision of the body of Christ, strong and weak ties are intermingled not only through physical connection in forming a community, but also through the same intermingling online.

Thompson is not dismissive of the physical component of the body of Christ imagery for the church; it is in fact an essential aspect of it. She argues, "While Paul's image of the church as the body of Christ has been and continues to be an animating vision for Christian identity, that concept is most fully understood when placed within the larger context of the incarnation, the belief that God entered in to our fleshy, material world through the body of a human being, Jesus."[38] Christianity, in other words, is a religion of physical bodies. More than that, it is not a religion of just any physical body, but rather one that proclaims that God is most clearly revealed in the body of one who walked among the rural villages of Galilee, dined with outcasts, healed the sick, and was brutally put to death by the reigning powers of his day. This centrality of bodies is essential to Christian identity and an understanding of the church.

Thompson at this point turns to Luther's theology of the cross and incarnation. "The take-home message of God becoming a body, for Luther," Thompson contends, "is that this human being, Jesus, was in complete alignment with God, embodying God's love in the world even unto death and, through his death and resurrection, making humanity worthy before God, something we are unable to do for ourselves."[39] Such embodying God's love in the world means turning towards our neighbor in love, and for Luther when we do that we inevitably enter into the suffering that is part of the existence of our neighbors. Unavoidably, turning towards our neighbors in love means opening ourselves to the hurt that permeates this world.

---

37. Hansen, "The Networking of Differences," 33. Quoted in Thompson, *The Virtual Body*, 50–51.

38. Thompson, *The Virtual Body*, 53.

39. Ibid., 55.

Thompson aims to extend this entering into the neighbor's suffering to connections forged online. Such connections mix strong and weak ties in new ways. She draws from her own experience of support following her diagnosis of cancer. She relates how through social media she could communicate information to those within her congregational community that would not have been possible to communicate through person-to-person conversations, and that this information gave rise to deeper conversations and development of stronger ties than would otherwise have been possible. At the same time, these same sites also cultivated important weak-tie connections. She gives examples of a mass being celebrated for her in India by a church with which she did not have a direct connection, and of non-Christian friends who were moved to pray for her, thus blurring the religious lines of who is in the church and who is outside of it. In these experiences, the presence of the divine is felt virtually, mediated through not only strong-tie connections but also weak-tie ones that extend the body of Christ beyond rigid boundaries of church in an invisible cyber-web.

As I have noted, Thompson employs an instrumental view of technology that I find problematic for its separation of our self-identity from the tools that we use. This gives us the impression that we can choose whether to employ digital tools helpfully or harmfully, as if we had true recourse to opt out from them. While she cautions about the importance of paying attention to what and how new technologies are created and whose interests they serve, this caution still leaves technology in the realm of tools along the lines of Tillich's framing and caution about tools.[40] As I have also indicated, I find Peters's embodied understanding of technology and Stiegler's understanding of technology as *pharmakon* to be more helpful constructions. We can also recall that Thompson is dealing with the nature of online content and the interactions that occur online rather than considering the infrastructural issues involved with those interactions. This allows her not to turn her attention towards cybersecurity issues. Nonetheless, she is helpful in relating an image of the church to the cyberdimension. Her concern with the body of Christ having a virtual reality in the fullest sense of that term along with being inextricably embodied is an invaluable contribution. In particular, the recognition that the church is called to a cruciform hierarchy that uncovers and honors that which the culture hides and dishonors is in complete congruence

---

40. Ibid., 16.

with how I wish to understand the role of the hidden or invisible church within the cyberdimension.

In this vein, I am appreciative of her suggestion that worship in the church must attend to the online dimension as well as cultivate an attention to the needs of others. She calls on the church both to clearly claim the importance of weekly worship as "the countercultural practice of sustained attention toward the weakest among us" as well as an expansion of worship to include an online presence.[41] She views worship as a cultivation of attentiveness not just for the sake of the individual but for the sake of the entire community. Liturgy provides a framework, she suggests, not only for being shaped to hear the good news of forgiveness but also to offer forgiveness and to live into the new life found in the gospel. Worship provides a disruption to ordinary time that provides a glimpse of our embeddedness in relations, with God and with others. Here we might recall my suggestion in the third chapter to draw on Luther's sense of repentance as a means of seeing our true humanity as one that resides in a matrix of relationships flowing from divine creativity. More specifically, liturgical time is intended to be cyclical, as a means of returning to prayer and ritual again and again and through it growing in the ability to give attention to our relationships and most particularly to the needs of others. Thompson continues that the cruciform life is most clearly seen in the Eucharist, in the physical gathering, sharing of the meal, and becoming the gathered body of Christ.[42]

At the same time, Thompson also insists that because Christians must see beyond their own worshiping communities to the needs of others, digital technology must also be an essential aspect of Christian worship. She considers appreciatively, for instance, live streaming worship as a means of building fellowship across physical barriers. She is particularly concerned with those who are ill, disabled, or displaced from the community and unable to attend. She recognizes limitations to participation online, either for socioeconomic reasons or physical limitations such as those who are blind or visually impaired, are challenges to understanding the body of Christ in a virtual manner. Nonetheless, it is an aspect of reality that cannot be ignored by the church.

Thompson's turn to liturgy finds some parallels in Calvyn C. du Toit and Gys M. Loubser's reading of Christian liturgy through the lens

---

41. Ibid., 90.
42. Ibid., 92.

of Stiegler's understanding of technology as *pharmakon*. They contend, "Christian liturgy, chalked as complex rather than complicated, incorporates transversality, temporality, and non-linear creativity, whilst not neglecting structure, Christian tradition, and embodiment."[43] They suggest that liturgy offers a different, slightly slower, tempo than the culture of the hyper-industrial world. We can recall that for Stiegler a rhythmic offset is the source of individuation of particular contexts that provide a unique openness to the consistence of life. Liturgy can thus be seen as a means of creating locally unique consistence. Such contextualizing cannot be separated from larger connections, du Toit and Loubser would add. Liturgies grow out of histories of connections, so that Reformed or Lutheran or Catholic liturgies each reflect historical affiliations but also allow communities to anticipate possible futures in particular ways based on that history.

Christian liturgy, then, for du Toit and Loubser, is ever new as new situations and new technics come to influence a community. They note, for instance, "For years, the Notre Dame and other cathedrals acted as memory nodes reminding city denizens and strangers of the memory residing in all infrastructure. Lay people read symbols on the cathedral's west-work, for instance, and reconstitute themselves with the living and through the dead."[44] The point here is that the technology of the cathedral functioned to shape both the liturgy that occurred inside and to communicate a message to the community surrounding it. As new technological infrastructures come along the church and its liturgy must adapt with it. Thus they contend, "What is needed . . . is a thoughtful, even prayerful, integration of new technics into Christian liturgy."[45]

They offer a few suggestions for guiding the answer to this challenge of integration of new technics. They suggest that the current technological situation is one that pushes to higher and higher speed and volume, which flattens the time required for developing a rhythm of individuation. In response they see Christian liturgy as a contemplative art that can elicit a "time of the question" by slowing down the frenetic pace. In a sense we can hear this suggestion as a framing of contemplative liturgy as performance art that disrupts the constant deluge of information. They also suggest incorporating prayers of thanksgiving for electronic devices

---

43. du Toit and Loubser, "Liturgical Pharmacology," 3.
44. Ibid., 6.
45. Ibid.

while also asking for guidance in using them wisely. A further suggestion is to have worshipers place their mobile devices in the offering and then have them returned when they receive the elements in communion as a means of helping people recognize their attachment to these devices and how those devices are both a gift and a responsibility. While these liturgical actions are but suggestions, their larger point is that liturgy is embedded in the infrastructure of technology, and so it should appreciatively acknowledge this even while it also disrupts the rhythms set by the technology.

Expanding on the idea of liturgy as disruption, liturgical theologian Dirk Lange has theorized on this point in engagement with Luther and poststructuralist theory. Lange suggests that the life, death, and resurrection of Christ represent an unrepeatable event. It is an event that cannot be reduced to writing, either. He contends that Luther faced the challenge of non-repeatability by turning to liturgical language. The cross represents a traumatic wound in which meaning is dissolved into a chaotic abyss. Lange writes of Luther, "If 'meaning' is not to be attained by climbing the metaphysical ladder to an ever more profound experience of God, if it is not reached through a mystical exercise that peels off the layers of visible existence to uncover the true, invisible reality, if 'meaning' is not hidden somewhere behind the words only to be deciphered through intense allegorical work, then how do we even begin to speak about meaning?"[46] This is a question that returns us to the beginning of this book and the question of the meaning of the cyberspace. How can we speak of meaning? What allows meaning to be mediated? Lange holds that for Luther meaning was found in the confrontation with the failure of meaning. This confrontation is known through prayer and liturgical action. These are actions of faith, which apprehends "that which is absent or inaccessible in every event, in everything, and which disrupts every context and subject—and resists theorization."[47] Faith is being grasped by the meaning that cannot be comprehended because it has been dissolved into the abyss. The meaning of the cross and the absence of God seen there cannot be theorized; there is no "hidden meaning" waiting to be accessed if only we can find the proper decoder ring. Rather the cross is a trauma that disrupts our pretensions of being able to grasp meaning. Yet in the remains of this destruction of meaning, liturgical language can

---

46. Lange, *Trauma Recalled*, 95.
47. Ibid., 116.

poetically weave a new creation that continues after the abyss of meaning. Such weaving not only gives voice to the impossible task of speaking of meaning and of God after the abyss of the cross, but it further adds something new as the liturgical poetics is repeated again and again. Lange further explains,

> Luther is continually thrown back on, confronted with, events, words, that elude systematization, and in that confrontation something returns. This "something" is first "experienced" as loss—as the displacement of event, context, and subject, the reality of an absence in everything. But it is also the discovery of an addition, the discovery that meaning is not to be found hidden behind things but that a new language for meaning is required.[48]

This addition is not a return to an origin, but rather a new framework of meaning. Lange contends that Luther's critique of the practice of seeing the mass as a return of the sacrifice of Christ comes from this sense of the impossibility of a return to the original event. The Eucharist is not about the original meaning of the event but about the loss of meaning through the event. This same critique then applies to a Zwinglian sense of the Lord's Supper as a memorial meal. The liturgical celebration of the Eucharist is a confrontation with the failure of meaning. It is a confrontation that celebrates a body, the unsystematizable body of Christ, absent and yet really present in the bread and wine but also in the gathering of the community.

To return to Thompson, the virtual aspect of the body of Christ is an absence that is really present. I would suggest that it is a virtual reality that is mediated through the bread and wine and the word, but also through the confrontation with meaninglessness that comes through suffering, such as Thompson's stories of confronting her cancer diagnosis. Such a confrontation occurs through the virtual communities established online as well. The body of Christ is a space of lifting up the lower or hidden parts—the marginalized and suffering—to draw again on Pauline imagery. The cyberdimension allows those otherwise unseen to be seen more readily and thus allows the hidden community of the church to reach out in new ways.

---

48. Ibid., 121.

The Postcolonial and Decolonial Church

Now that we have encountered these metaphors of the hidden church and the body of Christ, seen through a largely Lutheran lens, how might these configurations help us in understanding the movement of the dimension of Spirit within the cyberdimension? More pointedly, do they contribute to resistance against the colonization of the cyberdimension that we have encountered in previous chapters? We have seen that the trope of the hidden church might be seen as a counter-power assemblage, but does this not lead into the kind of direct confrontation that EDT (Electronic Disturbance Theater) warned about? Can we find in these images a way of thinking about resistance from the inside that might speak to the challenges of the cyberdimension? To address these questions, I suggest we turn next to postcolonial and decolonial thought and see how they may be useful in enriching our images of the church and the holy community. More specifically, let us first look at theologian Catherine Keller's framing of postcolonial thought as a resource for theology in her book *God and Power*, and then turn to decolonial theorist and poet Édouard Glissant's engaging of the decolonial imaginary.

Beyond Confrontational Binaries

Keller seeks to engage the theopolitics of empire in the postmodern context. That is, she seeks to resist the totalizing tendencies of dissolving the "*power of worship* into the *worship of power*," as she puts it.[49] As we have seen, there is considerable resonance here with my sense of the power of worship being a disruptive power. For Keller, her particular target is the "messianic imperialism" of the *Pax Americana* that leaves in its wake ecological disaster and cultural waste to those outside the American empire. Based in the early Christian resistance to the Roman Empire, she seeks a pluralistic political theology of the postcolonial multitude. At the same time, while appreciative of the aims of liberation theology in challenging social injustice and sin, she wishes to problematize some of its assumptions. In particular, she wants to nuance liberation theology's tendency toward uncritical acceptance of apocalyptic rhetoric and its binary divisions of oppressor and oppressed.

---

49. Keller, *God and Power*, viii.

She demonstrates how apocalyptic and eschatological thinking has been crucial to resistance and liberation movements. In particular, the image of the kingdom of God as an eschatological end towards which history is headed has often proved valuable in spurring the church towards working for making the justice which is to come a reality in the here and now. Contextual theology—whether Latin American liberation, Korean minjung, Black, Womanist, feminist, queer, or so forth—has lifted up previously buried identities as new marginalized subjects ready to oppose the various oppressions opposing them. The apocalyptic symbol of the righteousness of the kingdom of God gives a revolutionary edge to these theological formulations of the prophetic call to justice. At the same time, she notes that such images of a singular end to which the universe is aimed is itself a totality that mirrors the ideology of empire. "But the liberation hermeneutic pretends—partly of course for purposes of rhetorical strategy, of church pedagogy—that the Bible itself presents an unambiguously liberatory vision.... It does not notice how frequently the apocalyptic Lord of lords and King of kings, bringing on his white horse the empire of God, has inspired the sacred violence of the Christian empire."[50] Thus in its resistance to totality, liberation theology risks mirroring that which it resists. She cautions against destructive modes of resistance, as they simply further empower the "dialectic of domination."[51]

In particular, we can see her theological desire to deconstruct discourses of the omnipotence of the Almighty as directly linked to these concerns about apocalyptic mirroring. Keller contends, "Historically, divine omnipotence was only achieved as a mimicry of empire. It was intended to mock and compete with the already divinized forms of pagan empire."[52] Yet in doing so, she continues, it also gave subsequent Christian empires an internal contradiction of anti-imperialism and a propensity to authoritarian conceptions of God and political power. Indeed, we can see even in Luther's critiques of the visible church a bit of this critique of empire even while at other times he lapses into more authoritarian modes of thought. Keller's concern with divine omnipotence as a mirroring of imperial apocalyptic rhetoric parallels the concern I raised in chapter 3 about understanding divine transcendence as the god of the panopticon, surveying all and thereby legitimizing all forms of surveillance.

50. Ibid., 101.
51. Ibid., 44.
52. Ibid., 51.

At the same time, Keller is concerned with apocalyptic justification for a purity of resistance as becoming a defining trait or even addiction for certain strands of progressive Christianity. This addiction to resistance, she suggests, is particularly notable in the liberal Protestant tradition, where the protesting too easily becomes constitutive of the Protestant. She points to Chinese American feminist Rey Chow's contention that the predominance of a progressive Protestant preoccupation with protest on behalf of universal justice as a means of salvation for the victims of history fits Max Weber's analysis of Protestant thought as being the animating spirit of capitalism in mirroring capitalism's own drive towards universalism. Protest becomes its own constitutive meta-identity whose purity cannot be questioned. This idea of an ultimate unity in justice becomes its own totalizing force; "revolutionary-left ideology can become orthodoxy and push toward a totalitarian effect," as she puts it.[53]

Along these lines we can see a challenge to the traditional understanding of the metaphor of the invisible church. As we have encountered, it, at least as read by recent German theologians, assumes an eschatological unity. We may not be able to see who is in the true church or not, but the omnipotent God can, and all too often this true church becomes construed as those who are pure in their faith (even if still struggling with the old Adam). Keller might argue that these totalizing images come from the patristic church's absorbing the ideology of the Roman Empire. She asserts, "It is a hybridization of pagan philosophy with biblical metaphor that produced Christian theology as such and so provided the terms of orthodoxy ... theology learned from the *metaphysics* of the empire how to abstract from the *politics* of empire."[54] Systematic theology thus came to see itself as a collection of timeless propositions and was therefore blinded to its and the church's implication within the Western imperial colonialist project. Part of the adopted imperial ideology includes a tendency to yearn for a purity of understanding of insiders and outsiders within the church. Even more, the role of Caesar as the great head binding the empire together was replaced by a god of unlimited power as the head of the great empire of the kingdom of God as a totalizing force. Thus even the image of the body of Christ, which as we have seen drew on the widely known imperial image of the state as a body and thus was employed to further the cosmic aspirations of the empire, must

53. Ibid., 103.
54. Ibid., 100.

be seen to have some ambiguity in this regard. This is not to say that these two images are now useless, but rather that some reframing is required.

We might therefore say that Keller views apocalyptic thinking as *pharmakon*, in Stiegler's sense. Thus she argues for what she calls counter-apocalyptic thinking. This is not non-eschatological thinking, but rather questions an eschatological teleology of aiming towards ultimate unity. It is an eschatology that celebrates diversity as intrinsically valuable, as well as "attention *to and through* apocalypse" as a means of speaking of justice while avoiding the final judgments of totality.[55] Such thinking attempts to avoid mirroring apocalyptic totality while at the same time still working—impurely and ambiguously—with a passion for justice. She explains, "Here ethical discernment as to what is better and what is worse frees itself from the habit of apocalypse, the habit of good versus evil. It can cure itself first of all from the fallacy of the binary alternative that allows it to perceive no alternative to the either/or of absolute truth (good!) versus mere relativism (evil!)."[56] We might hear in this position resonance with the impure protest and improper naming that empowers collective action by subaltern resistance groups that we encountered in chapter 4. To further this resonance, Keller asks, "Might the irony of a *counter-apocalypse* decenter the [apocalyptic] pattern in its religious and secular, sexist and feminist forms? Parody may lend a lightening touch."[57] In this we certainly find resonances with Anonymous and digital forms of protest at their most effective. Counter-apocalypse can further be understood as being similar to the resistance from the inside that we have discussed in previous chapters. Counter-apocalypse seeks to avoid the binary of pure motives versus evil motives as well. Along these lines she points out that too often liberation theology has seen the biblical texts as purely texts of liberation. Yet as we have just seen with the image of the body of Christ and with our earlier encounter with Stephen Moore's postcolonial biblical hermeneutics, biblical texts can also be complicit in the thinking of empire. For Keller, the idea of purity of motives is not helpful. Rather she argues for valuing hybridity and coalition building as a means of finding a third way between the two poles of the binary. Thus

55. Ibid., 62.
56. Ibid., 103.
57. Ibid., 62.

she argues not for "*relativism* but *relationalism*" as a means of enacting counter-apocalypse.[58]

In this search for a theory that can engage the fluidity and indeterminate borders of postmodernity that Keller engages postcolonial thought. For her, postcolonial theory lifts up the multiplicity of the world in its irreducible diversity. At the same time, she is not interested in diversity as separation, but rather as the interwoven fabric of existence. She stresses that she is not interested in postcolonial theory as a means to dismiss the reality of colonialism or the importance of justice movements, but rather as a theological tool to supplement and nuance liberative and contextual theologies by "offer[ing] an internal challenge to the certainties and dichotomies that tempt every emancipatory discourse to render final judgment rather than justice."[59] Keller further explains that postcolonial thought is not thinking that assumes that colonialism is past. Rather it seeks to work within the colonial structures and their aftermath, growing within the pressures of empire to identify alternatives from within. Postcolonial thought deals with the in-between of contexts and lifts up their hybridity. Such hybridity reminds us of Ball's argument for a cyborg existence over against the data double. Postcolonial theory, then, is helpful for the constructive task of theology, according to Keller, in helping to think about the porous borders between contexts. For our purposes, this applies to the cyberdimension in that it crosses and redefines the boundaries that have traditionally marked differing contexts.

At the same time, Keller insists that we cannot assume that rigid boundaries are a thing of the past. In this she is arguing against Hardt and Negri, who contend that the time of the modern nation-state is over.[60] We have already seen other suggestions that the cyberdimension has made nation-states obsolete, notably from Barlow and Owen. Hardt and Negri were writing at the same time as Barlow, in the 1990s. Yet Keller, writing a half-decade later, points to the Bush wars in Afghanistan and Iraq as evidence that nation-states might not be finished yet. Now more than a decade on from Keller's text, this seems even truer. Indeed, we started the first chapter with Putin's attempts to reinscribe national sovereignty over cyberspace, and the increased nationalism of the Trump era makes the continuing relevance of the nation-state hard to argue against, even

---

58. Ibid., 110.
59. Ibid., 103.
60. Ibid., 118.

as I argue that it has become but one—albeit central—component of the reigning power assemblage.

Keller suggests that postcolonial theory can assist theology in its constructive task of engaging the world. Further, it calls theology forth to build coalitions for the sake of justice. Indeed, she sees such coalition-building as the formation of an *ekklessia* or community. It is a community built on a desire to love the depth, diversity, and otherness found in the world. As she puts it, "it is not a harmless churchy balance of love and justice that we need, but an *ekklesia* (community) of just love, an *eros* that readies us for deadly dangers and delightful surprises."[61] In fact, she goes so far as to suggest, "If desire partakes of the infinite *in* the finite, it may be the only way to counter the boundless greed of empire *for* the finite."[62] Such theologizing of the infinite within the finite as an alternative to the totalizing tendencies of the powers of this world is not far at all from a Lutheran theology of the *communicatio idiomatum*. Even more, we can recall my contention that repentance is a turn from drawing our identity from the calculable finitude of our actions to allowing our identity and actions to flow from the trace of the infinite within us. I would suggest that we understand Keller's coalitional community as an assemblage of the invisible church, but not one that seeks to counter the power assemblage of the cyberdimension, but rather one that invokes the presence of the infinite in its diversity.

Keller notes that the early church was willing to cross any boundaries with its message. Christianity, that is, has always seen itself as capable of address beyond the specificities of any context. It has always been intercontextual. Foundational to its border-crossing message is a message of love. Yet, she notes, love cannot be disembodied. It is always tied to the particular. The abstract concept of love is not love. Thus she notes that in the biblical traditions, the infinite may be addressed through the particular of "you." In this, she suggests, "The infinite might become intimate. It might become loveable. It might become Love."[63] The Christian notion of love, that is, is incarnated and radically imminent. Thus she suggests that in the postmodern situation—which, I might add, would include the cyberdimension—where there is no "outside" from which to speak objectively, Christian love can speak, incarnationally, from the

---

61. Ibid., 111.
62. Ibid.
63. Ibid., 133.

inside. For Keller this means that every relation and encounter partakes in the co-constituting of the world through the relationality of mutually vulnerable bodies: relationships, she insists, are constitutive of identity. Relationships cannot be separated from essence or be construed as "accidental" to identity. Such a relational and bodily focus deconstructs the imperial formulations of the "God of power and might."[64] It is on this basis of mutual vulnerability and incarnated love that coalitions for life may be formed.

In our search for consistence in the cyberdimension, such incarnational coalitions form the basis for considering what the hidden church might mean. This leads us to the question of how this love becomes incarnated in the particular of the cyberdimension. Can we speak of imminence within the diffuse reality of the cyberdimension? Is it possible to think of colonizer and colonized in a non-territorial dimension? Perhaps not, properly speaking. Yet can we not at least constructively engage what we hear from incarnational and postcolonial discourses and consider it improperly for the cyberdimension? Perhaps in a dimension where time and space are manifested differently incarnational love and territoriality might also be manifested differently. Before proceeding with this line of thought, let us turn more specifically to decolonial thought.

The Decolonial Dissolution and Relation

Glissant attends to a number of issues that have relevance to our discussion of the cyberdimension thus far. He deals with language and poetics, totality and relation, opacity and transparency, culture and time, to name but a few. As theologian An Yountae describes, Glissant's "longtime interest lies in articulating the inexhaustible power of the profound solidarity/relation from which the fragile name of the community is born."[65] As an entryway into these concepts, let us turn first to his discussion of computers. First published in French in 1990, *Poetics of Relation* predates the widespread availability of the Internet. Nonetheless, he was already able to see several ways in which computers would bring significant changes.

Glissant sees computers as amplifying the urgency of the question of the value of poetics that had already been raised by the focus on technology in modernity. As computers edge the world towards more data-based

64. Ibid., 51.
65. An, *Decolonial Abyss*, 90.

thinking, it raises the question of what kind of information a poem brings. Poems do not add data to human knowledge. Further, he adds, while the binary code of computers is a rhythm, it is not a poetic one. One might say it is a functional steady drumbeat but not a syncopated one along the lines of Stiegler's theory of culture. Glissant is not worried about the role of poems in this sense, as he suggests that poems do add something different from computers. "The poet's truth," he contends, "is also the truth of the desired other, whereas precisely, the truth of a computer system is closed back upon its own sufficient logic."[66] Thus computers form a closed system of internal logic through an accumulation of data, while poetics open in desire—just as Keller insists as well. Poetics push into the infinite, while computers analyze what is. This is not dissimilar from what we have already seen in our discussion of poetics. We can also see the challenge it presents to a Teilhardian system of pushing towards an Omega point of coalescing together rather than opening into infinity.

Yet Glissant sees a greater challenge coming from computers. They have sped up time. Speed, he argues, has become commonplace. This is an observation that has only become more true in the intervening decades. The challenge of this is that it "renders the sudden flash ordinary."[67] This is precisely the move that du Toit and Loubser suggest with their turn to liturgy as a "time of the question." For them liturgy brings a ponderousness into a technological word and seeks to infuse the pondering and the encounter with the divine into a world imbued with digital sensibilities.

Beyond this, computers for Glissant represent a vision of totality. Yet it is code totality, a totality regulated by the programming that sets its parameters—indeed an algorithmic totality. That is, it "evades the drama of languages." The multiplicity of languages is an important aspect of identity, to Glissant's mind. He sees languages as alive and mixing. Thus for example he insists on that there is not one French language, but rather many. He is particularly interested in Creole, a language of hybridity. Such a hybrid language is a construction of culture out of the broken pieces of many cultures with which the Caribbean is left. Yet computers reduce language to a handful of standardized ones—and, we may add, Western languages. Indeed he points approvingly at attempts to write

---

66. Glissant, *Poetics of Relation*, 82.

67. Ibid., 83.

new computer languages based on non-Western languages as a way of preservering some variety of thought within computing.[68]

In response to these issues of speed and language, Glissant sees an increase in oral poetry. Oral poetry is performed or enacted. It transcends reduction to data. It is an event, and often done in a performative ritual that could be seen as liturgical. We might think here of the community in Corinth hearing Paul's letters read aloud, mediating his absent presence. Beyond that, orality is invisible and yet embodied. The sudden flash of truth is not confined to an encounter with words on a page but rather through words heard in time. It is mediated by voice rather than text. Yet he does not see oral poetics as an alternative to computers but rather as a supplement. He writes, "The computer . . . seems to be the privileged instrument of someone wanting to 'follow' any Whole whose variants multiply vertiginously. It is useful for suggesting what is stable within the unstable. Therefore, though it does not create poetry, it can 'show the way' to a poetics."[69] That is, computers can make manageable the complexities of a vast system and find coherent patterns invisible to the human mind. Yet in doing so it will also thereby identify the diversities that do not fit the system; yet it cannot make sense of or hold together these multiplicities. That weaving and creating a quilt of meaning out of the various discarded ends of fabric is the role of poetics.

Glissant considers the energy of the world to be its poetic force. "This world of force," he says, "does not direct any line of force but infinitely reveals them."[70] This infinitely revealed poetics of the world is what he calls "Relation." Much like Keller's focus on relationality, Glissant's Relation is a way of speaking of identity without getting trapped into discussions of ontological essences. For Glissant the interrelations that occur in a poetics of Relation weave life together and become constitutive of community and identity. Such identity is not static but rather always provisional and continually arising. It is much like Keller's sense of coalitions. Relation is thus central to poetics and the decolonial reality. It offers a contrast to the thinking of totality. Relation is what constitutes identity. It is not ontology or an understanding of existence that is reducible to an essence. Rather, through relation identity and community are constituted. Such identities are fluid and provisional, poetically constructed through an interweaving of relationalities. In this, relation does not come from nothing but

68. Ibid., 109.
69. Ibid., 84.
70. Ibid., 159.

rather from shared knowledge. It emerges from interaction. In particular, Glissant sees this as occurring through language.

Language production, for Glissant, is inextricably tied to the production of cultures. In this he is critical of the elevation of written languages at the expense of oral ones. While there is a necessary role for "vehicular" written languages, the relationship between these languages and local linguistic expressions is complex. As an example, not only is there is there not a single French language, but there has never been one. There have always been multiple languages expressed under the multiple identity of "the French language." Further, a lingua franca, he avers, is always apoetical. It communicates what is necessary, but not what is vibrant and creative. Thus he contends, "We have come to realize that all literal literacy needs to be buttressed by a cultural literacy that opens up possibilities and allows the revival of autonomous creative forces from within, and hence 'inside,' the language under consideration."[71] A language is a weaving of a culture out of a particular reality. In this he sees the particular value of Creole languages as a hybrid stitching together of a unique cultural reality. Glissant speaks of Creole as a counter-poetics or forced poetics that attempts to stitch together meaning and identity from these fragments. It is a poetics of survival, one that he warns against too optimistically glamorizing. It is a means of speaking identity out of the abyss of namelessness. Creolization is a means of non-teleological movement in stitching together meaning in the circularity of chaos. We might frame it as a form of impure dissent.

Following this vein of thought, Glissant is particularly concerned about the ways that technology is reduced to using a handful of languages. "How is it possible to come out of seclusion if only two or three languages continue to monopolize the irrefutable powers of technology and their manipulation, which are imposed as the sole path to salvation and energized by their actual effects?"[72] The language of cyberspace—both in terms of the predominance of English in the content of the Internet but also in terms of computer programming languages built around Western modes of thought—function to make invisible those who do not learn the cyber lingua franca or transparent those who do. In response, Glissant advocates the development of ethnotechniques that allow contextual development. Chief among these is poetics and the promotion

---

71. Ibid., 104.
72. Ibid., 108.

of languages. Poetics renders the absolute as opaque and produces the possibility of creative consistence. He explains:

> On the other side of the bitter struggles against domination and for the liberation of the imagination, there opens up a multiply dispersed zone in which we are gripped by vertigo. But this is not the vertigo preceding apocalypse and Babel's fall. It is the shiver of a beginning, confronted with extreme possibility.[73]

We can see this poetic possibility as a counter-apocalyptic opening to the divine glory of radiant opacity.

This leads to his contrast between opacity and transparency. Opacity refers to an irreducible Otherness, a hidden excess. "It is that which cannot be reduced, which is the most perennial guarantee of participation and confluence," Glissant explains.[74] We can recall Mayra Rivera's discussion of Otherness in the Gospel of John that we engaged in chapter 3 and the contention there that the glory of God is found in a celebration of that which is not seen. We can now term such glory a celebration of opacity. For his part, Glissant points out that opacity should not be confused with obscurity. That which is opaque may or may not be obscure. He notes, for instance, that some aspects of his own identity are obscure, or hidden, and this is not problematic.[75] In this we can recall Luther's contention that a Christian's self is hidden or withdrawn. What is a greater issue than obscurity is the importance of opacity rather than the transparency of totality. The work of transparency is to expose, unearth, uncover, and lay bare what is. Transparency is the work of rendering the world systematizable or calculable. Opacity refers to the hidden excess of the incalculable. Thus we might think of big data and cyber-surveillance as attempts to render the opacity of life as transparent.

As we consider this for the metaphor of the invisible or hidden church, we might ask whether the invisible church as it was argued by the Reformers actually functions to render transparent. That is, while there is a certain opacity in that we cannot see the depths of infinity (faith) in the hearts of others, this is a transitory phase. We can be assured that at the end what seems opaque to us now will be rendered transparent.

---

73. Ibid., 109.
74. Ibid., 191.
75. He writes, "It does not disturb me to accept that there are places where my identity is obscure to me, and the fact that it amazes me does not mean I relinquish it." Ibid., 192.

The opacity is a function of our human limitation rather than something to be celebrated. Might we find a way to consider the invisible church a gathering of opacity without becoming transparent? Certainly we can think of the hidden church as obscure—a collection of obscure identities harbored together in their diffracted opacity within the church. Perhaps as paradox we can even speak of an invisibly opaque church as a means of considering the imperceptible but not transparent web of relation within an assemblage of irreducible identities.

All of these issues addressed by Glissant stem from a technological sensibility rooted in a linear understanding of time as progressing from a certain point towards a certain point. He sees this as fundamental to Western thinking because it is fundamental to Christian thought. That is, Christianity universalizes linear time with its division of before Christ and after Christ, thus creating a sense of a universal human history. Glissant sees this Christian narrative then being superseded (in linear fashion!) by the narrative of science, with its quest for human origins looking back, and amassing information and technology looking forward. "Both were concerned with transcending the old mythical filiation linked to the destiny of a community," he writes, "to go beyond this with a universalizing notion that would retain, however, the power of the principle of linearity and that 'grasped' and justified History," by which he means an all-enveloping linear narrative of history.[76] Indeed, might we not see a recombination of these two stories of history in Teilhard de Chardin's musings on the Omega point and Barlow's utopian cyberspace?

Glissant sees decolonial thought, in contrast, as cyclical. He draws here on the Plantation experience—that is, the communal experience of the plantation system—for how it produced a sense of time and memory. He explains, "Memory in our works is not a calendar memory; our experience of time does not keep company with the rhythms of month and year alone; it is aggravated by the void, the final sentence of the Plantation."[77] We will return shortly to what he means by the "void." For now, the point is that he uncovers in his Caribbean context a rupture in any ability to speak of a linear history. Rather there is memory that is left after the linear collapses. Scraps of memory must be picked up and reassembled—through the stitching together of poetics—in a manner that does not fit the technological and more specifically computer logic nar-

---

76. Ibid., 49.
77. Ibid., 72.

rative of linearity in advancement. In this I find a more helpful analysis and potent critique of the technological vision of progress than I do of Christian theology of time, though it is certainly a helpful deconstruction of many Christian accounts of Salvation History in its fully capitalized majesty.[78]

Memory thus becomes essential to the production of new culture(s). As An explains, "relation is the historically 'accumulated' element of exchange or sharing, which one embodies, engages, and lives out in community."[79] The embodied history of co-constitution of a community is the basis of culture. Culture for Glissant, contra Stiegler, is never singular but rather always multiple, varied, and hybridizing. Stiegler's and Tillich's discussions of culture fit Glissant's critique: "During the period when positivism was triumphant, culture (not yet cultures) was conceived of as monolithic, culture existing wherever the refinements of civilization have led to humanism. When conceived of in this manner, culture is presented as purely abstract, the very essence of this movement toward an ideal."[80] In contrast, Glissant sees cultures as diverse hybrids. He contrasts culture as a plantation monoculture with the diversity of a Creole garden.

Yet technology wants to instill a linearity of thought. As the cyberdimension becomes ever more present, it becomes more and more effective in this by inspiring a desire for newness rather than Otherness. Yet does Glissant's cyclical view of time not have a rather liturgical resonance? Not in the sense of him speaking of Christian worship, of course. Rather, there seems to be a resonant cyclical sense of history in the Lutheran vein of Eucharistic thought that we traced above. Might such a liturgical sensibility act to supplement and restrain the Christian apocalyptic tendencies?

Gurgling underneath all of these others concepts for Glissant roils chaos. More specifically, *chaos-monde* or abyss. As art critic Ulrich Loock explains, "Glissant's name for the relations between all things is the world, which appears threefold: as *tout-monde* (the world in its entirety), *écho-monde* (the world of things resonating with one another) and

---

78. While this is not the appropriate place for a full consideration of this issue, I will briefly suggest that Luther's use of the idea of the *communicatio idiomatum* is one theological formulation that can be used to construct a challenge to purely linear constructions of time from a Christian perspective.

79. An, *Decolonial Abyss*, 111.

80. Glissant, *Poetics of Relation*, 133.

chaos-monde (a world that cannot be systematized)."[81] Glissant's concern is with recognizing the experience of violent rupture and trauma in the reality of the Caribbean people while also speaking of how life goes on after the rupture. Central to him, then, is a retrieval of the middle passage. According to An, "It is also in this middle passage that the figure of the abyss is born. The abyss, as its etymological root of 'bottomlessness' indicates, represents the sense of groundlessness constituting the fabric of reality in the colonial world."[82] Yet this abyss is not an end; rather it gives birth to a people who braid for themselves a new identity after the abyss. To be sure, he notes those who never escape the abyss, but he also considers those who emerge. For them, the experience "quickened into this continuous/discontinuous thing; the panic of the new land, the haunting of the former land, finally the alliance with the imposed land, suffered and redeemed. The unconscious memory of the abyss served as the alluvium for these metamorphoses."[83] Thus what is central to Glissant's concerns is not the abyss itself but rather the crossing or mediating of it. Thus he meditates on the boat of the middle passage, to which we will return shortly, and the edge of the sea as the mixing and alternating between order and chaos. Through the encounter with the abyss of the middle passage, decolonial difference is encountered as an abyss of being. That is, it is a chaotic fragmentation that exceeds words. It is from this fragmentation that the decolonial self must emerge.

Within this image of chaos, An notes the importance of the image of the slave ship of the middle passage for Glissant. An points out that Glissant mentions it three times. Glissant speaks of dissolving in the bowels of the ship, into the deep, into the chaos:

> What is terrifying partakes of the abyss, three times linked to the unknown. First, the time you fell into the belly of the boat. For, in your poetic vision, a boat has no belly; a boat does not swallow up, does not devour; a boat is steered by open skies. Yet, the belly of this boat dissolves you, precipitates you into a nonworld from which you cry out. This boat is a womb, a womb abyss. . . . This boat is your womb, a matrix, and yet it expels you. This boat: pregnant with as many dead as living under the sentence of death.[84]

81. Loock, "Opacity."
82. An, *Decolonial Abyss*, 89.
83. Glissant, *Poetics of Relation*, 7.
84. Ibid., 6.

For An, Glissant, "shows us how passage might be envisioned in the abyss of the middle passage in which the experience of trauma is transformed into a newly conceived identity rooted in becoming and Relation."[85] Relation emerges from the remains of the trauma of the boat once all that once was has vanished. The ship forced this trauma and enforced a dissolution of what was, yet it is what must be returned to in the weaving together of what continues.

We may recall the centrality of the ship for Peters's discussion of technology. He argued that only with the invention of the technology of the boat was the ocean revealed to be a medium (at least for humans). The ship, we may further recall from the first chapter, is the artificial ground on which humans can stand in order to mediate the experience of the ocean. Rather than devoid of meaning, the ship reveals the deep to be but a reservoir of excess meaning. Turning from this ship to Glissant's ship of the middle passage, we can see this ship transversing the depths more complexly. While it represents the dissolution of meaning, it also functions as a site of access to the remains of meaning.

We might also recall the centrality of nautical imagery for cyberspace, with its docks and ports and surfing the net. Thus we can see in the cyberdimension the dissolution of what was and the need to weave anew a story of community and divinity. Yet this weaving ought not to be glamorized as a triumphant march of progress towards an apocalyptic goal of transparent unity. It is a traumatic passage into the abyss of the middle, where the certainties of what was cannot stand the excess of meaning now accessed. The powers of the old creation, as it were, clutch ever more frantically at the shores that have been left, even at the risk of wreckage among the rocks. Perhaps, then, we can add Glissant's middle-passage boat to this technological boat.

Yet these are not the only important boat images for our concern. The boat is also an ancient symbol of the church. Many church logos, including that of the World Council of Churches, use a boat or ship as part of their design. Church architecture, meanwhile, has often shaped the physical churches into the shape of a sea vessel, with its nave and so forth.

Theologically, the metaphor of the church as a ship dates at least to Tertullian. In fact, he calls the church a "little boat," referencing the small boat the disciples were in on the Sea of Galilee with Jesus asleep on board. As a storm rolled in and threatened to swamp them, Jesus rose up and

---

85. An, *Decolonial Abyss*, 111.

stilled the storm. Thus this boat became the locus of salvation for those disciples. So too, for Tertullian, the church is the location from which God's saving grace is made effective and so is a small boat amidst the towering waves of the world.[86] The small boat is not quite so grand as the ship, though perhaps the humility of the boat better fits Luther's sense of the hidden church rather than the grand galleon, barquentine, or other such full-rigged ship images employed by many church institutions.

Constructively, might we add that the boat, with its Glissantian ramifications, to our images of the church in the cyberdimension? To do so would mean seeing the boat not only as a metaphor of safety in the storm but also one of ambiguity, of horror and fragmentation in dissolving into the belly of the boat but also of being expelled by it into new shores where weaving anew after the trauma must take place. Certainly I would not—could not—universalize the ship of the middle passage, yet I also would not want its reality to be lost in easy discussions about the metaphor of the boat. As the boat of the middle passage symbolizes the dissolution of meaning but also the reweaving that must occur afterwards, so too does the liturgy of the church symbolize the poetic reweaving of meaning after the dissolution of meaning in the cross, as we have seen in Lange's interpretation of Luther.

Indeed, we have these three ships: the ship of the church, the ship of the middle passage, and the ship as technology that reveals the medium of the sea to be a medium. These ships cross the surface of the deep, mediating the deep as rich in meaning even if also ambiguous and dangerous. Might these images of the ship cross with one another, mingling their mediation without falling into transparency? Might we see the abyss as revealed as a space of meaning and possibility and new beginning rather than only as fearful and of loss through the technology of the ship? A technology, we must recall, that requires infrastructure to access the meaning it mediates. An infrastructure of construction techniques, of a language, of a word; infrastructures that mediate relation to the depths of meaning of the world around us, ourselves, and the excess of consistence. These represent infrastructures of the inorganic, the organic, the psychological, and the spirit dimensions of life.

The church as a ship becomes a mediator of making seen what is invisible in the abyss and a space where meaning is dissolved and identity is made invisible. Can the ship be an image of weeping as well as

---

86. Rankin, *Tertullian and the Church*, 67.

of meaning? A means for making sense of a permeating polyvalence of meaning? Truly, the ship of the church should not be reducible to one meaning. Rather, the ship is the opening to relation, a co-constituting through shared meaning and exchange of knowledge received in interpreting the deep of the sea. This boat of the church is an invitation into the imminent opacity of divinity shared in relation. Earlier, with Peters, we saw the ship as an artificial ground on which humans can stand in order to access the medium of the sea. Yet with Glissant we also find the ship to be a place of dissolution and disintegration of meaning from which new meaning must be rewoven. Glissant's dissolving is a metaphor of the teleological inadequacy of the technological narrative that we find in a Teilhardian framework of movement towards the Omega Point. Can the church draw from both of these ships in understanding its small boat?

In the first chapter, I asked whether the arrival of cyberspace might be a means by which the structures of the old creation could be challenged and cracked open so that in the new openings created something new might emerge. We can now reframe this question to whether the invisible church of cyberspace might be a metaphor of rewoven meaning in the wake of the attempts of reduction to calculability by the power assemblages. These attempts at reduction must be disrupted, but such disruption is not sufficient on its own. The poetic scraps must be rewoven, with spaces between the words for breath and ineffability. Such meaning can be mediated for Christians through the small boat of the church; particularly through its liturgy and its reaching out to the suffering in the world. The invisible church becomes a temporary artificial ground from which the meaning found in the abyss might be mediated opaquely. Such mediation of opacity is an embodied encounter, and not merely cognitive. It is allowing the song of what might be to emerge from the remains of what was, a hope of the Internet that could be while mourning the loss of the Internet that could have been and yet also acting in the Internet as it is.

The Hidden Church and the Dimension of Spirit

Can the metaphor of the hidden church allow a return to the exuberance of the early confidence in the infinite possibilities provided by the Internet? No, it cannot. However, it may provide a possibility for speaking of the infinite within the cyberdimension. Perhaps, even, we might dare to speak of the small boat as a locus of salvation in the cyber realm. That is, might the small boat of the church be a means of offering salve on the wound of reduction and proletarianization? Of mediating the depths of meaning in the cyberdimension in a manner that does not render transparent, but rather points to the infinite expanse of immanent opacity beyond surveillance? Such a vision is not so emphatic as a Barlowian or Teilhardian ideal. It does not deny or minimize the strength of the power assemblage of cyberspace, but rather teases at its pretensions like a trickster. The trope of the hidden church points out that there is more than what is seen of reality, including in the cyberdimension.

A renewed vision of the cyberdimension cannot see it as supplanting the other dimensions of existence. Indeed, we might see the problems of India's demonetization as stemming from an attempt to have digital currency supplant physical currency. This move caused problems because it failed to account for the inorganic and organic dimensions. It failed to see those who do not have Internet access or have limited access. In 2014, it was estimated that 4.4 billion people did not have Internet access, while it is difficult to say how many more had limited access. The India demonetization points to how easily these people are forgotten about or dismissed by the power assemblage. The hidden church cannot allow them to remain invisible in this way.

Those who are not online are not unaffected by the cyberdimension. From the effects of global warming directly connected to cyber activities to economic decisions that affect them, the cyberdimension has an impact on everything and everyone, whether they use Google or not. Indian theologian M. Peter Singh has written about the theological imperative to contend with the "digital divide" and its connection to issues of gender justice, particularly in his own context of India. Theologically, Singh understands cyberspace as a prophetic egalitarian vision of community that can be used to move the church to work to expand egalitarian community within the day-to-day lives of people, working to overcome digital and economic divides.[87] Within this, he affirms the ambiguity of information technology, advocating for theological dialogue on acceptable and unacceptable consequences of new technologies. He further insists, "Little attention has been given to the consequences of uneven technological diffusion for social inequality and so the information technology is far from achieving its potential reach and impact, and there are concerns

87. Singh, *Cybertheology*, Kindle location 5239.

that the digital divide is growing as the pace of change accelerates."[88] In particular he argues that the introduction of information technologies into the home as a substitute for office and factory work is in fact a type of worker exploitation because it only helps professionals and not working-class people, shop owners, or other forms of nonprofessional employment, particularly in village and rural settings.[89] He especially notes the importance of the informal sector of work, which represents 94 percent of working women in India. Thus he calls for a change in the economic paradigm in order to appreciate traditional occupations and techniques rather than seeing them as being made obsolete by information technologies.[90] He also ties these concerns to patriarchal visions of society that lead to an unwillingness to educate girls, including introducing them to computers. All of these issues, taken together, create a digital elite while the masses are left behind. Singh's writing predates the demonetization movement towards e-transactions, but helps to provide the context in which this move was so problematic.

In a similar vein, Lisa Parks notes the gendered effects of Internet access in the village she studied in Zambia. Her work focuses on attempts to introduce Internet access in the village of Macha. She notes the interpenetrating systems essential for Internet use. For instance, the water supply there is irregular, and so many women must carry water from central spigots home, often expending many hours of the day. Yet this task is necessary for life, including the lives of those who want to use the Internet, such as in a local private school. Thus Parks contends, "*this* water infrastructure—the movement of water performed by Machan women—supports *this* Internet access—children in a local private school."[91] Without the women performing this function, their children could not live, and so could not attend a school that can afford the cost of Internet access. Thus she continues, "Machan water carriers not only support and sustain their families but, in the logic of digital capitalism, their labor is implicitly commandeered to sustain populations on the cusp of becoming new markets for commercial Internet service providers . . . as market saturation peaks in industrialized parts of the world."[92] Even

88. Ibid., Kindle location 2202.
89. Ibid., Kindle location 2312.
90. Ibid., Kindle location 2542.
91. Parks, "Water, Energy, Access," 123.
92. Ibid.

so, she reports that through interviews she found that the bulk of these women had never heard of the Internet, thus demonstrating a gendering of the digital divide, just as Singh notes from the Indian context.

Parks points out how quickly Internet access became essential for those who had it. She quotes a hospital administrator that she interviewed: "I think the mobile phone is the center of information . . . without it, it's like life without blood. To a human being. Because I'll be paralyzed. I'll be completely paralyzed without this technology."[93] Parks notes, however, that the company providing Wi-Fi to the area went bankrupt in 2012, leaving only mobile phones as a means of accessing the Internet. Yet at the same time, we must be wary of thinking that giving Internet access to those without it is automatically a positive gift given to these "others." Parks points out that while most of the women had not heard of the Internet, this was in part because they were not interested in such technology and were content without it. To think that their existence is lessened by the lack of Internet access follows the logic of the power assemblage. Indeed, Parks suggests that this "foregrounds the reality that the digital divide may be as much an invention of Western humanitarianism and/or digital capitalism as it is a salient concern among Macha's rural residents."[94] Online access comes with a steep cost: giving up some of one's opacity and local individuation.

Cyberspace as a dimension of existence must, then, see the thorough interpenetration of dimensions within cyberspace. Spirit or consciousness cannot be divorced from the inorganic, organic, or cyber dimensions of reality. Spirit must occur in the midst of the interactions; it must have an immanent transcendence.

The hidden church as a metaphor of flourishing existence must likewise not be a distant hope of what might be or an unattainable vision of the Internet as we would have wanted it to be, even as it is not enough to settle for a cynical realism of the Internet as it is. In this we reach the limitation of the metaphor of unambiguous existence. A dream of cyberspace with no cybersecurity threats is not helpful in allowing persistence and consistence in a colonized cyberspace. A vision of a flourishing cyberdimension in which artistry has been reinfused into life, however, is one that calls forth the activity of poetic construction of life.

93. Ibid., 127
94. Ibid., 132.

Certainly I do not mean to suggest the metaphor of the hidden church as the only possible metaphor of flourishing within cyberspace. It is a small boat on a vast sea of meaning. It is not the only vessel afloat. Some of what is found in those waters might bring dissolution while others parts may convey hope; much undoubtedly ambiguously does both. All is mediated by the available technologies to reveal it as media. The hidden church speaks of this mediation from my own tradition as a means of speaking of the word of the infinite into the finitude of technology. It is a means of engaging the dimension of spirit.

In what ways, though, does this technology of the small boat engage a dimension dominated by the power assemblages of cyberspace? In Tillichian terms we can ask how the hidden church might engage the profanization of the cyberdimension, or in Glissantian terms weave decolonized poetry in the wreckage of the dashed hopes of the Internet that might have been.

Postcolonial biblical scholar Andrew Kinoti Lairenge provides some direction as he speaks of the postcolonial church as a mimic church. He draws inspiration from Paul in Galatians. He reads Paul as unconsciously mimicking the colonizing hierarchy of the Roman Empire in his urging the Galatians to mimic him, even while he is also rebelling against the empire. At the same time, by challenging Paul's authority, Paul's audience has undertaken to define themselves rather than as remaining a "colonized other." Lairenge writes, "In this case mimicry acts as an ambivalent space of colonial negotiations shrouded with domination, counter domination, and localized freedoms."[95] The Galatian church has a type of freedom through this ambivalence in that it is free to weigh the gospel as explained by Paul against that presented by others; they can mimic him in being free to rebel against him. In the same way, Lairenge views the African church as a mimic church, intended to be the same but not the same as mother churches from Europe and America. The African churches, Lairenge continues, can use this mimicry as a technique for subverting ecclesial hierarchies.

Such mimicry may be a way of subverting rather than mirroring power assemblages, of engaging in counter-apocalypse, to use Keller's framing. The church as coalition of the invisible of the cyberdimension can be viewed as a subversion or mimicry of the power assemblage. While the rhizome of the military cyber-industrial-digital-surveillance complex

---

95. Wafula et al., eds., *The Postcolonial Church*, 71.

continues to grow and consume cyberspace, so too can the networked rhizome of the invisible whose existence delegitimizes the powers of the cyber-complex also spread as a coalition of ironic mimicry and tricksters engaged in improper naming and impure protest by illuminating the spaces where creolized poetic speech can open to infinity within the closed logic of computers. The rhizome is *pharmakon*. Flourishing in the cyberdimension can be understood as the cultivation of opacity rather than being reduced to mirroring power.

Returning to Luther, we have seen that the hidden church is not something that we choose to enter, but rather we are brought into by faith. Being part of it is a response to God's action. The hidden church occurs rather than exists. It cannot be found here or there, just as the cyberdimension is not found here or there. We find ourselves already entangled within it. I have also suggested in chapter 3, following Luther's logic, that opacity flows from the indwelling of the infinite within us rather than through our actions. For this reason, for Luther repentance was not a matter of saying "Sorry" for the wrong things that we have done but rather is a matter of turning our trust away from our own actions, good or bad, and instead trusting in God. This repentance is at the heart of the life of the hidden church. So too, I have suggested, repentance in the cyberdimension comes in the form of a turn from being identified by our actions to a trust in the opacity of the infinite within us.

This, then, is at the heart of the hidden church of the cyberdimension. It is a trust in the ability of the infinite to indwell and propel poetic possibilities amidst the ones and zeroes of the cyberdimension as well as the complex layers of relation that formulate meaning from those ones and zeroes. Such an encounter with the infinite calls forth concrete action as a manifestation of the infinite as love in particularity, following Keller. Such love cannot be identified as statically here or there, but rather is found in a lifting up of those hidden in cyberspace, either through their exclusion from participation by the digital divide or those deemed outside the parameters of normalcy by algorithms. It is also found in the celebration of opacity inherent in true relationship with the depths of others, an opacity that may be found in anonymity or in rhythmic disruption. The hidden church of the cyberdimension finds itself swimming in the depths of excess of meaning found in all dimensions, accessed and interpreted uniquely through the medium of cyberspace.

Bibliography

An, Yountae. *The Decolonial Abyss: Mysticism and Cosmopolitics from the Ruins.* Perspectives in Continental Philosophy. New York: Fordham University Press, 2017.
Ashok, India. "Anonymous Hacker Group dupes Trump, Secret Service and FBI with latest 'Leak.'" *International Business Times*, March 22, 2016. http://www.ibtimes.co.uk/anonymous-hacker-group-dupes-trump-secret-service-fbi-latest-leak-1550942.
Augustine. "Reply to Faustus the Manichean." In *War and Christian Ethics: Classic and Contemporary Readings on the Morality of War*, edited by Arthur F. Holmes, 63–68. Grand Rapids: Baker Academic, 1975, 2005.
———. "To Count Boniface." In *War and Christian Ethics: Classic and Contemporary Readings on the Morality of War*, edited by Arthur F. Holmes, 61–62. Grand Rapids: Baker Academic, 1975, 2005.
Ball, Kirstie. "Organization, Surveillance, and the Body: Towards a Politics of Resistance." In *Theorizing Surveillance: The Panopticon and Beyond*, edited by David Lyon, 296–317. Portland, OR: Willand, 2006.
Barlow, John Perry. "A Declaration of Independence for Cyberspace." Electronic Frontier Foundation website. www.eff.org/cyberspace-independence.
———. "Selling Wine Without Bottles: The Economy of the Mind on the Global Net." Electronic Frontier Foundation website. https://w2.eff.org/Misc/Publications/John_Perry_Barlow/HTML/idea_economy_article.html.
Barth, Hans-Martin. *The Theology of Martin Luther: A Critical Assessment.* Translated by Linda M. Maloney. Minneapolis: Fortress, 2013.
Bayer, Oswald. *Martin Luther's Theology: A Contemporary Interpretation.* Translated by Thomas H. Trapp. Grand Rapids: Eerdmans, 2008.
Bazzichelli, Tatiana. *Networked Disruption: Rethinking Oppositions in Art, Hacktivism, and the Business of Social Networking.* Aarhus, Denmark: Digital Aesthetics Research Center, 2013.
Beard, Matthew. "Cyberwar and Just War Theory." Paper posted on academia.edu. www.academia.edu/8199528/Cyberwar_and_Just_War_Theory.
Bell, Daniel M., Jr. *Just War as Christian Discipleship: Recentering the Tradition in the Church Rather Than the State.* Grand Rapids: Brazos, 2009.
Birch, Charles, and John B. Cobb, Jr. *The Liberation of Life: From the Cell to the Community.* Denton, TX: Environmental Ethics, 1990.

Bloom, Alexander. "How the Web Affects Memory." *Harvard Magazine*, November/ Dececmber 2011. http://harvardmagazine.com/2011/11/how-the-web-affects-memory.

Boellstorff, Tom. *Coming of Age in Second Life: An Anthropologist Explores the Virtually Human*. Princeton, NJ: Princeton University Press, 2008.

Boesel, Chris, and S. Wesley Ariarajah, eds. *Divine Multiplicity: Trinities, Diversities, and the Nature of Relation*. New York: Fordham University Press, 2014.

Borgman, Eric, et al, eds. *Cyberspace-Cyberethics-Cybertheology. Concilium* 2005.1.

Breslow, Jason M. "With or Without the Patriot Act, Here's How the NSA Can Still Spy on Americans." *Frontline*, June 1, 2015. http://www.pbs.org/wgbh/frontline/article/with-or-without-the-patriot-act-heres-how-the-nsa-can-still-spy-on-americans/.

Briefing. "War in the Fifth Column." *The Economist*, July 1, 2010. http://www.economist.com/node/16478792.

Carletti, Giulia. "The Disruptive Power of Performance Art." *Uber Aura Magazine*. Accessed February 10, 2018. http://www.uberauramagazine.com/art/disruptive-power-performance-art/.

Carnegie Mellon University. "More Than Facial Recognition." Accessed March 9, 2018. https://www.cmu.edu/homepage/society/2011/summer/facial-recognition.shtml.

Carroll, Chris. "Cone of Silence Surrounds U.S. Cyberwarfare." *Stars and Stripes*, October 18, 2011. https://stripes.com/news/cone-of-silence-surrounds-u-s-cyberarfare-1.158090.

Chilton, Kevin. Testimony for "The Status of U.S. Strategic Forces Hearing Before the Strategic Forces Subcommittee of the Committee on Armed Services," House of Representatives, One hundred Eleventh Congress, First Session, March 17, 2009. Washington, DC: US Government Printing Office, 2010.

Chowdhury, Debasish Roy. "Note Ban: Will it Make India or Break Modi?" *South China Morning Post*, January 8, 2017. http://www.scmp.com/week-asia/politics/article/2060038/note-ban-will-it-make-india-or-break-modi.

Clarke, Richard, et al. *NSA Report: Liberty and Security in a Changing World*. President's Review Group on Intelligence and Communications Technologies. Project MUSE. Princeton, NJ: Princeton University Press, 2014.

CNN. "2016 Presidential Campaign Hacking Fast Facts." https://edition.cnn.com/2016/12/26/us/2016-presidential-campaign-hacking-fast.

Cobb, Jennifer. *Cybergrace: The Search for God in the Digital World*. New York: Crown, 1998.

Cobb Kreisberg, Jennifer. "A Globe, Clothing Itself with a Brain." *Wired*, June 1, 1995. http://www.wired.com/1995/06/teilhard/.

Coleman, Gabriella. *Hacker, Hoaxer, Whistleblower, Spy: The Many Faces of Anonymous*. Kindle ed. New York: Verso, 2015.

———. "The Latest Snowden Revelation Is Dangerous for Anonymous—And for All of Us." *Wired*, Feb. 4, 2014. https://www.wired.com/2014/02/comes-around-goes-around-latest-snowden-revelation-isnt-just-dangerous-anonymous-us/.

Corera, Gordon. "Can U.S. Election Hack Be Traced to Russia?" BBC News, Dec. 22, 2016. http://www.bbc.com/news/world-us-canada-38370630.

Conan, Neal. (Host), T. Jordan, C. Karasic, and O. Ruffin (guests). "Hacktivism." The Connection radio broadcast, July 30, 2001. National Public Radio. WBUR, Boston.

Critical Art Ensemble. *Electronic Civil Disobedience and Other Unpopular Ideas*. Brooklyn: Autonomedia, 1996. http://critical-art.net/books/ecd/ecd2.pdf.

Culp, Andrew. *The Dark Deleuze*. Minneapolis: University of Minnesota Press, 2016.

Deibert, Ronald J. *Black Code: Surveillance, Privacy, and the Dark Side of the Internet.* Toronto: McClelland & Stewart, 2013.
Delanda, Manuel. *Assemblage Theory.* Edinburgh: Edinburgh University Press, 2016.
Deleuze, Gilles. *Pourparler 1972–1990.* Paris: Editions de Minuit, 1990.
Deleuze, Gilles, and Felix Guattari. *A Thousand Plateaus: Capitalism and Schizophrenia.* Project Lamar. Translated by Brian Massumi. Minneapolis: University of Minnesota Press, 1987. http://projectlamar.com/media/A-Thousand-Plateaus.pdf.
Deleuze, Gilles, and Claire Parnet. *Dialogues II.* Translated by Barbara Habberiam, Eliot Ross Albert, and Hugh Tomlinson. New York: Columbia University Press, 2002.
Denning, Dorothy. "The Rise of Hacktivism." *Georgetown Journal of International Affairs,* September 8, 2015. https://www.georgetownjournalofinternationalaffairs.org/online-edition/the-rise-of-hacktivism.
Der Derian, James. *Virtuous War: Mapping the Military-Industrial-Media-Entertainment Network.* 2nd ed. London: Routledge, *2009.*
Deseriis, Marco. "Improper Names: The Minor Politics of Collective Pseudonyms and Multiple-Use Names." PhD diss., New York University, 2010.
Detrow, Scott. "Obama on Russian Hacking: 'We Need to Take Action. And We Will.'" *NPR Morning Edition,* December 15, 2016. http://www.npr.org/2016/12/15/505775550/obama-on-russian-hacking-we-need-to-take-action-and-we-will.
Dillenberger, John. *A Theology of Artistic Sensibilities: The Visual Arts and The Church.* London: SCM, 1987.
Dipert, Randall. "The Ethics of Cyberwar." *Journal of Military Ethics* 9.4 (2010) 384–410.
Douglas, Kelly Brown. *Stand Your Ground: Black Bodies and the Justice of God.* Maryknoll, NY: Orbis, 2015.
Dourish, Paul. "Protocols, Packets, and Proximity: The Materiality of Internet Routing." In *Signal Traffic: Critical Studies of Media Infrastructures,* edited by Lisa Parks and Nicole Starosielski, 183–204. Urbana, IL: University of Illinois Press, 2015.
Dubrofsky, Rachel E., and Shoshana Amielle Magnet, eds. *Feminist Surveillance Studies.* Durham, NC: Duke University Press, 2015.
Duhigg, Charles. "How Companies Learn Your Secrets." *New York Times Magazine,* February 16, 2012. http://www.nytimes.com/2012/02/19/magazine/shopping-habits.html.
Du Toit, Calvyn C., and Gys M. Loubser. "Liturgical Pharmacology: Time of the Question, Complexity, and Ethics." *Hervormde Teologiese Studies/Theological Studies,* 72 (1) a3214. https//:dx.doi.org/10.4012/hts.v21i1.3214.
Edwards, Jim. "Ford Exec: 'We Know Everyone Who Breaks The Law' Thanks To Our GPS In Your Car." *Business Insider,* January 8, 2014. http://www.businessinsider.my/ford-exec-gps-2014-1/?r=US&IR=T#tZjLIxXhGg3qUiJg.97.
Electronic Frontier Foundation. "History." Accessed March 2, 2018. https://www.eff.org/about/history.
Gibson, William. *Neuromancer.* New York: Berkley, 1989.
Gladwell, Malcolm. "Small Change: Why the Revolution Will Not Be Tweeted." *The New Yorker,* October 4, 2010. https://sites.tufts.edu/alquestaeng1fall2017/files/2017/08/Small-Change-Why-the-Revolution-Will-Not-Be-Tweeted-by-Malcolm-Gladwell.pdf.
Glissant, Édouard. *Poetics of Relation.* Translated by Betsy Wing. Ann Arbor, MI: University of Michigan Press, 1997.

Gorman, Siobhan, and Jennifer Valentino-DeVries. "New Details Show Broader NSA Surveillance Reach." *The Wall Street Journal*, August 20, 2013. http://www.wsj.com/articles/SB10001424127887324108204579022874091732470.

Grau, Marion. *Of Divine Economy: Refinancing Redemption*. London: T&T Clark, 2004.

———. *Refiguring Theological Hermeneutics: Hermes, Trickster, Fool*. New York: Palgrave Macmillan, 2014.

Greenberg, Andy. *This Machine Kills Secrets: Julian Assange, the Cypherpunks, and Their Fight to Empower Whistleblowers*. New York: Plume, 2012.

Greenwald, Glenn. *No Place to Hide: Edward Snowden, the NSA, and the U.S. Surveillance State*. New York: Metropolitan, 2014.

Gude, Hubert, et al. "Mass Data: Transfers from Germany Aid US Surveillance." *Der Spiegel*. Aug. 5, 2013. http://www.spiegel.de/international/world/german-intelligence-sends-massive-amounts-of-data-to-the-nsa-a-914821.html.

Gurnow, Michael. *The Edward Snowden Affair: Exposing the Politics and Media Behind the NSA Scandal*. Indianapolis: Blue River, 2014.

Habermas, Jürgen. "Civil Disobedience: Litmus Test for the Democratic Constitutional State." *Berkeley Journal of Sociology*, 30 (1985) 95–116.

Hansen, Guillermo. "The Networking of Differences that Make a Difference: Theology and Unity of the Church." *Dialog: A Journal of Theology* 51.1 (Spring 2012) 31–42.

Haggerty, Kevin D. "Tear Down the Walls: On Demolishing the Panopticon." In *Theorizing Surveillance: The Panopticon and Beyond*, edited by David Lyon, 23–45. Portland, OR: Willand, 2006.

Haggerty, Kevin D., and Richard V. Ericson. "The Surveillant Assemblage." *British Journal of Sociology* 51, 605–22. doi:10.1080/00071310020015280.

Harding, Luke. *The Snowden Files: The Inside Story of the World's Most Wanted Man*. New York: Vintage, 2014.

Hayless, N. Katherine. *How We Think: Digital Media and Contemporary Technogenesis*. Chicago: University of Chicago Press, 2012.

Heim, Michael. *The Metaphysics of Virtual Reality*. New York: Oxford University Press, 1993. Scribd. https://www.scribd.com/document/124737823/The-Metaphysics-of-Virtual-Reality.

Holmes, Arthur F., ed. *War and Christian Ethics: Classic and Contemporary Readings on the Morality of War*. Grand Rapids: Baker Academic, 1975, 2005.

Home, Stewart. "Multiple Names." *Festival of Plagiarism*, London, 1988. The Seven by Nine Squares website. www.thing.de/projekte/7:9%23/multiple_names.html.

"How BAE sold cyber-surveillance tools to Arab states." BBC News, June 15, 2017. http://www.bbc.com/news/world-middle-east-40276568.

Huchingson, James E. "Dimensions of Life: A Systems Approach to the Inorganic and the Organic in Paul Tillich and Pierre Teilhard de Chardin." *Zygon* 40.3 (September 2005) 751–58.

Hutnyk, John. "Proletarianization." *New Formations*, 77 (October 1, 2012) 127–49. doi:10.3898/NEWF.77.08.2012.

Ieven, Bram. "The Forgetting of Aesthetics: Individuation, Technology, and Aesthetics in the Work of Bernard Steigler." *New Formations*, 77 (October 1, 2012) 76–96. doi:103898/NEWF.77.05.2012.

Jüngel, Eberhard. *Theological Essays II*. Translated by Arnold Neufeldt-Fast and J. B. Webster. London: Bloomsbury T&T Clark, 2014.

Kearney, Richard. "God After God: An Anatheist Attempt to Reimagine God." In *Reimagining the Sacred: Richard Kearney Debates God*, edited by Richard Kearney and Jens Zimmermann, 6–18. New York: Columbia University Press, 2016.
———. *The God Who May Be: A Hermeneutics of Religion*. Indianapolis: Indiana University Press, 2001.
Kearney, Richard, and Jens Zimmermann, eds. *Reimagining the Sacred: Richard Kearney Debates God*. New York: Columbia University Press, 2016.
Keefe-Perry, L. Callid. *Way to Water: A Theopoetics Primer*. Eugene, OR: Cascade, 2014.
Keller, Catherine. *God and Power: Counter-Apocalyptic Journeys*. Minneapolis: Fortress, 2005.
King, Martin Luther, Jr. "Letter from a Birmingham Jail." African Studies Center, University of Pennsylvania. https://www.africa.upenn.edu/Articles_Gen/Letter_Birmingham.html.
Klein, Adam G. "How Anonymous Hacked Donald Trump." *The Conversation*, March 31, 2016. http://theconversation.com/how-anonymous-hacked-donald-trump-56794.
Koepsell, David R. *The Ontology of Cyberspace: Philosophy, Law, and the Future of Intellectual Property*. Chicago: Open Court, 2003.
Kolb, Robert, and Timothy J. Wengert, eds. *Book of Concord*. Translated by Charles Arand, et al. Minneapolis: Fortress, 2000.
Kroll, Jason. "Free Kevin, Kevin Freed." *Linux Journal*, January 21, 2000. http://www.linuxjournal.com/article/5052.
Lange, Dirk G. *Trauma Recalled: Liturgy, Disruption, and Theology*. Minneapolis: Fortress, 2010.
Laurent, Samuel. "The Holy Spirit, the Story of God." In *Divine Multiplicity: Trinities, Diversities, and the Nature of Relation*, edited by Chris Boesel and S. Wesley Ariarajah, 193–216. New York: Fordham University Press, 2014.
Leigh, David, and Luke Harding. *WikiLeaks: Inside Julian Assange's War on Secrecy*. New York: PublicAffairs, 2011.
Levin, Sam. "Facebook told advertisers it can identify teens feeling 'insecure' and 'worthless.'" *The Guardian*, May 1, 2017. https://www.theguardian.com/technology/2017/may/01/facebook-advertising-data-insecure-teens.
Lewis. James A. "Thresholds for Cyberwar." Center for Strategic and International Studies, September 2010. http://csis-org/publication/thresholds-cyberwar.
Lieberman, Daniel F. *The Evolution of the Human Head*. Cambridge, MA: Harvard University Press, 2011.
Loock, Ulrich. "Opacity." *Frieze*, November 7, 2012. https://frieze.com/article/opacity.
Luther, Martin. *Luther's Works*. Edited by Jaroslav Pelikan and Helmut T. Lehman. 55 vols. Philadelphia and St. Louis: Fortress and Concordia, 1955–86.
Lyon, David. *Surveillance After Snowden*. Cambridge, UK: Polity, 2015.
———. *Surveillance Studies: An Overview*. Cambridge, UK: Polity, 2007.
Lyon, David, ed. *Theorizing Surveillance: The Panopticon and Beyond*. Portland, OR: Willand, 2006.
Magnet, Shoshana Amielle. *When Biometrics Fail: Gender, Race, and the Technology of Identity*. Durham, NC: Duke University Press, 2011.
Manning, Russell Re, ed. *The Cambridge Companion to Paul Tillich*. New York: Cambridge University Press, 2008.
Maxwell, Glyn. *On Poetry*. Cambridge, MA: Harvard University Press, 2012, 2016.

Mayer, F. E. "The Proper Distinction Between Law and Gospel and the Terminology Visible and Invisible Church." *Concordia Theological Monthly*, XXV.3 (March 1952) 177–98.

McAteer, John. "When Jesus Himself Wanted to Explain to His Disciples What His Forthcoming Death Was All About, He Didn't Give Them a Theory, He Gave Them a Meal." Video ut Intellectum, May 13, 2011. https://filmphilosopher.wordpress.com/2011/05/13/when-jesus-himself-wanted-to-explain-to-his-disciples-what-his-forthcoming-death-was-all-about-he-didnt-give-them-a-theory-he-gave-them-a-meal/.

McCaughey, Martha, and Michael D. Ayers, eds. *Cyberactivism: Online Activism in Theory and Practice*. London: Routledge, 2003.

Meyer, David. "Cyberspace Must Die. Here's Why." *Gigaom*, February 7, 2015. https://gigaom.com/2015/02/07/cyberspace-must-die-heres-why/.

Miller, Donald L., ed. *The Lewis Mumford Reader*. New York: Pantheon, 1986.

Mills, Elinor. "Social Engineering 101: Mitnick and Other Hackers Show How It's Done." *c/net*, July 21, 2008. https://www.cnet.com/news/social-engineering-101-mitnick-and-other-hackers-show-how-its-done/.

Moltmann, Jürgen. *God in Creation: A New Theology of Creation and the Spirit of God*. Translated by Margaret Kohl. Minneapolis: Fortress, 1993.

Moore, Stephen D. *Empire and Apocalypse: Postcolonialism and the New Testament*. Bible in the Modern World. Sheffield, UK: Sheffield Phoenix, 2006.

Mumford, Lewis. "Art and Technics." In *The Lewis Mumford Reader*, edited by Donald L. Miller, 348–61. New York: Pantheon, 1986.

Myers, Ched. *Binding the Strong Man: A Political Reading of Mark's Story of Jesus*. 20th anniv. ed. Maryknoll, NY: Orbis, 2015.

Nakashima, Ellen, et al. "U.S., Israel Developed Flame Computer Virus to Slow Iranian Nuclear Efforts, Officials Say." *Washington Post*, June 19, 2012. https://www.washingtonpost.com/world/national-security/us-israel-developed-computer-virus-to-slow-iranian-nuclear-efforts-officials-say/2012/06/19/gJQA6xBPoV_story.html?utm_term=.008bf0f05bda.

Nalapat, Madhav. "Sukhoi Likely Downed by Cyber Weapons." *Sunday Guardian Live*, May 27, 2017. http://www.sundayguardianlive.com/news/9573-sukhoi-likely-downed-cyber-weapons.

Obama Presidential Policy Directive/PPD-28. January 17, 2014. https://obamawhitehouse.archives.gov/the-press-office/2014/01/17/presidential-policy-directive-signals-intelligence-activities.

O'Harrow, Robert, Jr. "The Outsourcing of U.S. intelligence raises risks among the benefits." *The Washington Post*, June 9, 2013. https://www.washingtonpost.com/world/national-security/the-outsourcing-of-us-intelligence-raises-risks-among-the-benefits/2013/06/09/eba2d314-d14c-11e2-9f1a-1a7cdee20287_story.html.

Olson, Parmy. *We Are Anonymous: Inside the Hacker World of LulzSec, Anonymous, and the Global Cyber Insurgency*. New York: Back Bay, 2012.

The Open Web Application Security Project. "SQL Injection." Updated April 10, 2016. https://www.owasp.org/index.php/SQL_Injection.

Owen, Taylor. *Disruptive Power: The Crisis of the State in the Digital Age*. Oxford: Oxford University Press, 2015.

Paletta, Damian, et al. "Cyberwar Ignites a New Arms Race." *The Wall Street Journal*, October 11, 2015. http://www.wsj.com/articles/cyberwar-ignites-a-new-arms-race-1444611128.

Parks, Lisa. "Water, Engergy, Access." In *Signal Traffic: Critical Studies of Media Infrastructures*, edited by Lisa Parks and Nicole Starosielski, 115–36. Urbana, IL: University of Illinois Press, 2015.

Parks, Lisa, and Nicole Starosielski. "Introduction." In *Signal Traffic: Critical Studies of Media Infrastructures*, edited by Lisa Parks and Nicole Starosielski, 1–30. Urbana, IL: University of Illinois Press, 2015.

Parrella, Frederick. "Tillich's Theology of the Concrete Spirit." In *The Cambridge Companion to Paul Tillich*, edited by Russell Re Manning, 74–90. New York: Cambridge University Press, 2008.

Peters, John Dunham. *The Marvelous Clouds: Toward a Philosophy of Elemental Media*. Chicago: University of Chicago Press, 2015.

Pilkington, Ed. "Chelsea Manning Released From Military Prison." *The Guardian*, May 17, 2017. https://www.theguardian.com/us-news/2017/may/17/chelsea-manning-released-from-prison.

"Putrajaya Ramps Up Request." *Malay Mail Online*, December 26, 2016. http://www.themalaymailonline.com/malaysia/article/putrajaya-ramps-up-request-for-facebook-users-data-in-first-half-2016.

Rankin, David. *Tertullian and the Church*. Cambridge: Cambridge University Press, 1995.

Raschke, Carl. *GloboChrist: The Great Commission Takes a Postmodern Turn*. Grand Rapids: Baker Academic, 2008.

Raza, Talal. "MOIB warns against the use of Inpage; says the software is being exploited by Indian Intelligence Agencies." *Digital Rights Monitor News*, October 13, 2017. http://digitalrightsmonitor.pk/moib-warns-against-the-use-of-inpage-says-the-software-is-being-exploited-by-indian-intelligence-agencies/.

Razumovskaya, Olga. "Russia Moves Some Servers to Russian Data Centers." *The Wall Street Journal*, April 10, 2015. http://www.wsj.com/articles/google-moves-some-servers-to-russian-data-centers-1428680491.

Rivera, Mayra. *The Touch of Transcendence: A Postcolonial Theology of God*. Louisville: Westminster John Knox Press, 2007.

Reuters. "Latin American countries call summit over diversion of Evo Morales's plane." *The Telegraph*, July 4, 2013. http://www.telegraph.co.uk/news/worldnews/southamerica/bolivia/10158924/Latin-American-countries-call-summit-over-diversion-of-Evo-Moraless--plane.html.

Ruffin, Oxblood. "Old School Hacker Oxblood Ruffin Discusses Anonymous and the Future of Hacktavism." *Radio Free Europe/Radio Liberty*, April 26, 2013. https://www.rferl.org/a/hacker_oxblood_ruffin_discusses_anonymous_and_the_future_of_hacktivism/24228166.html.

Sanger, David. *Confront and Conceal: Obama's Secret Wars and Surprising Use of American Power*. New York: Crown, 2012.

Sauter, Molly. *The Coming Swarm: DDoS Actions, Hacktivism, and Civil Disobedience on the Internet*. New York: Bloomsbury Academic, 2014.

Savage, Charlie. "Chelsea Manning Tried Committing Suicide a Second Time in October." *New York Times*, November 4, 2016. http://www.nytimes.

com/2016/11/05/us/chelsea-manning-tried-committing-suicide-a-second-time-in-october.html?_r=0.
Schacter, Daniel L., and Donna Rose Addis. "The cognitive neuroscience of constructive memory: remembering the past and imagining the future." *The Royal Society Publishing*, May 29, 2007. http://rstb.royalsocietypublishing.org/content/362/1481/773.short.
Schlink, Edmund. *Theology of the Lutheran Confessions*. Translated by Paul F. Koehneke and Herbert J. A. Bouman. St. Louis: Concordia, 1961.
Schlor, Veronika. "Cyborgs: Feminist Approaches to the Cyberworld." In *Cyberspace-Cyberethics-Cybertheology*, edited by Eric Borgman, et al., 60–67. Concilium. London: SCM, 2005.
Schneier, Bruce. *Data and Goliath: The Hidden Battles to Collect Your Data and Control Your World*. New York: W. W. Norton, 2015.
Segal, Adam. *The Hacked World Order: How Nations Fight, Trade, Maneuver, and Manipulate in the Digital Age*. 2d ed. New York: PublicAffairs, 2017.
Shoichet, Catherine E. "Bolivia: Presidential plane forced to land after false rumors of Snowden onboard." CNN, July 3, 2013. http://edition.cnn.com/2013/07/02/world/americas/bolivia-presidential-plane/.
Siddiqui, Sabrina. "NSA chief: Trump 'has not ordered disruption of Russia election meddling.'" *The Guardian*, February 27, 2018. https://www.theguardian.com/us-news/2018/feb/27/trump-russia-meddling-mike-rogers.
Singer, P. W., and Allan Friedman. *Cybersecurity and Cyberwar: What Everyone Needs to Know*. Oxford: Oxford University Press, 2014.
Singh, M. Peter. *Cybertheology*. Kindle ed. N.p.: Indian Society for Promoting Christian Knowledge, 2014.
Smith, Andrea. "Not-Seeing: State Surveillance, Settler Colonialism, and Gender Violence." In *Feminist Surveillance Studies*, edited Rachel E. Dubrofsky and Shoshana Amielle Magnet, 21–38. Durham, NC: Duke University Press, 2015.
Soldatov, Andrei, and Irina Borogan. *The Red Web: The Struggle Between Russia's Digital Dictators and the New Online Revolutionaries*. New York: PublicAffairs, 2015.
Spadaro, Antonio. *Cybertheology: Thinking Christianity in the Era of the Internet*. Translated by Maria Way. New York: Fordham University Press, 2014.
Spinello, Richard A. *Cyberethics: Morality and Law in Cyberspace*. 4th ed. Burlington, MA: Jones and Bartlett Learning, 2011.
Starosielski, Nicole. "Fixed Flow: Undersea Cables as Media Infrastructure." In *Signal Traffic: Critical Studies of Media Infrastructures*, edited by Lisa Parks and Nicole Starosielski, 53–70. Urbana, IL: University of Illinois Press, 2015.
Starr, Barbara, and Zachary Cohen. "Pentagon Considers Changing Nuclear Retaliation Rules." CNN, January 18, 2018. http://edition.cnn.com/2018/01/18/politics/pentagon-nuclear-posture-review-draft/index.html.
Stiegler, Bernard. *The Decadence of Industrial Democracies: Disbelief and Discredit, Vol. 1*. Translated by Daniel Ross and Suzanne Arnold. Cambridge, UK: Polity, 2011.
———. *For a New Critique of Political Economy*. Translated by Daniel Ross. Cambridge, UK: Polity, 2010.
Szoldra, Paul. "The Anonymous 'War' on Donald Trump is a Complete Disaster." *Business Insider*, April 1, 2016. http://www.businessinsider.my/anonymous-war-donald-trump-fail-2016-4/?r=US&IR=T#OEOmcQWjUOQZMFLO.97.

Teilhard de Chardin, Pierre. *The Future of Man*. Translated by Norman Denny. New York: Image Books Doubleday, 1959. https://ia801409.us.archive.org/21/items/TheFutureOfMan/Future_of_Man.pdf.

———. *The Phenomenon of Man*. Translated by Bernard Wall. London: HarperColophon, 1959, 1965, 1975.

Thompson, Deanna A. *The Virtual Body of Christ in a Suffering World*. Nashville: Abingdon, 2016.

Tillich, Paul. *Systematic Theology Vol. 1*. Chicago: University of Chicago Press, 1951.

———. *Systematic Theology Vol. 3*. Chicago: University of Chicago Press, 1963.

———. *Theology of Culture*. Edited by Robert C. Kimball. Oxford: Oxford University Press, 1959.

Trozzo, Eric J. *Rupturing Eschatology: Divine Glory and the Silence of the Cross*. Emerging Scholars. Minneapolis: Fortress, 2014.

Tolokonnikova, Nadezhda. "As I Serve My 'Deuce' in Lockdown." In *Comradely Greetings: The Prison Letters of Nadya and Slavoj*, translated by Ian Dreiblatt, 63–70. New York: Verso, 2014.

———. "I Write You from a Special Economic Zone." In *Comradely Greetings: The Prison Letters of Nadya and Slavoj*, translated by Ian Dreiblatt, 53–56. New York: Verso, 2014.

———. "When You Put on a Mask, You Leave Your Own Time." In *Comradely Greetings: The Prison Letters of Nadya and Slavoj*, translated by Ian Dreiblatt, 85–92. New York: Verso, 2014.

Tolokonnikova, Nadezhda, and Slavoj Zizek. *Comradely Greetings: The Prison Letters of Nadya and Slavoj*. Translated by Ian Dreiblatt. New York: Verso, 2014.

US Executive Office of the President. "Big data: Seizing opportunities, preserving values." May 1, 2014. http://www.whitehouse.gov/sites/default/files/docs/big_data_privacy_report_may_1_2014.pdf.

Veigh, Sandor. "Classifying Forms of Online Activism: The Case of Cyberprotests Against the World Bank." In *Cyberactivism: Online Activism in Theory and Practice*, edited by Martha McCaughey and Michael D. Ayers, 71–96. London: Routledge, 2003.

Wafula, R. S., et al., eds. *The Postcolonial Church: Bible, Theology, and Mission*. Alameda, CA: Borderless, 2016.

Walzer, Michael. *Just and Unjust Wars: A Moral Argument with Historical Illustrations*. 4th ed. New York: Basic, 1977, 2006.

Watkins, Eli. "White House Officially Blames North Korea for Massive 'WannaCry' Cyberattack." CNN, December 20, 2017. http://edition.cnn.com/2017/12/18/politics/white-house-tom-bossert-north-korea-wannacry/index.html.

Wildiers, N. M. *Introduction to Teilhard de Chardin*. Translated by Hubert Hoskins. New York: Harper and Row, 1968.

Wink, Walter. *Engaging the Powers: Discernment and Resistance in a World of Domination*. Minneapolis: Augsburg Fortress, 1992.

Yadron, Danny. "FBI confirms it won't tell Apple how it hacked San Bernardino shooter's iPhone." *The Guardian*, April 26, 2016. https://www.theguardian.com/technology/2016/apr/27/fbi-apple-iphone-secret-hack-san-bernardino.

Yorgasan, Ethan. "The Gospel in Communication: A Conversation with John Durham Peters." *Dialogue: A Journal of Mormon Thought*, 40.4, 29–46.

Zechner, Manuela, and Bue Rübner Hansen. "Unchained Melodies of the New Proletariat." Review of *For a New Critique of Political Economy*, by Bernard Steigler. *Generation Online*, accessed February 28, 2018. http://www.generation-online.org/other/stieglerreview.htm.

Zetter, Kim. *Countdown to Zero Day: Stuxnet and the Launch of the World's First Digital Weapon*. New York: Crown, 2014.

Zizek, Slavoj. *The Parallax View*. Cambridge, MA: MIT Press, 2006.

———. *Organs Without Bodies: On Deleuze and Consequences*. London: Routledge, 2004.

———. "A New and Much More Risky Heroism Will Be Needed." In *Comradely Greetings: The Prison Letters of Nadya and Slavoj*, translated by Ian Dreiblatt, 93–112. New York: Verso, 2014.

———. "Is Our Position Utopian?" In *Comradely Greetings: The Prison Letters of Nadya and Slavoj*, translated by Ian Dreiblatt, 45–52. New York: Verso, 2014.

Name/Subject Index

Absent presence, 36–38, 48, 143, 235, 250
Air gap, 13, 15
Algorithm, 25, 57, 112–17, 127, 138, 142, 199
Anonymous, 145–47, 153–157, 161–62, 164–71, 175–77, 179–81
Anonymity, 16, 83, 154, 168–169, 176, 180, 191, 201, 263
Anti-virus, 12–13, 62, 65
Assange, Julian, 191–92, 194–95, 201
Assemblage, 112, 119–24, 127, 154, 232, 236, 247, 253
    Surveillant, 119, 127, 129, 138, 141, 168, 173, 189, 197, 219
    Power, 18–19, 127, 137–38, 141, 146, 151, 157–64, 166–70, 175, 177, 179–80, 182n98, 189, 191, 202–3, 206, 210, 215–216, 218, 221, 224, 232, 247, 258–59, 261–62
    Counter, 123, 232, 242, 247
Attribution problem, 57, 72, 80, 81, 83, 86, 88, 97, 99, 123, 128
Augustine, 88, 91–96, 99, 100
    Evils of war, 88, 92, 98–99
    Invisible church, 225–226
    Just War, 91–93, 95, 98, 100

Barlow, John Perry, 17, 22–27, 35, 38–40, 55, 56, 58, 129, 144, 155, 184, 222, 246, 253
    Civilization of the Mind, 26–27

Declaration of Independence for Cyberspace, 22–23, 38
Barth, Hans-Martin, 227–29, 232
Beard, Matthew, 84–89
Bell, Daniel M., 18, 80, 89–98, 100
Bentham, Jeremy, 117
Boat, *see* Ship
Body of Christ, 20, 225, 232–38, 241–42, 244–45
Bush, George W., 63, 68, 201, 246

Certificate authorities, 15
China, 22, 73, 77–79, 88, 158, 198–99
CIA Triad, 7
Civil Rights Movement, 149, 161–64, 177–78
Clarke, Richard, 62
Cobb, Jennifer, 38–42, 44–47, 55n86
Colonialism, 125–126, 189, 246
Common good, 62, 84, 93, 99, 100, 140–44, 160, 186, 224
Common Sense Ontology, *see* Cyberspace, nature of
Common space, *see* Cyberspace, as a common space
Consciousness, 55, 207, 261
    and divinity, 44, 46, 54
    and technology, 45
    collective, 42–44
Consistence, 132, 133, 136, 140, 171, 173, 175, 179, 182–85, 207–8, 220, 222, 239, 248, 252, 257, 261
Copycat attacks, 63, 65

Counter-apocalypse, 245–46, 252, 262
Critical Art Ensemble, 148, 150, 154, 166, 167
Cryptography, 14, 65, 192
Cult of the Dead Cow, 151–52, 162
Cyber Command, 63n6, 74, 78, 86n78
Cyber defense, 9–10, 12–16, 61–62, 75, 83
    Authentication, 9
    Identification, 9–10, 83
Cyberattacks, 10, 12–13, 60, 68–71, 75–87, 95, 100, 145
Cyber-complex, 64, 111, 127, 141, 158, 180, 189, 214–15, 262–63
Cybersecurity, x, 2, 4–5, 7–9, 12, 17–18, 45, 55–59, 61, 72, 77, 128, 130, 147, 185, 225, 261
Cyberspace, *see* Internet; Cyberdimension
    As a common space, 155, 160–61, 176, 180
    As a military realm, 77n50, 84, 101, 104, 111, 115, 146, 158–60, 173, 180, 185
    As privately held, 25–26, 105–6, 160, 170, 180
    connotations of the term, 17
    the nature of, 21–25, 28, 35, 37–42, 44, 46, 55, 200, 204, 214, 221, 224, 259, 261
    Cyberwar, x, 1, 7, 18, 27, 56, 59–63, 67–90, 94–101, 146, 150
    Arms race, 67, 78, 84, 87–88, 99
    Cyberweapons, ix, 18, 62–64, 67, 70, 75, 78, 83, 86, 90, 95, 99–101, 111, 146, 224
    Estonian Cyberwar, 70
    Offensive mind-set, 62, 75–78
    Operation Orchard, 70
    Stuxnet, 8, 60–70, 87

DDoS, 11, 12, 19, 71–73, 86, 148–53, 159, 161–63, 175, 177–79, 219
Data, 102–3
    Big data, 18, 103, 106–8, 112–16, 126, 128, 132, 139–41, 168, 189, 252
    Data brokers, 109, 111
    Data double, 129, 131, 136, 138–40, 142–43, 167, 169, 185, 246
    Data mining, x, 10, 18, 57, 59, 83, 104, 106–10, 116, 128–29, 135, 139, 141, 144, 168, 198, 214
    Metadata, 104–5, 107, 126, 197–98
Deleuze, Gilles, 119–24, 154, 167n59, 170, 204–5
Demonetization, 223–24, 259–60
Der Derian, James, 75–76, 97
Deibert, Ronald J., 72, 75, 84, 105, 158, 162
Digital activism, 19, 59, 149, 152, 154, 162, 166, 175–79, 185; *see* Hacktivism
Digital divide, 30, 224, 259–62, 263
Dillenberger, John, 172, 183, 214
Dimension, 17, 21, 38, 47–55, 61, 85, 101, 121, 163, 224–25
    Cyber, 17, 19–20, 55–59, 70–71, 84, 100, 103, 108, 110, 137–43, 147, 150, 155, 158, 163, 171, 173, 184–85, 189, 204–5, 215, 221, 224, 234, 241, 246–48, 256, 258–63
    Historical, 48–50, 52–53
    Inorganic, 17, 34, 42–43, 47–51, 67, 259, 261
    Multidimensional unity, 53, 55, 59
    Organic, 17, 34, 47–51, 101, 121, 169, 257, 259, 261
    Psychological, 48, 50, 52–53, 257
    Spirit, 19–20, 21, 48, 50–59, 67, 84, 99, 101, 103–4, 121, 133, 136, 139–43, 147, 157, 161, 171–72, 182, 183, 185–86, 205, 210, 216, 221–22, 225, 242, 257, 261–62

NAME/SUBJECT INDEX   277

Dipert, Randall, 80–84, 88–90, 94–95, 97, 99–100
Disruption, 147, 152, 163–66, 169, 171, 175, 178–80, 183–86, 205, 212–15, 217, 235, 238, 240, 258, 263
Dolphins, 31–35
Dourish, Paul, 28–29, 56, 58

Electronic Civil Disobedience (ECD), 150–51
Electronic Disturbance Theater (EDT), 148–50, 154, 159, 161, 166, 176, 242
Ellsburg, Daniel, 190–93, 196
Embodiment, 10, 33, 37, 44, 52, 55, 130, 137, 155, 170, 210, 216, 221, 236–37, 239, 250, 254, 258; *see* Technology, as embodied
Encryption, 7, 14–15, 169, 191, 200
Enforced normality, 115–17, 126–27, 142
Excess, 18–19, 37, 121, 135–36, 138–41, 167, 171–72, 183, 195, 205, 208, 217, 220–21, 224, 228, 252, 256–57, 263

Fake news, ix, 182
Fiber-optic undersea cables, 29–30, 35, 197
Five Eyes, 197
Foucault, Michel, 18, 117–18, 141

GCHQ, 159, 197, 200, 202
Glissant, Édouard, 20, 124, 135, 225, 242, 248–58, 262
Glory of God, 18, 143, 231, 252
Grammatization, 207–8, 218
Grau, Marion, 19, 216–20

Hackers, 10–13, 61–66, 147, 151, 155, 166n57, 176–77
    Patriotic hackers, 71–73, 87, 95, 125
Hacktivism, 8, 19, 59, 73–74, 125, 145–47, 151–54, 157,
166, 179, 189; *see* Digital Activism
Hayless, N. Katherine, 105, 114, 183
Hidden Church, 19, 20, 59, 157, 225, 228–34, 238, 242, 244, 247–48, 252–53, 257–63
Huchingson, James E., 53–55
Human identity, *see* Subjectivity
Hyper-industrial, 109, 131, 137, 214, 239

Improper name, 168–69, 180, 186, 220, 245, 263
Impure dissent, 117, 219, 251
Incarnation, 236, 247–48
India, 22, 78, 88, 223–24, 234, 237, 259–61
Individuation, 130, 132n85, 208, 211–12, 214–15, 239, 261
Industry and culture, 136, 137, 143–44, 166, 171, 215, 222
Infrastructuralism, 17, 30–38, 221, 224
Internet, 24, 56, 58, 84, 103, 155, 160–61, 191, 199, 201, 225, 258
    Functioning, 2–5, 10, 28–29, 111
    Organization, 5–6, 15–16, 22–23, 109–10, 204
    Packets, 3–4
Irony, *see* Parody
Israel, 60, 62, 65, 66n16, 68, 70
Invisible Church, *see* Hidden Church

Jüngel, Eberhard, 133–139
Just War, 18, 80–100, 140
    Christian discipleship (CD), 89–91, 95–96, 98, 100
    criteria, 80, 90–91, 93–94, 96, 99
    Jus ad bellum, 80, 94
    Jus in bello, 80, 94
    Public Policy Criteria (PPC), 89–91, 93–95, 100
Justice, 8, 27, 45, 90–100, 157, 161, 174, 192, 243–47

NAME/SUBJECT INDEX

Kearney, Richard, 131–32, 136
Keller, Catherine, 20, 225, 242–50, 262–63
Khora, 44
King Jr., Martin Luther, 126, 164–66, 175, 222
Kingdom of God, 27, 50, 52–53, 58, 91, 101, 155, 157, 173–75, 231, 243, 244
Koepsell, David R., 24–28, 57–58, 160

Laurent, Samuel, 182–86, 221
Leaks, 15, 63, 146, 188, 190–94, 196, 201–2
    Apache helicopter attack, 194
    Pentagon Papers, 190, 193
    Wikileaks, ix, 191–94, 201
Liturgy, 238–40, 249, 257–58
Lulz, 153–54, 175, 181
Luther, Martin, 133–35, 219, 225–32, 234, 236, 238, 240–43, 252, 254n78, 257, 263
Luther Blissett Project, 167, 181
Lyon, David, 107, 111–12, 116, 125–26, 140, 142

Mail art, 167
Malaysia, ix, 30n22, 76n47, 112
Malware, 11–13, 16, 61, 64–67, 75, 87, 149, 159
    APTs, 78
    botnets, 11–12, 71, 79, 149–50
    WANK, 147
    worms, 8, 11, 147
Manning, Chelsea, 19, 193–96, 201, 203
Maxwell, Glyn, 19, 183–84, 205, 208, 212
McAteer, John, 156, 173–74
Media, 21, 28–31, 33–37, 39, 41–42, 46, 52, 56–57, 110, 122, 127, 161, 210, 262
    elemental, 35
    immersive, 39
Memory, 104–5, 206–7, 211, 214–15, 254–55
Military philosophy, 80–81, 89

Mnemnotechnical retention, 207, 211, 215
Moltmann, Jürgen, 133
Moore, Stephen, 156, 245
Myers, Ched, 155–56
Myth, 26, 220–22

Narrative, 170, 172, 183, 217, 221–22, 253, 258
    of cyberspace, 22, 185–86, 204, 215
    thought, 105, 114, 183
    understanding of the Holy Spirit, 182–83, 204
Nashi, 71, 73
Nation-state, 61, 65, 72, 84, 89, 95, 98, 155, 246
Neoist, 167–69, 181
Nomadic, 121–22
Noosphere, 20, 42–44, 54
NSA, 15–16, 63–64, 66n16, 69, 74, 76–79, 86n78, 103, 104n5, 111–12, 126, 194–202
Nuclear weapons, 8, 60, 67, 85–87, 99, 124, 147, 152

Obama, Barack, 63, 68–70, 75, 86, 201
Omega Point, 42–43, 45, 47, 54, 55, 249, 253, 258
Opacity, 18, 20, 135–36, 183–84, 224, 248, 253, 258–63
Owen, Taylor, 57n88, 113–14, 154n24, 155, 158, 163, 175, 179, 246
Ownership, 10, 26–27, 160; *see* Cyberspace, as commonly held
    in the old sense, 26

Palantir, 113, 199
Panikkar, Raimon, 221
Panopticon, 18, 117–19, 125, 127, 141–42, 244
Parody, 19, 154, 156–57, 174–75, 179–81, 185, 245
Patches, 11, 13, 62–63, 65, 69, 79
Peace of God, 97

Performance art, 19, 150, 166, 168, 170–75, 181, 185, 219, 239
Peters, John Durham, 17, 31–39, 42, 44–45, 52, 57, 130, 136–38, 206n74, 210, 216, 221, 224, 237, 256, 258
Pharmakon, 208, 211–12, 237, 239, 245, 263
Platonism, 25, 28, 40, 44, 46, 56, 204, 224
Poetics, 135, 138, 172, 183–86, 204, 212, 220, 241, 250–52, 257–58, 261, 263
  And computers, 248–50
  Black/printed space, 183
  White/blank space, 19–20, 183–84, 204, 208, 224
  Poetic force, 250
  Poetry, 19, 33, 172, 183–84, 186, 212, 250, 262
Postcolonial church, 262
Presumption for justice, 95–96
Privacy, 83, 102, 116, 140–43, 198
Process thought, 40–41
Programmable Logic Controllers, 66
Proletariat, 109–10, 207–9
Putin, Vladimir, 17, 22–23, 26, 58, 71, 205n71

Rahner, Karl, 172
Raschke, Carl, 123
Repentance, 135, 185, 238, 247, 263
Rhizome, 119–24, 141, 154, 262–63
Rhythm, 19, 30, 183–84, 205, 212, 214–16, 239–40, 249, 253, 263
Rivera, Mayra, 18, 138–43, 252
Ruffin, Oxblood, 152, 162
Russia, 21–23, 71–72, 77, 84, 86, 125, 158, 164, 196, 203, 205, 219
Russia election interference, 72, 86

Sacrament, 38, 44, 46, 143, 157, 229–32
Schneier, Bruce, 102–4, 107–10, 115, 127
Ship, 20, 34, 255–59, 262
Singh, M. Peter, 259–61

Smith, Andrea, 18, 116–17, 125–27, 129, 138, 142–43, 166, 176, 179, 215
Snowden, Edward, ix, x, 16, 19, 60, 63, 69–70, 75–76, 79, 110–11, 159, 188–90, 195–204
Social sorting, 116, 140
Spadaro, Antonio, 42–46
Stiegler, Bernard, 19, 109–10, 127, 131–33, 136–39, 143, 166, 169, 171, 206–16, 218, 220, 232, 237, 239, 245, 249, 254
Strong ties, 232–33, 235–37
Subjectivity, 27, 30, 41, 57, 108, 128–33, 137, 139, 170
Surveillance, 10, 16, 18, 74, 101–4, 107–19, 124–30, 136–44, 154, 158, 166, 176–77, 190–91, 195–96, 199–201, 214, 252, 259
Swarm, 20, 110, 127, 167, 185–86, 235–36

Techniques, 32–33, 206n74, 251, 257, 260
Technology, 19–20, 36, 57, 100–101, 122, 138, 141, 164, 210–11, 213, 215, 221, 233, 238–40, 253–54, 262
  Bernard Stiegler's definition, 137, 206, 208, 215
  Creates media, 57, 262
  Embodied, 32–33, 37, 129–30, 210
  John Durham Peters' definition, 32–35, 38, 44, 57, 136–37, 206n74, 216, 221, 256
  Paul Tillich's definition, 51–52, 137
  Theology of, 37, 42, 44, 221, 239
Teilhard de Chardin, Pierre, 17, 40, 42–47, 53–55, 249, 253, 258–59
Telephone Cable Channel, 29, 58
Terra nullis, 125
Tertullian, 256–57
The electrohippies, 148–50, 154, 160–62, 176

Theology of art, 171–175
The Onion Router (TOR), 15–16, 191–92
Theopoetics, 186, 221
Theosphere, 47–48
Thompson, Deanna, 20, 225, 232–38, 241
Tillich, Paul, 2, 17, 21, 32, 36–38, 46–59, 108, 121, 136–37, 139, 141, 144, 167n56, 171–73, 183, 209, 223, 225, 237, 254
Time
    In cyberspace, 36
    cyclical, 238, 253
    Linear concept, 253–54
    Liturgical, 238–40, 249, 254
Tolokonnikova, Nadezhda, 19, 203, 206, 219
Transparency, 20, 183, 248, 252, 257
Trickster, 19, 186–87, 190, 216–20, 222, 259, 263
Trump, Donald, 86n78, 145–46, 154, 180, 182
Trust, 5–7, 14–16, 65, 131, 133, 142, 263

Ultimate concern, 173
United States of America, ix, 1, 6, 22, 62–63, 65, 68, 70–71, 74, 77–79, 86n78, 111, 114, 148, 152, 158, 160, 161, 176, 188–90, 197–99, 201–3

Virtual body of Christ, 20, 232
Virtuous war, 75

Walzer, Michael, 84–86, 99
Weak ties, 232–33, 235–37
Weblining, 115–16
Whistleblowing, 59, 110, 190–91, 195–96, 203, 206, 215–16, 222
Windows Update, 65
Wink, Walter, 174–75, 181
Word of God, 37, 134, 157, 229

Zero day, 11, 61–66, 69, 76, 88, 99, 111
Zizek, Slavoj, 19, 124, 136, 203–6

www.ingramcontent.com/pod-product-compliance
Lightning Source LLC
Chambersburg PA
CBHW021655230426
43668CB00008B/626